Not My Type

Not My Type

AUTOMATING

SEXUAL RACISM

IN ONLINE DATING

Apryl Williams

Foreword by **Safiya Umoja Noble**

STANFORD UNIVERSITY PRESS
Stanford, California

Stanford University Press
Stanford, California

Library of Congress Cataloging-in-Publication Data
Names: Williams, Apryl, author.
Title: Not my type : automating sexual racism in online dating / Apryl Williams.
Description: Stanford, California : Stanford University Press, 2024. | Includes
    bibliographical references and index.
Identifiers: LCCN 2023020279 (print) | LCCN 2023020280 (ebook)
    | ISBN 9781503635043 (cloth) | ISBN 9781503635050 (paperback) |
    ISBN 9781503637610 (ebook)
Subjects: LCSH: Online dating--Social aspects--United States. | Racism—United
    States. | Sexism—United States. | Computer algorithms—Social aspects—United
    States.
Classification: LCC HQ801.82 .W554 2024 (print) | LCC HQ801.82 (ebook) |
    DDC 306.730285—dc23/eng/20230518
LC record available at https://lccn.loc.gov/2023020279
LC ebook record available at https://lccn.loc.gov/2023020280

Cover design: Jason Anscomb
Cover photography: Shutterstock

For all those searching for love, that they may find it within.

Contents

Foreword BY SAFIYA UMOJA NOBLE ix

Acknowledgments xv

INTRODUCTION 1

1 A New Sexual Racism? 27

2 Automating Sexual Racism 50

3 I'm Just Not Comfortable with Them 82
   The Myth of Neutral Personal Preference

4 I've Always Wanted to Fuck a
   Black or Asian Woman 112
   Being Racially Curated in the Sexual Marketplace

5 Safety Thirst 138
   Who Gets to Be Safe While Dating Online?

CONCLUSION
All You Need Is Love
(and Transparency, Trust, and Safety) 165

Appendix 181

Notes 183

Bibliography 211

Index 235

We are living in a time where headlines about algorithmic discrimination are commonplace. So-called Artificial Intelligence systems are pervasive across every major industry. Algorithmic sort-and-display advertising systems are used to segment and micro-target consumer groups in a way that seems normal, and maybe even helpful, to the everyday person. It's impossible to interact with any major internet platform without experiencing a moderated environment where decisions have been predetermined about what we will see, and how we will experience it, under a regime of surveillance. The illusion of privacy in our most intimate of choices like sexual intimacy, coupled with the buying and selling of our online behavior across global companies, is not widely understood by the public, which makes this book both timely and important for scholars, journalists, policymakers, and people who use these platforms. Even less apparent are the values upon which these systems "see" us, or rather, make statistical predictions and data profiles about who we are in order to match us (as the product) with other products (people)—another important reason why we need this book.

In fact, we are living through a time of profound social, political, and economic change marked by increased technological participation and mediation. No part of our human experience is immune from digital extraction or manipulation, including our sexual intimacies, especially when we are actively sharing ourselves on digital and social networks. But these experiences, as Apryl Williams so deftly documents, are tied to larger social structures, and part of the historical moment that we need to better understand. As I was reading this book, I was reminded of critical theorist and sociologist C. Wright Mills, who signaled to us that we must look between the "personal troubles of milieu and the public issues of social structure" to understand the traps we experience yet struggle to articulate or make sense of easily.

Online dating applications and platforms are one such set of "traps" that tell us as much about our own personal biography of choice, taste, desire, and imagined possibility as they do larger histories and frameworks of racist ideologies of want, desirability, acceptability, and normativity. It is in the illusion of private choice, in the "swiping" left or right, under the pretext of personal taste that the cultivation and practice of sexual racism cedes from obvious view. We struggle to understand how we are shaping, and are shaped by, a technological apparatus like an online dating system that is designed for profit at all costs, even if it relies upon harmful tropes and ideologies to succeed. Apryl Williams has gifted us research that moves between these frames—the personal and the structural—so we can better understand the implications of a narrowing set of possibilities through digital and statistical matchmaking.

To deploy the "sociological imagination" that Mills wrote about in 1959 requires an intellectual curiosity about the everyday, the banal, the entertaining, the private, and even the most intimate of human conditions and desires. Such curiosity is at the heart of many information and internet scholars, digital sociologists, media and communications researchers, political economists, and psychologists who have been asking hard questions about the role of networked technologies, or "the internet" as we know it, in remaking economies, culture, communities, and individual behavior. These types of scholars know by looking closely at the experiences of people on the internet, and we put these reported and observed experiences in the context of rapid shifts from industrial and manufacturing work to data-driven and technological work, or in the context of structural systems of power and dominance. We look at digital cultures. We study the dynamics of human behavior, optimized at scale by platforms that are small and intimate, or large and encompassing of billions of people. We who work in these fields are often attendant to the profoundly uneven ways that technology is developed and deployed around the world, and we seek to research and write about it in real time. Almost as quickly as we can study and learn, the artifacts of and capital investments in technology shift again.

These scholarly inquiries into digital systems and cultures are important. They explain the contours of history and society that are imbued in the technologies that come into existence. They help us understand the logics upon which some novel technology like dating apps rest, and why it will be used in ways that should be fairly unsurprising, such as to ensure or enforce White supremacist or ethnic purity standards. When Professor Williams asked me to write the foreword for this book, *Not My Type: Automating Sexual Racism in Online Dating*, I knew it would be an important work that looks at the granular, specific ways that online dating companies practice algorithmic (and human) sorting, and it would tell us more about the personal, private troubles we need to understand, like maintaining systems of sexual racism—or even better, how we can imagine dismantling such systems. Indeed, this book helps us better understand the particulars that inform a broad set of digital technologies that are remaking human interaction in an era marked by ungovernable digital automation.

The issues raised in this book are not just about the values and contradictions of people who use platforms. Discrimination and ideologies of supremacy may be a dimension of the cultural values that users of dating platforms hold, but Williams sheds greater light on how algorithmic discrimination is fundamental to the business logics, models, and success of these companies too. There is a business case that shows demonstrable profit, or these practices could not thrive and stockholders would not approve. Williams is providing the details so we can unpack and possibly influence the choices tech companies make. This is the kind of original research that is important to those of us working in the fields of internet and digital media studies, communications, information studies, and computer and data science. By looking at such a popular phenomenon as online dating, we get to see how spectacular and powerful this ecosystem is in influencing our intimacies.

For the technologists among us, Williams has situated human–computer interaction and digital architectures and interfaces as a set of sociological practices that are imbued with a host of power relations by telling us how these systems work. This is often the most overlooked dimension of technology design—the social dimension that replicates harmful practices of racism, sexism, and oppression of sexual and religious/faith minorities and other potentially vulnerable people. For the humanists and social scientists, policymakers and activists, this book is more of the evidence we need to embolden the change we so desperately need in the tech industry. Indeed, an entire cottage industry of "ethical AI" has emerged because of the work of people like Apryl Williams who have shone a light on something seemingly easy and uncomplicated. I am grateful to be in a community of scholars doing this kind of work. It is vastly improving research in the academy and work coming out of Silicon corridors around the world.

What this book also does is the important work of framing the facts, figures, and reports coming from users and makers of online dating technologies. So many people wonder how online dating works, how and why they see the people they see in their applications, and maybe even wonder what "the algorithm" is doing. Here is where Williams deftly deploys the sociological imagination by reminding us that personal troubles must be brought into the public, where we might come to realize that these problems are not simply our own but part of a larger system of oppression. The stories she compiles are the details that illuminate the complicated intersection between individual experiences and histories of structural racism and sexism.

The following passage from Williams illustrates why we need her careful study of online dating platforms and serves as a clarion call to understand these systems in the context of historical racism and sexism:

> Sexual racism existed long before dating platforms came to be. But they hide the overtly racist logics of sexual racism, helping to conceal them as personal choice. Further, dating platforms automate sexual racism, making it hyperefficient and routine to swipe in racially curated sexual marketplaces. Because dating platforms hide the underlying racist sorting and ranking algorithms, people more readily believe that their private racism is a neutral, harmless personal choice with few social implications. Hence automated sexual racism is perceived as more progressive than the outright anti-miscegenation laws, one-drop rules, and racial terrorism that prevented and discouraged interracial coupling in the past.

It is here that Williams makes the mundane, naturalized practice of online dating a matter we should think about more carefully. This book will take a reader on a journey through a history of race and racism, while educating us on how power systems are embedded in online dating applications. I consider this book to be illustrative of the very real and difficult work of making the invisible value structures of algorithmic and machine learning systems visible, at a time when we so desperately need these kinds of data literacies.

Apryl Williams' careful study has been worth the wait and will change the way we think about the racial politics of statistical sorting, one swipe at a time. It is essential reading as we grapple with how everyday entertainment apps are affecting our behavior and worldviews, and how our worldviews are in turn making their way into software design.

Safiya Umoja Noble, PhD

UNIVERSITY OF CALIFORNIA, LOS ANGELES

Acknowledgments

I first began thinking about algorithms in online dating platforms after hearing the cofounder of OkCupid talk about ranking systems and attraction at a conference back in 2015. At that time, I was still a graduate student. As I swiped and clicked my way through matches on various dating platforms, I constantly thought about how those systems might be racialized. Jenny Davis, who also attended this conference plenary and who shared my indignation, suggested "you should write a book about it—but after you finish your dissertation," and here we are. Around that same time, PJ and Jessie Patella-Rey invited me to speak about my budding ideas on their podcast, the *Peepshow Podcast*. I have such gratitude for those friends who believed in this work in the half-baked form it was in back then. Since that time, Safiya Noble gifted the world with *Algorithms of Oppression*, and Ruha Benjamin with *Race After Technology*. Suddenly, my ideas, which I still had doubts about, now had validity. These sister-scholars had given me a blueprint for completing the work I had envisioned. They paved the way with their work and cheered me on with bright eyes every time we had opportunities to speak about it. And when Safiya agreed to write the foreword for this book, I was so honored to continue in this work with her and with all of those who fight for Black liberation, Black joy, and Black abundance.

Over the seven years it has taken to get this book from inside my head to out into the world, I've met many people who have helped shape it—and who have shaped me in the process. As an avid user (and critic) of dating platforms, I was very surprised to have met one of those people on Tinder, of all places. And even more surprised when we held our "deleting dating apps from our phones" ritual together, shortly after we both sensed we wouldn't need them anymore. My partner Jonathon, you have sustained me in many ways through the final leg of this journey—at times, quite literally providing sustenance by bringing tea and snacks to my bedside table, and at other times sustaining my spirit when I was feeling overwhelmed by the immense task of piecing this book together, sacrificing your own sleep to keep me company on the long writing days that occasionally lasted until 3 am. Without you, I would have given up on dating platforms altogether, casting them aside as not worth fixing. But because of *us*, I believe it's worth taking the time to figure out how they can be made better—even if that means starting over with new platforms, new code, and new design that use equitable, reparative algorithms.

And then there are my other partners—partners in love, in life, in joy—who have all also helped carry me to the finish line of bringing this work to life. Of these, I don't think there's anyone quite as familiar with my chaotic writing style as Kendra Albert who served as my weekend writing partner, sounding board, first pass editor, and occasional stand in for Google when I had questions about various interpretations of the law. When we met at the big yellow house where Harvard's Berkman Klein Center used to be located, I knew we'd be friends, but I could not imagine how much we'd learn from each other. Many of the ideas I present in this book, I conceived after our conversations. Most directly, Kendra coined the term "algorithmically conservative," which I use in my Conclusion—an idea that we are both excited to return to when time allows.

Another of these partners in life, Afsaneh Rigot quite literally made it possible for me to do this work. When I first began amassing resources, she sent me a thorough overview of the literature she was familiar with and shared insight about her experience working with dating platforms. Then, she risked her own social capital to introduce me to insiders at dating companies. Without her generosity of spirit, I would not be privy to goings on inside the online dating industry and would have far less to write about. Thank you for being my partner in the struggle.

To the friends and family who have been partners in joy, old and new, who celebrated the drafting of every chapter and every book project update— Adriana, Beatriz, Shantal, Janay, Jess, Nicole, Michael, Émilie, Guadalupe, Gabe, Jenny, Paige, Jari, Amy, Alex, Keesha, Graham, Emily, Mom, Dad, my baby sister Aliyah, and my brother, Aaron—you all have supported me, often reminding me of who I am when I forget.

There are also many research collaborations that have helped me work through the problems in the online dating industry that I write about here but none more fruitful than my collaborative project with Ronald Robertson and Hanyu Chwe. When I first came to them wanting to figure out how dating platforms' algorithms decide who is attractive, I had a clunky project in mind that would rely on users donating their own data they had downloaded from various dating sites. Ron and Hanyu's vision for an audit-style experiment was way more effective than my plan. Our interdisciplinary team pushed the boundaries of how this kind of work is done, and I am forever grateful for the time we worked together.

Of course, my biggest debt of gratitude is to the participants who took time to meet with me and my research assistants, during the height of the pandemic, as most of these interviews were conducted during the spring and summer of 2020. I have such fond memories of our conversations, because often, we were just two people connecting in a world of such uncertainty to laugh and commiserate over online dating struggles. I am deeply thankful to those who shared so freely with me about their experiences and hope that I have honored your words and maintained a narrative that is true to your perspective and experience.

Though I have been fortunate in many ways, I am immensely lucky to have been helped by brilliant students who served as my research assistants throughout this process. Sydney McDonald, an undergraduate at Harvard University, spent a semester transcribing and cleaning interviews while I was a fellow at the Berkman Klein Center. Rachel Keynton, an advanced graduate student in the Department of Sociology at the University of Notre Dame, conducted all of the interviews with White-identifying participants and helped transcribe several of those interview transcripts. Tinate Zebedayo, who was at the time a master's student in social work at the University of Michigan, helped code, amass, and structure my data tables. Lastly, Mel Monier, an advanced graduate student in the Department of Communication and Media at the University of Michigan, helped me in the final stages to get this book to production by serving as my copy editor when I was down to the wire on a deadline.

I am also fortunate to have been well supported by colleagues at several institutions and organizations while I conducted this research. I am incredibly grateful for the other members of my 2019–2020 cohort of fellows at Harvard University's Berkman Klein Center for Internet and Society. We endured a difficult year together, yet Baobao, Mutale, Momin, Leo, Julie, Afsaneh, and I have found ways to meaningfully support one another's work over the years. Beyond that cohort, the community of people at the Berkman Klein Center and the Cyberlaw Clinic have enriched my worldview. And though there are too many to name, you know who you are.

Likewise, my colleagues at the University of Michigan have been generous with their time, sharing insight, reading drafts, and offering feedback where needed. In 2021, though I had just joined the faculty at the University of Michigan the previous year, my department chairs at the time, Lisa Nakamura and Nojin Kwak, advocated for me to take a research fellowship at the Technology Ethics Center at the University of Notre Dame. I was able to draft all but two chapters of this book during that time—a process that would have taken much longer had my attention been divided by the many demands of junior faculty life. It was also during this time that Christian Sandvig helped me find some creative solutions for tech's black box problem by suggesting I look for dating companies' patents. Finding Match Group's patent was a game changer for this work, and I am indebted to Christian for that suggestion.

Some colleagues know how to offer encouragement when needed most, on the long road that is the book-writing process. Hollis, Megan, Devon, Sarah, and Germaine—thank you for being colleagues and friends. Last but certainly not least, in the short time that I have been a Senior Fellow in Trustworthy AI at the Mozilla Foundation, I have had the opportunity to work with some of the most passionate, committed people I've encountered in the tech world. I am constantly amazed by the impactful, behind the scenes work going on at the Mozilla Foundation and consider myself lucky to be part of a tech organization that is trying to move the world toward equity.

Finally, I could not have produced this work without my copyeditors Jennifer Gordon and Stephanie Moodie, my editor Marcela Maxfield, and the entire team at Stanford University Press. Thank you for taking on this project and for believing in its power.

Not My Type

Introduction

In August of 2015, I was in Chicago meeting with several thousand fellow sociologists at our annual conference. That year, everyone was abuzz with statements made by Aziz Ansari (this was before he was "canceled," the first time, for sexual misconduct) at the conference plenary, "Modern Romance: Dating, Mating, and Marriage." I was more taken with a comment made by another panelist, Christian Rudder, cofounder and former president of OkCupid. Rudder joked, "If you think your matches are ugly, it's probably because you're ugly," as he explained the mechanics of OkCupid's matching and sorting algorithm. He stated that matches reflect a mathematically generated score that is a combination of several factors: attractiveness scores, how often users send and respond to messages, and how much traffic a particular person generates on the app. I began to wonder how these scores take for granted the social norms that underlie such sorting. In the simplest terms, algorithms are a set of rules, directives, or mathematic calculations. Online dating algorithms are simply programmed to predict or mimic expected behavior using data gathered about an existing user base. The hidden assumption is that these mathematically based systems can predict attraction and attractiveness, while eliminating, to some extent, user bias. Even if they can successfully predict these socially constructed concepts (which is debatable), should we trust artificially intelligent systems to pick whom we might see on intimacy platforms?[1]

Dating apps are said to mimic modern dating practices. Traditional, offline dating experiences were largely based in networks. Individuals met people in areas that they frequented in their neighborhoods, at the local bar, the grocery store, and so on. People also used to (and still do) date friends of friends. When speaking to some of my senior colleagues about this book, they always liked to remind me that there was more social pressure to stay together in the past. The fact that you had mutual friends in the same networks meant that you had more incentive to try to make it work. At first glance, a sorting algorithm might not seem like such a bad idea, especially when users are led to believe that their matches are curated based on a matchmaking questionnaire like the ones featured on OkCupid and eHarmony. While this is in part true, it may also be desirable to browse through the entire "universe" of users in an area.

Matching and sorting algorithms are designed, to an extent, to replicate these offline dating processes. The early days of Tinder provided an extra layer of "security" in that the user would be presented with matches that had some relation to people in their network by connecting to their Facebook account. The user is led to believe that location parameters can guide them toward either a more traditional experience (if the location settings are set to within 5 miles of where they are located) or toward a less traditional experience (if the user sets their location settings to within 250 miles). The offline courtship and dating game would not traditionally allow for a long-distance first introduction. In some ways, intimacy apps widen the universe of users with whom we have the opportunity to interact. But through other, more opaque processes, dating apps can limit and make decisions for users about would-be partners based on race and attractiveness before the user ever sees prospective partners. These factors restrict whom we would encounter in ways that are unnatural for some.

If your networks are racially and socioeconomically homogeneous (White, heteronormative, and wealthy), you might seek to replicate these parameters in the context of your online dating options. However, if you are hoping that your quest for the perfect match might include all the diversity of the human experience, you might be better off searching elsewhere because implicit in the attractiveness scores used to train algorithms are all of the social norms and beliefs about beauty and desire that society believes to be most admirable: peak feminine attractiveness is White, blonde, symmetrical, and thin. The pinnacle of masculine desirability is White, tall, and athletically toned with a chiseled jawline. In short, an algorithm might decide that you are too attractive (or not attractive enough) for a particular match before you or the person on the other end ever has a chance to awkwardly meet and decide for yourselves—especially if someone in the equation does not exist within the framing of normative beauty and desire.

The OkCupid founder's "joke" actually revealed a harsh truth of the online dating industry. Their algorithms optimize bias and pre-sort potential matches based on your own physical features. Their decisions about whom you might be attracted to (and whom you may attract) are largely influenced by how you look, how attractive the algorithm deems you to be, and how often other highly attractive individuals have interacted with your profile. Of course, in the minds of those at online dating companies, they are doing you a favor by quickly eliminating those you might not find attractive (or whom you may not attract). Their ultimate truth, though, is that sending you too many "unattractive" matches may turn you away from their service, causing them to lose out on profit. The question then is, should they do this?

Though biologists debate the degree to which attraction is biological, social scientists commonly hold the perspective that what is considered attractive substantially differs from culture to culture, across continents. Attractiveness, beauty ideals, and the racialized and gendered norms that coexist alongside and *shape* these concepts shift over time. Moreover, we perform beauty, and the reception of that performance is audience specific. In the United States (and across the globe) racism further complicates beauty and attractiveness norms. Sociologist Patricia Hill Collins argues that the authority to define beauty norms and gender ideas is an instrument of racialized power.[2] Gender scholar Judith Butler further informs that ideals about beauty and attractiveness are entangled with expectations about the performance of gender, masculinity and femininity.[3]

If these socially constructed racialized beliefs about attractiveness, femininity, and masculinity are so deeply entrenched in our society, how can the algorithms that govern our online intimacy experiences claim to avoid them? Or is it the case that they rely specifically on this human bias as a measure for sorting? How do algorithms perpetuate the ideas that undergird our learned beliefs about race, gender, and attractiveness? This book presents a deep exploration of these entangled ideas and concepts, centering on the larger question of how algorithms used by intimacy platforms impact the online dating experience of anyone who is not the archetypal White, male-presenting, straight guy.

The problem, though, is that straight White dudes and White women are the users for whom the dating companies build their platforms, despite evidence that dating sites are increasingly used more by Black users and other folks of color than White daters.[4] Designing for the normative user presents a problem for the rest of us whose experiences differ greatly.[5] One very important difference is how White daters and daters of color experience race and racism while using dating platforms. Most White users of dating apps—whether gay, bisexual, pansexual, or straight—find it acceptable to express racial preference in a partner.[6] In 2014, the most up-to-date statistics provided by OkCupid showed how people tend to select matches in accordance with racial preference. Figure I.1 shows that Black, Latina, and White women rate Asian men as 13, 14, and 12 percent less attractive than other men on the platform, respectively. Black men are rated as 27, 16, and 8 percent less attractive than other men by Asian, Latina, and White women, respectively. Asian women rate Asian men as 24 percent more attractive than other men, and Black women rate Black men as 23 percent more attractive than other men.[7] These numbers demonstrate the sociological principle of homophily—the idea that like attracts like. We would expect members of one racial category to rate more highly the attractiveness of other members of that same racial category.

However, homophily does not account for such strong negative bias against members outside of one's racial or ethnic group, suggesting that racial preference is not meaningless. The first graph indicates that Black women are rated as less attractive by members outside their racial group, while the same does not hold true for Asian and Latina women. This racially

FIGURE I.1   OkCupid match data from 2014, showing how men and women in each racial category rate each other's attractiveness.

2014 OKCupid Match Data

Men Rating Women	ASIAN WOMEN	BLACK WOMEN	LATINA WOMEN	WHITE WOMEN
ASIAN men rating	15%	-20%	2%	3%
BLACK men rating	2%	1%	2%	-6%
LATINO men rating	4%	-18%	10%	4%
WHITE men rating	9%	-17%	3%	6%

Women Rating Men	ASIAN MEN	BLACK MEN	LATINO MEN	WHITE MEN
ASIAN women rating	24%	-27%	-15%	18%
BLACK women rating	-13%	23%	-3%	-6%
LATINA women rating	-14%	-16%	18%	12%
WHITE women rating	-12%	-8%	1%	19%

Source: OkCupid no longer hosts the data shown in the figure, which I originally found at http://blog.okcupid.com/index.php/race-attraction-2009-2014/ The same data are available at Reddit: https://www.reddit.com/r/OkCupid/ comments/n1hdmm/okcupid_quickmatch_scores_based_on_race/

disparate effect is, in part, the result of racial tropes and racist stereotypes that position Black women as hypersexual and undesirable for long-term relationships.

While White people may feel that their racial preferences are neutral, harmless expressions of desire and compatibility, most people of color find these racialized choices to be overtly racist. This kind of racism has a name:

sexual racism. Often concealed as private, meaningless personal preference,[8] I define *sexual racism* as personal racialized reasoning in sexual, intimate, and/ or romantic partner choice or interest. In broader societal context, sexual racism connotes a set of beliefs, practices, and behaviors at the intersection of what is considered acceptable racialized gendered performance. This theoretical framing is important for understanding how dating and intimacy platforms allow sexual racism to flourish because they rely on White normative standards of attraction, desirability, and gender aesthetics to program sorting and matching algorithms. At times, dating companies' attractiveness ranking algorithms even seem to rely on the logics of eugenics: the closer one is to White ideal beauty aesthetics, the higher one's attractiveness score. By concealing this process and underlying logic from users, the companies help perpetuate the belief that there is an unbiased normative standard for beauty and that any preferences we have are morally neutral and should remain unquestioned. Hence, dating platforms automate sexual racism and White supremacist beliefs about beauty and desirability by failing to disclose the use of racialized ranking and sorting systems and by allowing users to target and racially fetishize people of color.

I argue that we should hold online dating companies accountable for their part in automating and legitimizing sexual racism, transphobia, and violence against minoritized people. While online dating seems to be a benign digital tool used to pursue mating, dating, and society's ultimate goal of marriage, sociologists understand that mating and marriage are opportunities for racialized social control (especially within the racial historical context of the United States). Put simply, the political overlaps with the personal in our choices about with whom we date, couple, and partner. Narratives of sexual racism help to define, structure, and justify racial distinctions in other arenas of power and structured social control.[9]

When we think about race and racism in the United States, we must consider the legacy of widespread anti-miscegenation laws that were created during slavery to prevent interracial coupling and marriage. This legal form of discrimination legitimated the prevailing cultural logic of the time that the White race was pure and should not mix blood with those outside the race. Anti-miscegenation laws were directly rooted in early faulty beliefs about biological White racial superiority. Though the 1967 Supreme Court decision in *Loving v. Virginia* indicated that such laws were unconstitutional, these logics about interracial relationships prevail and reveal themselves in contemporary iterations of the White power movement, White nationalist alt-right discourses, and the fear of White genocide.[10] At the time of their conception, anti-miscegenation laws were thought of as morally sound, and it was believed that they promoted a societal good by keeping the races pure. We now understand such rules to be structured, racist limits of inherent human freedoms. I wonder if, in the future, we will feel the same way about matching algorithms that use race and ethnicity as a sorting point in online dating platforms.

In my quest to further understand how race is entangled with attractiveness, desirability, and sorting algorithms, I encountered a popular article in which the author relates learning about how Tinder viewed their attractiveness and desirability.[11] Upon learning how Tinder scored them, they were subsequently horrified about the process, which demonstrated that their perceived attractiveness was not reflected back to them by Tinder's user base. Turns out, OkCupid is not the only company to use a rating and scoring system based on attractiveness scores, similar to that which was outlined by Rudder, OkCupid's founder. In fact, Match Group represents a conglomerate of online dating companies including Match.com, OkCupid, Plentyof Fish, Tinder, and Hinge, to name a few. Though Match Group states that they do not share data across brands for commercial purposes, they do "share data between brands for limited and critical purposes, including for corporate audit, analysis and consolidated reporting, [and] to comply with applicable law,"[12] so it is reasonable to assume that they all use similar matching, ranking, and sorting algorithms as I demonstrate in detail later.

To better understand the rationale behind these automated sorting and matching processes, I read Rudder's book, *Dataclysm*.[13] In my naiveté, I fully expected him to lay out all of OkCupid's matching algorithm secrets. There were no such secrets. Instead, I was shocked by how clearly he was able to demonstrate that race does indeed play an explicit role in users' perceptions of attractiveness. In Rudder's own words, "When you're looking at how two American strangers behave in a romantic context, race is the ultimate confounding factor."[14] Worse, his data demonstrate that it is particularly hard out there for Black women. On average, as OkCupid's most recently released data show, Asian men rated Black women as 20 percent less attractive than other women, Latino men rated Black women as 18 percent less attractive than other women, and White men rated Black women as 17 percent less attractive than other women.[15] These calculations are based on thousands of active OkCupid users that Rudder claims accurately reflect the general population of internet users—except that OkCupid's users are reported to be *more* educated, progressive, and urban than the general internet user. Throughout the rest of Rudder's chapter on race, he explains that although 84 percent of people on OkCupid answered no to the question, "Would you consider dating someone who has vocalized a strong negative bias toward a certain race of people?" their actions substantially differ from their expressed beliefs. To be clear, the question is really, "Are you okay with dating a racist?"

OkCupid's publicly released data show that the number of users answering yes to this question had been declining up until 2013 when we began to see a slight uptick in those responding yes to the question. The commotion stirred by the blog posts and Rudder's book *Dataclysm* caused a lot of people to start asking questions about racism in online dating. *Salon* relayed one particularly insightful interview with Rudder about the racial trends discussed in his book. "So men are sexists, and we're all racist?"[16] the reporter prompted. Rudder responded,

> "The more you look at the data, the more it does confirm the cynics' intuition about humanity. People online are free to act out their worst impulses with very little incentive to act out their best. I guess it just goes to show how politeness or propriety keeps us decent human beings. Offline, society actually has a very good effect on behavior in a very large sense."

Rudder's comment suggests that people on dating sites (people online) are both sexist and racist because there's no one to shame them into hiding these "impulses." In a seemingly deliberate manner, Rudder does not explicitly state that race plays a role in people acting on their "worst impulses." Yet later in the interview, he was asked about which data points were the most significant to him.[17] Rudder responded,

> "Well, the most obvious thing is racial messaging patterns. We asked people about race and everybody is like, yeah, interracial marriage is to-

tally great. . . . We also asked people questions like, 'Would you ever date someone who told a racist joke?' and the answers are very liberal in the way you would expect. . . . But then you go out and look at what people do or who they choose for themselves, and you see that this is just not the case. Race is a huge factor and certain types of interracial relationships—I wouldn't say are taboo, but certainly in the aggregate they are less desirable."

Rudder's insight supports the idea that even well-meaning "liberal" individuals cannot avoid or entirely unlearn socialization that prescribes myths of racialized personal preference.

Unfortunately, OkCupid stopped releasing data-driven reports of racial matching rates in 2014 and has since deleted the original blog post containing this data (see Figure I.1) and the graph of user responses (Figure I.2). Still, screen captures of these reports and accompanying analysis remain in internet infamy. An archived Reddit thread with over 600 comments discusses the racialized nature of match rates at length. One Reddit user commented,

FIGURE I.2   Percent of OkCupid users from 2008 to 2014 who answered yes to various questions regarding dating and racial preferences.

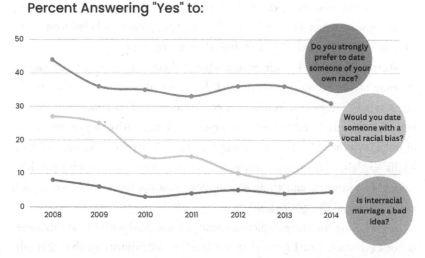

Source: Data were originally retrieved from the OkCupid blog: http://blog.okcupid .com/index.php/race-attraction-2009-2014/ Their blog no longer hosts this data.

"It talks about how it's about racism. Is it racist that I am not sexually attracted to some races?"[18] My undergraduate students who are racially, ethnically, and socioeconomically diverse often ask this question.

When we talk about personal preference in partners, it is important to understand that none of our internal belief systems, personal choices, or desires develop in a vacuum.[19] We are all products of socialization into the norms, beliefs, and ways of thinking of our larger society. This includes whom we think we should *not* be attracted to. Bryan, an interview respondent who identified as Chinese and Vietnamese, told me that his friends told him to stay away from dark-skinned Black women because they were "ghetto" and "ratchet." If someone is repeatedly told by their peers that dark-skinned Black women will act in a certain way, then they will likely internalize that view—often without introspection. The internalization of racial stereotypes may color who we find attractive, both sexually and generally. Of course, for many social reasons, we might seek partners who share political ideologies or religious beliefs. Yet, those social imperatives do not need to exclude potential partners on the basis of race or ethnicity. For example, Spanish-speaking students share that they'd like to date another person who speaks Spanish. This does not have to mean that they only date Spanish speakers with particular skin tones. Having personal preferences for shared culture or values with a person with whom you may potentially share your life is not wrong, but we should ask why some people are excluded from those categories simply on the basis of their race or skin tone.

Returning to the Reddit poster, what if there's just no sexual attraction to some races? Sexual attraction and desire are also shaped by the images, stereotypes, and beliefs individuals consume from their communities, parents, and friends. Further there is no biological imperative to pair with those of one's own race because race is itself a social construct.[20] As Sylvia Chan-Malik explains, "It's important to ask yourself why you like who you like, since this awareness can allow you to move past the flattened, stereotypical meanings racial categories hold."[21]

Unlearning the stereotypical meanings associated with racial categories is not easy work. But I hope that this book will demonstrate that this self-introspection is desperately needed in our dating lives. This task is vitally important because individuals' personally held beliefs about racial preference spill over into other areas of our lives whether we intend for it to or not.[22] Where online dating is concerned, these beliefs intersect with sorting and matching algorithms that are also rooted in racialized constructions of beauty. There is a compounding effect: personally held racial views + algorithmic bias based in historical constructions of race, gender, and attractiveness = a hyperracialized experience for all of us who use dating platforms. But this experience disproportionately impacts users of color. As I began to explore this compounding effect more thoroughly, an experience presented me with a more personal view.

Just a few days before my twenty-ninth birthday in 2019, I had journeyed to California to celebrate with a friend when an excited Tinder match asked if we could chat on FaceTime for a bit, so we could get to know each other. For the record, this individual is a White man, and you'll see why this is pertinent information soon. My friend didn't mind if I took the call as she was also curious about this potential suitor. When the call connected and his face appeared on the screen, I thought to myself, he's a little odd but cute. We'll see where this goes. By the end of the conversation, my attitude had shifted.

We chatted awkwardly for a few moments. My friend interrupted to ask what his name was. I laughingly explained to my match that I am notoriously bad at remembering names and had forgotten his. His response, though, was no laughing matter: "Let's put it this way: you can just call me master." My friend and I looked at each other with the same unspoken thought: things were about to get weird (and probably a little racist). She took the phone from my hand so she could question him directly. "What does that mean? Is your last name Master?" she asked with incredulity in her voice. I chimed in with, "Are you a dom—like the dominant type?" He responded sheepishly, "No, I was just joking." Not wanting to have my birthday celebrations ruined by what I believed to be casual racism, I hurried him off the phone and told him I would call him back when I returned to where I was living at the time, on the East Coast (where we had originally matched).

I called him back for some clarity on the situation two weeks later. I hoped, in vain, that he would offer some explanation for his "joke." I said, "If I ask you a question, can you just be honest with me?" He nodded in agreement, so I cautiously proceeded. "Was that a race joke?" He averted his eyes, looking down, and said, "No, it was just a stupid joke." I pressed, "Okay, but what kind of stupid joke?" He couldn't give me an answer, and with that I decided that the joke was indeed based in the increasingly popular fetish rooted in master–slave sexual role playing. In these situations, I typically delete the offender's number from my phone, report it on Tinder, and block the person. In this case, I was curious to see if he would follow up to try to defend his response in the following weeks. He never did, strengthening my personal feelings and sociological insight about the incident.

I never committed his name to memory and still don't know it. What I do know, based on interviews with seventy-three respondents of color, is that this is not a one-off experience. As I pondered why he might have thought such a joke was acceptable, I resolved that even if the joke had been about any other possible social arrangement, casually telling a Black woman to call a White man "master" is never a good idea and, at the very least, is not socially acceptable. I'd like to think that within the cultural context of the United States, such an interaction is widely perceived to be taboo. Though there are spaces for race play fetishes where people of color grant consent for these interactions, most of us are not willing participants in this sexual taboo. The nature of taboos is that people don't talk about such intimate perspectives during the first meeting with a potential partner. Something must have been communicated along the way that this is acceptable behavior.

Sociologists love to throw around the term "social forces" to connote a vague set of rules, norms, and social factors such as economic activity and systemic structure that exert power on individuals and society. What were the social forces present in the social arena of online dating that precipitated such a joke? Many scholars have argued that the temporal nature of online dating—with a focus on images directing users to make a quick decision based on appearances rather than the entire depth of a person—forces individuals to commoditize each other. When we become commodities, instead of whole persons, others see only our sexual value. Within this framework, the bodies of Black, Latina/o, Asian, Middle Eastern, and Native/Indigenous individuals are often targets for racial fetishization and are used as sites of sexual tourism. This experience economy, a type of social force, can trigger such racialized interactions wherein individuals seek out people of color because they are perceived as offering a fetishized type of sexual experience.

By their nature, online dating platforms show users a wide variety of options that they may not experience in their offline lives, especially if their networks are racially and socioeconomically homogeneous. Some users may be drawn to online dating platforms to explore racial taboos because they cannot find partners with whom to explore these ideas offline.

Black Feminism + Critical Algorithm Studies

In this book, I frame the internet as a network of networks in which users engage with an endpoint that represents an amalgamation of implicit cultural norms and beliefs. Algorithmically driven matchmaking and sorting are part of this system. Using this perspective, birthed from the growing field of critical internet studies, I conduct a deep, multimodal study of internet dating and intimacy applications with consideration given to all of the various inputs and outputs that are involved in this network: developers, technologists, conglomerate corporate stakeholders, and everyday users of these technologies like you and me. I explore the racial and gender biases that are programmed into intimacy applications and platforms (by mostly White programmers) that sequentially turn into expressions of automated eugenics, where the most similar and desirable users are paired together. In turn, I also probe the common and popular culture discourse surrounding the ideas of race, sexual racism, and interracial dating in intimacy platforms and applications. In the words of Jeremy Hunsinger, a scholar in communication studies, a critical internet studies approach is underpinned by intervention and answers the questions: What is the research intervening in? Where is the locus of the intervention? Hunsinger also suggests that scholars must bring forth the implicit framings that guide our work.[23]

Black feminism is the critical, reflexive lens with which I view the problems facing algorithms used in intimacy applications. It offers the hope of intervention for users, programmers, developers, and other relevant stakeholders. Black feminism's main purpose is to resist oppression. Intersecting oppressions, such as the positionality of being both woman and Black, or more apropos to this study, the position of being the least desired online dating demographic for Asian men precisely because they are both Asian and man, necessitate a Black feminist response. In this book, it is my goal to analyze the intersections of race and gender bias within a complicated system of intimacy platforms. One of the core tenets of Black feminism and other Black liberation ideologies is that these concepts actively work to dismantle inequality for all people groups—not just Black feminists. No one is free until we are all free. Hence my intervention works to highlight the combining social processes of marginalization and to position alternative frameworks that may help usher in freedom—bit by bit, swipe by swipe.

Black feminist thought encapsulates a body of critical social thought produced by Black women in response to historical oppression in the United States and in colonized and formerly colonized locales around the globe. Though Black feminist thought predates mainstream feminism, it addresses gaps in normative systems of knowledge because critical Marxist thought (as primarily written by White men and applied to White women) did not adequately address the unique oppressions experienced by women of color. As Patricia Hill Collins notes, "For African-American women, the knowledge gained at intersecting oppressions of race, class, and gender provides the stimulus for crafting and passing on the subjugated knowledge of Black women's critical social theory."[24] My personal approach to Black feminism leans heavily on the principals outlined by Collins in *Black Feminist Thought*: namely that Black feminism works to address the oppression and exploitation of all oppressed people groups—not solely the state of Black womanhood in the United States. As such, I position my critical internet studies approach in conversation with voices from other oppressed groups. I incorporate queer theory, Latina and Latino critical theory (LatCrit), and critical Indigenous theory when discussing the impact of online dating on these groups.

Because one aspect of the complex puzzle of algorithmic bias in online dating includes systems of evaluating attractiveness that are rooted in historical and contemporary representations of women of color as they relate to mainstream conceptions of attractiveness and beauty, Black feminist thought lends itself particularly well to my theorization of intimacy platforms. Traditionally, the American idea of a solid family structure is built on the "cult of true womanhood" or the idea that women should possess four values: piety, purity, submissiveness, and domesticity.[25] Historically, Black women were positioned as outsiders to true womanhood. They were not viewed as fully woman because White owners of enslaved people worked hard to position them as subhuman, providing cognitive dissonance that allowed them to distance themselves from the atrocities being committed under American chattel slavery. Black women were legally considered property and thus were literally commodities to be bought, sold, and traded.

Long after slavery was abolished in the United States, the sentiments and social constructions of Black women stuck around. Similar to the way that cognitive dissonance operated in the days of slavery, prevailing myths or stereotypes about Black women exist to justify treating Black women differently than other women. Collins calls these prevailing stereotypes about Black women "controlling images." Controlling images include stereotypical frames and tropes that you know when you see, though you may not be able to name them. For example, the Jezebel trope relies on stereotypes of Black women as hypersexual, sexually immoral, and exotic (think of nearly every barely clothed Black woman in hip-hop music videos). The mammy trope lies at the other end of the spectrum and includes the belief that large-bodied, dark-skinned women are so devoted to pleasing White masters and employers that they neglect to care for their own families. Further, their dark skin and large body size supposedly make them so sexually undesirable that they are often depicted as asexual (for a historical example, think Aunt Jemima on your syrup bottle; for a more contemporary example, think Madea from the Tyler Perry films). These stereotypes emerging from the intersection of a racialized and gendered bodies also extend to depictions of other women of color. The "spicy Latina" stereotype depicts Latina women who are exotic, curvy, loud, and hypersexual (for instance, Sofía Vergara in *Modern Family*), while Asian women are commonly purported to be meek, submissive, and quiet in public but sexually voracious and exotic in the bedroom (for example, the unnamed Vietnamese sex worker from *Full Metal Jacket*).

Safiya Noble, author of *Algorithms of Oppression*, remarks that these poisonous controlling images and toxic representations of Black femininity and sexuality remain a driving economic force in another algorithmically determined sector: the pornography industry.[26] Mireille Miller-Young informs that the fetishization of Black women, underscored by these controlling images, has created a robust market that relies on the tropes of Black bodies.[27] The large profits from the porn industry spill over into the search results users are presented with on Google. Because Google's search results are driven by profit, not the desire to provide accurate information to users, their algorithms position more profitable search results at the top. Noble finds that these results are often racially biased. In a notable example, she illustrates that a search for "Black girls" returned "HotBlackPussy.com" as the first result back in 2010. Since that time, Google's algorithms have changed to no longer include pornography as the top result. But the example provides ample evidence that Google is profit driven and does not provide "neutral" information to users.[28]

These racialized stereotypes and controlling images also extend to men of color, including the Black brute trope suggesting that Black men are hypersexual, with uncontrollable animalist urges to rape White women. This trope has roots in Reconstruction when racialized stereotypes and fear were used to maintain social control over Black men after the prevailing mechanism of control, slavery, had been abolished. Further, although the Asian American community is made up of fifty-two diverse and distinct ethnic groups, racialization in the United States dictates that these groups be treated according to similar controlling images.[29] Yen Ling Shek explains, "Racist images collapsed gender and sexuality so that Asian American men appeared to be both hypermasculine and effeminate."[30] The "yellow peril" trope frames Asian American men as the ultimate hypermasculine other, driven by desire for communist conquest, and suggesting that, due to their ties and loyalty to home countries, they will never fully assimilate into U.S. society. Asian men were intentionally framed as a threat to U.S. society and to White women in particular: "In order to prevent miscegenation, the intermingling of race, from occurring, popular images of Asian men as sexually deviant, asexual, effeminate, or luring White women to their opium dens were created."[31] These controlling images remain prevalent in today's depictions of Asian American men, though they often take on more subtle tones.[32]

While the analysis of this book does not center on controlling images, it is important to understand that they play a vital role in the construction of what is considered to be attractive in mainstream U.S. society and that they were circulated as means of social control both overtly and covertly in media. Now these controlling images are so normative that they have seeped into internet dating culture without challenge.

Whiteness and Technology

I have used online dating platforms in seventeen U.S. states, seven countries, and on three continents. I considered myself an online dating expert long before writing this book. The curious sociologist in me became increasingly preoccupied with the intersection of algorithmic manipulation and sexual racism in online dating. Is it possible to pinpoint where one ends and the next begins? Probably not. But that is one of the purposes of my exploration: to demonstrate how our preexisting ideas about race are reified through the use of algorithm-driven intimacy platforms in a fluid process that is difficult to disentangle.

To try to untangle where human social behavior mingles with automated sexual racism, we have to understand that the culture in which these algorithmic systems are conceived and implemented is shaped by Whiteness. In his book *Artificial Whiteness: Politics and Ideology in Artificial Intelligence,* Yarden Katz asserts that algorithms that drive contemporary computing systems will always bear the mark of elite Whiteness because these systems were initially created by the mid-twentieth century American military-industrial-academic complex.[33] Due to their origins, algorithmic systems will always conceptualize the normative user as White and masculine. More importantly, social thought around algorithms mimics the ideological adaptations of Whiteness. Whiteness and automation are both contested and adaptive. The labels applied to the science of algorithmic implementation and Whiteness have been redrawn numerous times, especially when their own aims are better served.[34] Algorithmic systems are technologies of Whiteness. And Whiteness is itself a technology of colonial and racist power created to substantiate claims of racialized social order. Thus, systems that automate sexual racism do so intentionally, by design.

Race is also a socially constructed technology.[35] In that way, racism then is a social tool. The ideas that we associate with Whiteness and Blackness are all meaningless if not understood in our particular socio-historic context. The current iteration of Whiteness has been defined by demonstrating who is "not white."[36] All aspects of acceptability in society have been defined by Whiteness, including suitable expressions of love and desirability. Sexual racism is a tool that is used to demarcate the bounds of appropriate White racial politics in sex, love, and romantic relationships. Though we no longer live in a world where racial segregation or outright racism or bigotry are socially tolerable, sexual racism thrives as a last outpost of overt, explicit racist thought—yes, even among liberal-thinking, well-educated daters.

Though dominant political ethos would have you believe that White liberals are sufficiently educated to have no need for the tool of racism, that's simply untrue. Many sociologists and social psychologists have documented that White individuals who believe themselves to be free of racist thoughts or notions of White racial superiority still espouse subtly racist beliefs.[37] This is all the more true regarding sexual racism. White supremacy is at the heart of sexual racism. Central to the idea that racialized partner preferences are a neutral and/or biological fact is the underlying belief that the White race is somehow distinct from all others. Race is not biologically significant, which means that the phenotypic traits that we associate within one racial group can be found in every other racial category. Curly kinky hair is not found only in Black people, and almond-shaped eyes are not found only in Asian people. Yet, the White race promotes the idea that Whiteness takes one form (intentionally and/or unintentionally). In truth, who is considered White is contested and ever changing. Sexual racism is a key part of that evolution: designating who is considered acceptably White and who must remain on the outside of—and in opposition to—Whiteness.

Technology enthusiasts purport that digitizing or automating older social mechanisms and rituals such as dating can rid us of social ills such as racism. But other scholars have already pointed out numerous examples for which this idealist thinking fails to hold true.[38] More to the point, they demonstrate that algorithm-driven technologies and platforms that are part of our everyday lives can and do rely upon preexisting racial biases. Further, White programmers and developers build these preexisting biases into algorithms that control systems, and those systems impact our lives. According to Noble,

> Artificial intelligence will become a major human rights issue in the twenty-first century. We are only beginning to understand the long-term consequences of these decision-making tools in both masking and deepening social inequality. . . . Part of the challenge of understanding

algorithmic oppression is to understand that mathematical formula-
tions to drive automated decisions are made by human beings. While we
often think of terms such as "big data" and "algorithms" as being benign,
neutral, or objective, they are anything but. The people who make these
decisions hold all types of values, many of which openly promote racism,
sexism, and false notions of meritocracy, which is well documented in
studies of Silicon Valley and other tech corridors.[39]

Algorithms play an integral role in many aspects of our lives. From
voting to healthcare to incarceration and enhanced policing mechanisms, algorithms are increasingly incorporated into existing mechanisms of control
in society.[40] Their covert nature and the ease with which they run in the
background of our social media platforms and dating apps can obscure the
fact that they maintain, uphold, and support systematic inequity and bolster
White supremacy.[41] The companies who employ these technologies do so
with relative impunity and without transparency, which is cause for concern.
At the very least, we should question whether or not we, as consumers and
platform users, have the right to regulate how and when algorithms are used
in the technologies we use, especially racialized systems, and particularly in
online dating platforms. Further, we have to realize that what happens in
the tech world ripples into other sectors. Ruha Benjamin, professor of African American studies at Princeton University, argues that tech companies
create social policy through their actions because of the powerful position
they occupy in the economy and within the social imagination.[42] That means
that if online dating companies routinely build and implement racially
biased algorithms, they offer legitimacy for the use of biased algorithms in
every crevice of our social lives—even the most intimate parts. Because the
tech industry is largely unregulated in the United States, it means that these
insidious racially biased algorithms can be, and likely are, shared across
industries—driving social segregation and compounding inequity.

Although many proponents of algorithm-driven technologies argue that
they eliminate human bias, critical perspectives contend that algorithms re-
instate and camouflage bias with shiny new technologies.[43] Benjamin refers
to this obfuscation of algorithmic inequity as the "New Jim Code": "innovation that enables social containment while appearing fairer than discrim-

inatory practices of a previous era . . . [it] entails a crucial sociotechnical component that hides not only the nature of domination, but allows it to penetrate every facet of social life."[44] As critical race theory questions the relationships between race, power, and concepts such as liberal order,[45] critical algorithm studies and critical internet studies examine the mechanisms of implicit normative Whiteness in every layer of algorithm-driven technologies and internet culture. In Benjamin's conceptualization, "discriminatory design" refers to a theoretical perspective that positions the coding process in which social biases are built into technological systems, including the laws and policies that govern their usage.[46]

Algorithm-driven technologies contribute to structural inequity that is made up of many interconnected algorithm-based systems in which individuals are reduced to numbers and data points without regard for their humanity. If it sounds somewhat circular, that is because the process is cyclical. As Kathy O'Neil demonstrates,

> Employers, for example, are increasingly using credit scores [a score that is algorithmically calculated] to evaluate potential hires. Those who pay their bills promptly, the thinking goes, are more likely to show up to work on time and follow the rules. In fact, there are plenty of responsible people and good workers who suffer misfortune and see their credit scores fall.[47]

In short, a credit score is an algorithmically driven assessment of projected performance. The *belief* that low credit scores equate to poor job performance leads to many qualified applications being passed over for jobs. The underlying assumptions that drive this belief are rooted in classical White American, neoliberal bootstrap mythology that suggests individuals should be able to work, save, and earn their way to good credit. This myth of meritocracy ignores that good credit is afforded to those who do not rely on credit cards or those who do not face moments of leaving bills unpaid because they do not have the financial security that intergenerational wealth affords—a safety net. Centuries of legal and political disenfranchisement have all but guaranteed that people of color are systematically excluded from wealth-building tools like home ownership and investing, which means that White credit seekers have been able to accrue creditworthiness through the passing of intergenerational wealth and stability.[48] As a result of financial insecurity, individuals turn to emergency options that often include predatory and exploitative lending, further lowering their credit scores. In this way, algorithms and the employers who rely on them reproduce structural inequity, rewarding White individuals for White privilege.

The insurance industry also has roots in seemingly innocent algorithmically derived assessments of risks and mortality rates. In practice, insurance rates are connected to credit score–generating algorithms that are rooted in structural and historical inequality.[49] Under the guise of proxies for reasonable driving behaviors, insurance companies make judgments about risk based on past credit behavior.[50] For example, "in Florida, adults with clean driving records and poor credit scores paid an average of $1,552 more than the same drivers with excellent credit and a *drunk driving conviction*."[51] These interconnected mechanisms create a web of algorithmically driven decisions that do not consider the socio-historical geopolitics of where people reside. When data about people are amassed, decisions can be easily divorced from the individuals whom these decisions impact.

I argue that algorithmically driven swipe-based dating applications encourage the same type of distance that leaves us unaware of the social consequences they engender. When we treat others as datafied sexual commodities based on limited bits of information we receive from a few pictures on a profile, we are forced to make quick decisions based on the social cues with which we are presented, and race can play a role in our decision making. Dating platforms increase the efficiency by which humans sort by race and ascribe meaning to categorizations by automating sexual racism. Intimacy platforms are profit driven, and dating companies know that the commoditization of sexual racism sells. That's why some dating platforms use paywalls to hide the ability to sort by race along with other categories, such as education and religion.

If we are to ever realize the so-called equitizing nature of the internet, we need to interrogate the implicit biases inherent in it and the algorithms that drive it. Namely, we must recognize that the internet is a space in which Whiteness is the default. All other racial categories are positioned in opposition to Whiteness. In the case of online dating, that means recognizing that all conceptualizations of attractiveness are also framed as they oppose White

European attractiveness aesthetics and mainstream (White) discourse on beauty ideals. In other words, internet culture and algorithmic culture were created by and for White people who have an interest in maintaining the status quo of power relations.[52] Hence, this book speaks to the lived experiences of women of color who are instructed to call White men their master in a trend of commoditized racial sexual fantasy as it also speaks to the idea that algorithms make the consumption of racialized bodies easier and more efficient. These algorithms that we have allowed to occupy such immense presence in our intimate lives automate sexual racism by creating a racially curated sexual marketplace.

Racially Curated Sexual Marketplaces

Racially curated sexual marketplaces are digital spaces where Black, Brown, Asian, Indigenous, and other people of color are commoditized as sexual objects because of their race. All people can shop for particular racialized, sexual experiences. But these automated racially curated sexual marketplaces most often benefit White individuals who will pay to play.[53] David, a White interview participant, shared that he prefers Hinge over Tinder because it allows for racial filtering:

> So Tinder is very like, "Here's everyone. Here's Blacks and Whites and Chinese and all this stuff." And I'm like, "I'm not into like half of them." So most of it was just like swiping just to like spend time. And so that's why Tinder kind of like got thrown out. Hinge was just that much better because it just seemed like a little upper class. Just, it was like a Lexus to a Toyota, I guess.

Though sometimes hidden behind a paywall, racial filters on dating platforms incentivize racial exclusion and/or targeted racial fetishization. These racially curated sexual marketplaces allow individuals who have been influenced by racist tropes to quickly sort and target folks of color based on beliefs that they might be more sexually adventurous. Controlling images present in media that we consume about love, romance, and dating inform our beliefs about who is datable and marriageable whether we recognize it or not. For example, in David's case, though he wanted to filter out Black and Chinese women from his dating experience, he also stated that he had race-based sexual fantasies. He relayed elsewhere in the interview (which you'll have a chance to read in Chapter 3) that his ideal partner would have "big boobs" and would be blonde and fit. In David's *public-facing* life, he was seeking the ideal type within the White racial frame of desirability.

David's story demonstrates an important distinction. Within the frame of Whiteness, personal racialized preference is acceptable, or even encouraged, while seeking a long-term mate. Often White individuals are encouraged by their families and communities to seek partners who are White. Race-based sexual fantasies are relegated to flings or sexual tourism. For many, the racially curated sexual marketplace created by racial filters on dating apps is designed for play and private experiential consumption of the racial other rather than for seeking public-facing, long-term dating relationships. There is no biological imperative to date within one's racial or ethnic group. Personal racial partner preference is shaped by our society and more directly the communities in which we grow up. Hence, racially curated sexual marketplaces on dating platforms extend the normative framing that pure Whiteness is the most desirable dating, mating, marriage, and reproductive outcome. Though interracial dating is no longer taboo, it is certainly not universally accepted.[54] By creating racially curated sexual marketplaces, dating platforms reinforce the idea that racial preference is a morally, socially neutral desire. It also extends and streamlines users' ability to engage in racial sexual tourism with limited social repercussions.

Looking Ahead

I have sought to present a Black feminist, critical internet studies perspective on algorithmic bias in online dating platforms, and this book follows in the tradition of resisting the oppression and fetishization of Black, Latinx, Asian, and Native nonbinary people, women, and men. Toward these aims, I draw from semi-structured, race-matched interviews that I conducted with a research assistant, Rachel Keynton, in 2019 and 2020 with 100 users of online dating platforms (see the Appendix for the demographic breakdown of the respondents). These respondents come from a variety of racial backgrounds, with respondents self-identifying as Black or African American, Native or Indigenous, Asian, Latina/o/x or Hispanic, Middle Eastern, and White or Caucasian. Rachel and I conducted interviews with respondents from all over the United States in both rural and urban areas; we were helped by Sydney McDonald, an undergraduate research assistant, who transcribed interviews as they were completed. I also include data from a social-psychological experiment that I conducted on a popular swipe-based dating application in collaboration with two colleagues, Ronald Robertson and Hanyu Chwe, who at the time of this research were advanced graduate students in the Network Science Institute at Northeastern University. Lastly, my data include a systematic review of patents and policies from Match Group to present the reader with a more thorough understanding of how online dating technologies are automating sexual racism.[55]

Taken together, these sources of data demonstrate that there is indeed explicit racial bias in online dating platforms—both in the algorithms that are used in sorting and within the personal dating ethos of dating app users. But these sources of data are not nearly as meaningful without contextualizing the social world from which racialized algorithmic processes emerged. Hence, this book is arranged in a manner that will allow readers to have a thorough grasp of the background social forces at play and to draw their own conclusions when presented with compelling data. All of the chapters are connected to or support the central theme of this book: sexual racism harms those on the receiving end, and dating platforms automate sexual racism through the use of racialized algorithmic sorting and ranking systems. Further, by concealing the use of racialized algorithmic systems and by creating racially curated sexual marketplaces where people of color are targets of racial fetishization, dating platforms normalize sexual racism.

I begin with a socio-historical account of the legal history of interracial relationships in the United States because these social factors influence our contemporary views about attraction and acceptable gender performance as it relates to desirability. Moving on to algorithm-driven dating platforms, I show how they are automating existing, historical sexual racism through structured gamified interfaces, automated eugenics, and the illusion of racial neutrality in matching algorithms. This is followed with an in-depth examination of the myth of race-neutral personal preference and racialized beliefs about interracial dating based on interviews with twenty-seven self-identified White/Caucasian users of online dating platforms. These interviews, conducted by my White–identifying research assistant, Rachel Keynton, present an unfiltered view of the logics of sexual racism, demonstrating that sexual racism is not simply a product of algorithmic dating technologies but an individual belief system that converges with covert (and, at times, overt) White supremacist logics.

I then amplify the voices of users of color as they describe encounters with racism, discrimination, xenophobia, and fetishization. I use data from seventy-three interviews conducted with frequent users of online dating platforms who identify as Black/African American, Latinx/Hispanic, Indigenous/Native, and Asian to clarify how intimate racialized views, choices about interracial dating, and racial bias in automated sorting converge to produce lived experiences of sexual racism for users of color.

Next, I look at incidents of violence of racial fetishization discussed by those I interviewed for this book. In this chapter, I focus on safety mechanisms available to users of dating and intimacy platforms and call for expanded protections to minimize harm for all users, not just normative White users. While my ultimate goal in conducting this research is to amplify the voices of marginalized users and help readers to become more informed about their own biases, a secondary goal is to hold online dating companies accountable for their part in continuing to create environments where racial bias thrives.

This work concludes by highlighting the resiliency of people of color who use dating platforms, while also asking why they must be resilient. In this final word, I lean on Ruha Benjamin's framing of the New Jim Code to discuss how everyday technologies contribute to social inequity.[56] I also rely on my colleague Afsaneh Rigot's formulation in *Design from the Margins* to craft strategies for activating change in system design.[57]

My hope is that our evaluation of online dating includes a close and critical examination of the technologies that govern the process and the social forces that guide our interactions with each other. I invite readers to think beyond traditional boundaries of algorithm studies by asking how the automating of sexual racism contributes to racial processes in the United States, including the racialization of dating. I also encourage readers to reflect on the implications of racial preference in dating as it speaks to dominant racial attitudes in the United States. Finally, I invite readers to ask if the ease and convenience of online dating is worth the harms caused by the processes that are automating sexual racism.

ONE

A New Sexual Racism?

In an interview, Kevin a self-identified Asian man, shared,

> A lot of people conflate being Asian with like, K-pop artists, and I'm not
> even Korean. I'm actually Chinese myself, so it's kind of weird because
> it's like usually the attention is flattering, but every time it's like—they're
> not trying to get to know me as a person, it's just like, "Oh, you're Asian,
> you must like this Asian thing," or "Oh, you're Asian, you must have a
> small penis."

When I probed a bit more, Kevin confided that he often confronts stereotypes about his penis size and believes that is a reason why he does not receive
more matches on dating platforms. Kevin's perspective affirms numerous
studies about perceptions of Asian masculinity.[1] Informed by this scholarship, I believe that there's more to the discrimination he faces as an Asian
man on dating platforms. Because Kevin is not a White man, his performance of masculinity will always be questioned, notated as non-normative
when compared to others on dating platforms. Kevin's experience highlights
the need for an intersectional approach to sexual racism because he is othered not solely on the condition of his non-Whiteness. His non-Whiteness

converges with existence in a body marked by a non-normative representation of masculinity; hence how we view gender and race are both central to understanding sexual racism.

What Is Sexual Racism? An Intersectional Response

In its simplest form, I define *sexual racism* as personal racialized reasoning in sexual, intimate, and/or romantic partner choice or interest. Yet, the lived experiences of the people I interviewed for this book demonstrate that sexual racism is experienced at the intersection of stereotypes about persons with "ethnic" phenotypes and how they are believed to adhere to masculinity and femininity scripts. In broader societal context, sexual racism connotes a set of beliefs, practices, and behaviors that demarcate and define acceptable racialized gendered performance. This theoretical framing is important for understanding how dating and intimacy platforms allow sexual racism to flourish because they rely on simplistic normative standards of attraction, desirability, and gender aesthetics to guide how sorting and matching algorithms are programmed. In this chapter, I explore seemingly neutral boundaries of personal choice and desirable physical aesthetics that inform individual user preferences and the feedback loop this presents for algorithms used in dating platforms.

Foundational to sexual racism is that Whiteness is always defined as the normative expression of sexuality, healthy desire, and acceptable gender role tropes. Because race and gender are both societally constructed ideas, they are always changing. Hence, what constitutes sexual racism is also changing. At the core of these practices are implicit and sometimes explicitly stated racialized beliefs about how women, men, and nonbinary people perform femininity and masculinity in relation to their perceived racial identity. This performance is always also marked by its relationship to the standard of White masculinity. Sexual racism enacted on dating platforms reproduces racial and gendered hierarchies that exist in other areas of society.[2] Sexual racism is a covert choice that appears to reside at the level of personal preference about phenotypical features such as skin tone, body size, lip thickness, nose width, eye shape, penis size, and the size of one's behind. As another interview respondent said, "Everyone's got a type." While it may be true that we are drawn to some physical features more than others, it is a myth that patterns of desirability are innate. Our so-called personal preferences are very much shaped by the beliefs about racial and gender politics of our communities, families, and friends.

Gender and race are both historical and ongoing sites of social domination and inequity. Using an intersectional perspective to untangle how our personal choices collide with larger forces of structural racism and sexism presents a clearer view of the processes that allow sexual racism to flourish on dating platforms. The matrix of domination as defined by Patricia Hill Collins is a complex social system of privilege and power.[3] I like to think of it more as a web because the domains of power in which social domination and oppression are experienced are interconnected and exert social pressure on individuals and social structures. I use the four domains of power— interpersonal, structural, hegemonic, and disciplinary—to situate how sexual racism impacts us all, on dating platforms but also in other aspects of our everyday lives. Scholars often use Gramsci's concept of hegemony to convey the "winning and holding of power" and the use of that power to subordinate, control, and regulate cultural meaning.[4] Sexual racism is an expression of a dominant cultural meaning about race and gender. Racialized meaning has been assigned to femininity and masculinity. Concurrently, meaning and value about racialized bodies as they exist within a particular gender is also implicitly understood. Social forces of power have created hegemonic or totalizing, racialized scripts about gender performance that deeply permeate our perceptions of each other in contexts of dating, intimacy, and marriage.[5]

Sexual racism is thus rooted in the matrix of domination and oppression in that suitors make choices about potential marriageability and desirability based on whether the person on the screen before them can conform to societally constructed racialized and gendered expectations of masculinity, femininity, desirability, and attractiveness. That is why when one is suspected to deviate from traditional racialized gender scripts, individuals typically respond with racist or misogynistic remarks.[6] For example, in Frances Shaw's review of misogyny in online dating spaces, one man repeatedly sent "Bitch

I said hi" when women did not respond as quickly as expected—because racism and/or misogyny are attempts at reinstating traditional racial and gender power differentials.[7]

Some groups, more than others, are routinely reminded that they do not conform to gender role expectations. Asian men are believed to have particular racial traits that would preclude them from performing the expected American idealized masculinity, namely the prevailing stereotype that Asian men have small penises and tend to be less muscular, less dominant, and unassertive.[8] On the flip side, Black men are believed to deviate from these same gender role scripts in almost the opposite manner. They are perceived to be too sexually aggressive with sexual appetites that are beyond control and without constraint, and with large penises capable of destructing White virtue.[9] In both cases, assessments of Asian and Black masculinity are measured against the standard of White heterotypical masculinity in the United States. A man cannot be so feminine that he lacks heteropatriarchal Christian standards of being the head of the household, but he also cannot be so sexually aggressive that it might lead him to be a reckless adulterer.[10] Hence, the only way to win at performing masculinity in Western contexts is to get as close as possible to straight White heteropatriarchal performances of masculinity. Suitors on dating platforms subconsciously (or consciously) assess a potential match's ability to conform to the scripts of traditional masculinity or to the cult of feminine virtue, and both are results of the totalizing power of White racial framing.[11]

Though it may seem overly simplistic to reduce sexual racism to one's limited ability to adhere to prescribed gender roles, that is because racism often appears to be a non-factor. In the case of sexual racism, we have been led to believe that people simply have innate attractions and desires that are unchangeable. The truth is that what we believe to be desirable is shaped by our society—a society that relies on racist thought to uphold White normative belief systems. Sociologist Joe Feagin argues that White Americans have, for four hundred years, established the rules of social life as well of those of political and economic power.[12] This means that Whiteness or the ideals of White superiority have deeply permeated values central to American life. There is an ever-present racist undercurrent that works to maintain White supremacy—even (or especially) where gender and politics of desirability are concerned. Online dating platforms may mask these racial politics through the allure of playful elements, but the undercurrents of sexual racism have always been present in society.

Virginia Ain't for Lovers—Sexual Racism Yesterday and Today

There is a long history of legal and extralegal attempts to define and constrain gendered expectations as they converge with race. In the past, there were explicit campaigns to portray Black people as savages in order to define the White race as ethically and morally superior.[13] By framing Black enslaved people as sexual savages, devoid of impulse regulation, White owners of enslaved people perpetuated the ruse that they were socially and biologically superior. The same reasoning was applied to most acts of imperialist or colonial domination and elimination, of which we are now all too familiar, including Native and Indigenous peoples in the United States, Mexico, and Canada, throughout Central and South America, Asia, and Australia as well as Black people in Africa and throughout its diaspora.

During the trans-Atlantic slave trade, forced intraracial and interracial rape of Black individuals (men and women) was perpetrated by owners of enslaved people under the guise of economic incentive—to grow a labor force.[14] These practices were widespread and normative. Under the faulty logics of eugenics, "the best" individuals, with the ideal physical physique and most successful reproductive histories, were forced to "mate." Or, in other cases, owners treated Black women who were enslaved as property and used them to satisfy sexual desires as they saw fit, later selling off their own offspring to increase profit.[15] This subjugation supported slavery as an economic force and introduced Whiteness as the hegemonic standard through routine sexual terrorism. After slavery, the legitimate means of forced intraracial rape were limited. However, rape of Black women and men largely continued as a method of maintaining social control during Reconstruction, along with lynching.

White men routinely raped Black women and men as a practice of demonstrating dominance and, in an attempt to justify extralegal lynching and other forms of racial terrorism, they also spread the myth that White women were routinely raped by Black men.[16] In public displays, Black men were murdered, hanged, and/or mutilated, often with their genitals cut off and distributed to crowd members (including young children) for souvenirs. These public acts of racial terrorism served to remind Black onlookers of their precarity in the moment but also symbolized White hatred for Black sexuality.[17] Specifically, the physical act of cutting off genitals served to remove the perceived threat of Black sexuality and masculinity.

During the period of widespread slavery, Reconstruction, and subsequent periods of extralegal lynching, the early seeds of contemporary sexual racism were sown. Prevailing thought of the day dictated that Blackness occupied an inherently evil type of sexuality. Lynching operated as a method of social control for Black observers but also for White participants. Witnessing such violent outcomes for violators of the social rules prohibiting interracial relationships meant that even White sympathizers might be too scared to speak out about the current logic of sexual racism. Further, the collective consumption of lynchings ensured that all participants took part in the rituals and beliefs communicated by the brutal act—ultimately providing further impetus for the narrative of White supremacy.

Even before the time of widespread lynching as a mechanism of social control, there was already federal and state-level legislation that attempted to define and demarcate boundaries of acceptable racialized sexual attraction. As early as 1691, a Virginia law prohibited interracial marriage: "As long as there are negro slaves in Virginia and bad White women, we shall have a free mulatto population."[18] Notice here how morality and racialized sexual politics are conflated. Good White women do not have sex with Black people—only bad White women engaged in interracial sexual relations. The law goes on to say:

> For prevention of that abominable mixture and spurious issue which hereafter may increase in this dominion, as well by negroes, mulattoes and Indians intermarrying with English or other White women by the accompanying with one another . . . and any English woman being free shall have a bastard child by any negro or mulatto she shall pay the sum of fifteen pounds sterling . . . or be disposed of for five years . . . and such a bastard shall be bound out as a servant.[19]

The state and social organizations have always had an interest in defining the rules of sexual racism in order to maintain the myth of White supremacy.[20] Importantly though, there is little mention of punishment for men in these laws, as was often the case because the emphasis was put on women to be virtuous. Purity, civility, and desirability have always been both racialized and gendered. Hence, when we think today of who is considered desirable (and how dating platforms determine desirability scores), we should think about why a certain aesthetic or gendered preference is regarded as more desirable than another.

The cult of true womanhood dictated that women must conform to prescribed social standards of piety, purity, submissiveness, and domesticity to meet the performance of true womanhood.[21] These ideals were (and still are) ascribed by White racial framing.[22] At the time that these standards were at peak popularity, they could only be performed mostly by the rich. Yet, emerging middle-class and working-class White women were encouraged to conform to these just-out-of-reach standards. Because only a few could attain that standard, a focus on Black women's sexuality emerged as a way to conceal gendered power dynamics that impacted all women.[23] Simultaneously, Collins argues, citing Barbara Omolade, that Black women's sexuality has been legally constructed as public property. The resulting controlling images or racialized and gendered myths about women of color still linger today.

> "White men used their power in the public sphere to construct a private sphere that would meet their needs and their desire for [B]lack women, which if publicly admitted would have undermined the false construct of race they needed to maintain power. Therefore, the history of [B]lack women in America reflects the juncture where the private and public spheres and personal and political oppression meet."[24]

Accordingly, sexual racism also lies at the juncture of personal, private, public, and political power in the matrix of domination.

The *interpersonal domain* of power speaks most directly to sexual racism as it is experienced in our intimate and romantic lives.[25] The interpersonal domain of power refers to how our experiences, values, and ideals exert power and subordination over others. Much of our social lives are communicated nonverbally through contextual understanding of symbolism and meaning. There was not a collective memorandum that Whiteness is to be desired, but, as stated previously, our cultural meaning dictates that Whiteness is the clean, virtuous, desirable normative standard. When we act on these implicit norms and beliefs through everyday interactions, we reaffirm and further normalize them. In doing so, people in the dominant group can oppress or discriminate against those in marginalized positions. In intimacy, and on dating platforms, this looks like dating profiles that say "no fats, no femmes, and no Blacks or Asians" (referring to a sexual or romantic preference for normative bodies, a masculine performance of gender, and a preference for everyone but Black and Asian people).[26] Alternatively, this can look like a fetishization of Black and Latina women for their figure (an aside, not all Black and Latina women have curvy figures!). Because women of color are treated as sexual commodities rather than human beings with full emotional capacity, power is exerted on them within the interpersonal domain of power. This is not to say women of color do not resist this aspect of sexual racism. Yet, these micro-level expressions of sexual racism contribute to alienation of self and may result in negative health outcomes for people of color who use online dating platforms.[27]

The *structural domain* of power organizes oppression and discrimination in society. Local, state, and federal governments contribute to shaping institutions that subordinate people with marginalized identities.[28] The structural domain pertains to sexual racism because of centuries of state-level effort to define and limit sexual relationships along racial divisions. The earliest U.S. Americans explicitly worked to maintain separation of races in public and private spheres.[29] Anti-miscegenation laws were widely observed in the United States until *Loving v. Virginia* in 1967 established such laws as unconstitutional. Now, many celebrate Loving Day in remembrance of that victory but also as a reminder about how the government limited human freedom to choose whom people could marry (based on race).

Yet this celebration belies the racist, insidious truth: that the effort to curtail interracial relationships was largely an exercise in eugenics. The desire to limit interracial marriage and sexual relations was about maintaining racial purity as evidenced by principles such as the one-drop rule.[30] One drop of Black blood was enough to demarcate one as Black, instead of multiracial or any other way one might choose to identify. During slavery, the one-drop rule was particularly useful to owners of enslaved people but was enforced haphazardly based on hair texture, skin tone, and other phenotypical features. Importantly, an enslaved person's racial status was determined through their mother. If their mother was enslaved, the child was assumed to be both Black and enslaved, no matter the father's racial background. The same was not always true for mixed-race children born to White women, especially if the children were light enough to "pass." Hence Black women were at once othered by their gender and race; and their offspring suffered repercussions accordingly within the structural domain of power.

At the time of the nation's founding, Thomas Jefferson largely advanced myths of racial purity connected to one-drop ideologies. (Perhaps Jefferson was so taken with the ideas of racial purity because he was ashamed of his relationship with Sally Hemings, a woman enslaved at Monticello who bore his children.) One-drop rules were based in the faulty belief in biological distinctions in race. The eugenics movement of the time, including the one-drop rule, gave birth to race-based legislation. One-drop rules were used to determine who was or was not an enslaved person, who could own property, who could vote, and who was allowed certain social mobility. Post-slavery, in southern states, anyone with one-quarter, one-eighth, or one-sixteenth (depending on the state) Black blood was legally determined to be Black.[31] Du Bois wrote at length about the color line because the principles of hypodescent were such a defining feature of the structural domain of power for Black people in his day.[32] I provide this historical account of the structural domain of power because, though seemingly only related to race, the underlying ideology of hypodescent is that race is sexually passed and reproduced. Thus, sex and gender are a central site where meaning about race is negotiated.[33] Sexual racism is firmly rooted in hypodescent ideologies. These rules were the means by which the structural domain of power subordinated women of color (Black and "mulatto") in the past.

The *hegemonic domain* of subordination refers to cultural myths that are regarded as normative and dominant; they go unquestioned. The impacts of previous harms inflicted under the structural domain of power are rooted in our culture and gain popularity through the hegemonic domain. Though it is no longer acceptable for the government to enforce practices of sexual racism, the damage has been done. The foundation has been laid for large conglomerates like Match Group to extend hegemonic power by building White hegemony into algorithmic sorting systems. While we are seeing increasing rates of interracial marriages and partnerships, the undercurrent of a hierarchy of racial desirability remains.[34] Collins's formulation of the hegemonic domain of subordination encourages us to ask about the cultural factors that allow sexual racism to persist as a largely socially accepted personal practice.[35] Media, the internet, religious institutions, schools, universities, and many other organizations socialize us into belief systems.

Over time, racist images were/are accepted as normative—though the past several decades have seen pushback against disparaging, hypersexual representations of people of color in media and in online spaces.[36] Still, feminist scholars point to controlling images that portray and reproduce racialized myths about sexuality and gender.[37] Power is both perpetuated and concealed through existing cultural arrangements, such as the controlling image of the Black mammy, which portrays Black women in caretaker roles who are too busy caring for White children and "too dark-skinned" to be sexually attractive (think Hattie McDaniel in *Gone with the Wind* and Viola Davis in *The Help*). Additionally, consider the angry Black woman stereotype, which positions "angry" Black women as hostile and overly aggressive in a way that marks them as unfeminine and questions why they are always so "angry" about injustices they experience (think Serena Williams in real life media coverage).

The *disciplinary domain* of power manages and reproduces large-scale inequities produced in the structural domain of power and maintained by the hegemonic domain. The disciplinary domain holds large organizations and companies responsible for reproducing inequity through explicitly or implicitly biased practices and norms. Where sexual racism in online dating is concerned, the disciplinary domain of power can be seen most clearly in the design of dating platforms and the programming of their algorithms. In Chapter 2, I present an in-depth investigation of how platforms are automating sexual racism, helping to further normalize it as a reasonable aspect of society within the disciplinary domain of power.

For a brief example demonstrating how tech companies extend the disciplinary domain of power in other areas of social life, I review how Amazon attempted to make their hiring practices more equitable, aided by algorithmic technology. Amazon developed a recruitment tool that used algorithms to sort job seekers based on "optimal fit" for open positions. In an effort to decrease bias, programmers decided to remove social identity categories such as race and gender. By the end of 2015, it was clear that the recruitment algorithm assigned better scores to men and lower scores to women applicants. The system, although adopted to decrease bias, failed because it had been trained on the company's previous years of hiring data, which were over-representative of men. Amazon had inadvertently trained its AI system to prefer men as candidates. This error was so prevalent that the system downgraded applicants with any indication that they were woman or femme identified: a degree from a women's college, affiliation with women-focused organizations, and feminized linguistic patterns. Even with an attempt at correction, the company was so deeply entrenched in structural inequity that the algorithm continuously found proxies for gender, no matter how many times they attempted to correct for it.[38]

The disciplinary domain of power and subordination relies on centuries of systematic injustice within the structural domain of power to perpetuate existing hegemonic structures. The case with Amazon demonstrates that an intervention rooted solely in addressing biased outcomes without addressing underlying structured power disadvantages will always fail. Likewise, sorting algorithms used in dating apps perpetuate sexual racism, but they do not create it. They are, however, guilty of affording an ease of participation. Dating platforms connect the interpersonal, structural, hegemonic, and disciplinary domains of power, reinforcing widespread beliefs about race, gender, desirability, and attraction.

Race in Hegemonic Gender Performance

Where the matrix of domination works well for unpacking the racial underpinnings of sexual racism, I turn to queer gender theorists and other feminist scholars to explore gendered power relations throughout this book. Because bodies are always gendered and racialized, an intersectional perspective elucidates how sexual racism has power to marginalize gendered bodies of color in intimate spheres.

Within the matrix of domination, bodies are often constrained by how others decode our outward expression of gender. Hence raced and gendered bodies have power but are forced to operate within a particular frame of what society affords to a performance of gender as it relates to that society's conception of race and gender. Early sociologists largely examined gendered power relations through a sex roles framework and spoke of gendered performance.[39] I write here about the way we do gender whether by expression or performance, in ways that are real, ascribed, and avowed for each individual. Unfortunately, others do not always evaluate us based on our chosen gender identity. Judith Butler writes at length about the hegemonic power of gendered categories: "the body . . . is a mere instrument or medium for which a set of cultural meanings are only externally related."[40] Bodies are not born with a gender. They are born with genitals that have cultural meaning ascribed to them. One comes to intrinsically know what our culture views as standard performances of femininity and masculinity. People may choose to adopt outward expressions of gender that conform to an accepted gender expression, but how others decode these expressions relies heavily on other social signifiers such as body size, muscularity, and race.[41] Specifically, because of the history in the United States, gender will always be decoded in light of race. Whiteness is the site in which we assume the normative, ideal gender type, whether masculine or feminine.[42] All other expressions of masculinity and femininity will be viewed as existing outside the norm because they exist outside of Whiteness.

R. W. Connell first used the language of hegemonic masculinity when she introduced the concept of multiple masculinities, implying that there are myriad ways to perform masculinity but limited socially acceptable masculinities.[43] Similarly, there are unlimited expressions of femininity, and other scholars have adopted the framing of emphasized or hegemonic femininities to convey that some femininity scripts are preferred.[44] The prevailing expressions of masculinity and femininity are a hegemonic force because they have the power to define what is normative, desirable, and accepted.[45] Gender exists within a social power hierarchy, with White cisgender heterosexual men atop that hierarchy. The existence of hegemonic masculinities and femininities necessitates the existence of subordinated masculinities and femininities—those whose expressions of gender are marginalized. Hegemonic masculinity privileges masculine gender expression that aligns with acceptable forms of aggression, being the best (at everything apparently), individuality, muscularity, and a strong jaw line.[46] Likewise, hegemonic femininity includes feminine gender expressions that align with body work including fitness, hair, makeup, and upkeep of fashion, and also include submissiveness and purity.[47]

Importantly, scholars note that hegemonic femininity is conceptualized as a counterpart to hegemonic masculinity. When women do not conform to hegemonic femininity, they are viewed culturally as insubordinate or as occupying the space of pariah femininities.[48] These alternative femininities appear to be expressions of gender that are associated with traditional masculine roles such as assertiveness, individuality, and achievement. Curiously, the framing of alternative femininities seems to perpetuate myths of binary gender. The ongoing scholarly discussion of hegemonic gender performance is just starting to include the idea that hegemonic masculinities and femininity are themselves rooted in hegemonic patriarchy.[49] In reality, anybody can perform masculinity and femininity. The concepts of the masculine and feminine are fictive binaries created by those with social power to maintain patriarchal ideals.

Even as contemporary gender scholars work to broaden conceptualizations of gender and gendered experience, this work still fails to fully realize how gendered performances are shaped by race. If nonhegemonic and subordinated gendered bodies are disciplined through their gender expression and Black, Brown, Asian, and Indigenous bodies through their racial or ethnic presentation, then people existing at the intersection of these two hegemonic regulators are doubly disciplined. Sexual racism attempts to render alternative gendered bodies of color as docile bodies. Foucault,[50] though rightfully criticized by feminist scholars,[51] provides some tools for understanding how sexual racism disciplines users of online dating platforms to engage with racialized and gendered bodies existing outside of normative desirability standards. Docile bodies are those that are vulnerable to social discipline and sanctioning. For example, a White man telling a Black woman that he's "always wanted to experience sex with a Black girl" represents an attempt at him upholding existing power dynamics—where it is acceptable for White men to demand sex from Black women on their own terms. Bodies are rendered docile, because they may be used or "improved," in this case, moved closer to a desirable and normative expression of racialized and gendered interaction by individuals and/or by a dating site's ranking algorithm.

In this example, the Black woman is viewed as docile as Whiteness tries to discipline her toward an existing power arrangement. When she pushes back, she resists that discipline. But non-White bodies cannot ever be fully mapped to normativity as White gendered performance is the standard of gender normativity.[52] Because normative gendered performance and normative racialized beliefs inform desirability and attraction, it may be appropriate to think of sexual racism as a panoptic form of discipline.[53] On dating platforms, discipline is experienced by people of color when they diverge from normative gender performances. They are met with statements like "You're not as cute as you think you are"[54] because despite self-confidence, they are always marked as other. Non-White individuals who fail to meet standards of hegemonic gender performance are disciplined by other users. And in some cases, repeated discipline under this panoptic force becomes internalized, and users regulate their own racialized gender performance.[55]

According to women of color with whom I spoke, this can look like constructing dating profiles to be as conforming as possible, being sure not to appear as a gendered other. For example, Brianna, a Black woman, spoke about making sure her natural, curly hair was straightened in every profile photo. She also made sure her makeup was not too visible as she felt men desired a more effortless performance of femininity. Although Brianna's hair may be straightened for photos, it will not be straight forever, as is the nature of curly, kinky hair. On the other hand, some suitors may be particularly attracted to natural, kinky hair because it represents sexual exoticism. Brianna provides a simple but compelling example for the case of understanding sexual racism as rooted in both racism and hegemonic gender roles. In her hair's natural state, Brianna is prohibited by her biology from maintaining this conformity to normative (White) gender expression (one in which straight hair is the unmarked default expression of feminine beauty but is largely unachievable without chemical intervention for many women of color). Yet she has been disciplined by other users, dating platforms, and society to believe that she must continue to align with racial and gendered normativity to be considered a desirable match. This internalized sexual racism appears to be relatively widespread in popular culture.[56] Despite its pervasiveness, scholars have not devoted the same attention to sexual racism as other forms of discrimination. In the next section, I consider why this may be, beginning with the question: Is sexual racism really racism?

Is Sexual Racism Really Racism?

Yes.

In a study designed to determine if men with same-sex attraction viewed sexual racism as problematic, researchers find that 64 percent of their respondents felt it was okay to designate racial preference in a dating profile, leading the authors to report that most men in their sample did not feel that sexual racism was truly racism. Denton Callander and colleagues, scholars of sexual health, offer that a key distinction lies in users' understanding of intentional offense: "While the majority of men we surveyed saw racism as a problem on sex and dating web services, over 70% disagreed with the idea that indicating a racial preference online is a form of racism."[57] These scholars reason that because it is hurtful to be labeled racist, individuals may want to distance themselves from the idea that having a racial preference in intimacy partners is racist. In my view, the desire to distance oneself from the thought of being racist suggests that the practice in question is likely racist. According to Callander and colleagues, a majority of their sample were White men.[58] The large presence of White men in the sample compels me to believe that they exhibit White fragility.

Robin DiAngelo's framing of White fragility indicates that White people will do almost anything to distance themselves from the thought that they might be racist. To avoid talking about race, they may shut down altogether when forced to confront their racism.[59] Perhaps the belief that sexual racism is not really racism comes from the same cognitive dissonance that allowed White owners of enslaved people to purport that they worshipped a loving God who created all of humanity with equality while owning, torturing, and terrorizing an entire group of people based on their supposed lack of humanity. It follows, then, that the White men in their study would feel they have the power to define what is *really* racism, as White men occupy a hegemonic space via their Whiteness, even if they are queer. In the same study, 43 percent of men reported being uncomfortable with indicated racial exclusion in dating profiles (while 46 percent reported being unbothered). Let's take a closer look at the 43 percent who likely represent people of color in their sample: "When these proportions were stratified by men's past experiences of racial exclusion online, those who *had not* experienced racial exclusion were less bothered by seeing it online than those who had experienced it."[60] Of course, those who had not experienced the impact of sexual racism are less likely to think of it as racism.

Callander and colleagues point to education level as a main mediator impacting how individuals perceive distinctions in racism and sexual racism; however, it is insightful that Black and Latino men in their sample tended to diverge from racial tropes while White men tended to enforce them.[61] In related studies, scholars have found that Black and Latino men with same-sex attraction are less likely to ascribe to racialized and gendered scripts, regardless of education level—again suggesting that White people do not think of sexual racism as racism because they do not experience it.[62] Redoubling my point, gay men in Callander and colleagues' study, who lived in queer communities or communities with relatively higher rates of diversity were less tolerant of sexual racism.[63] Hence, sexual racism is more tolerated when most (or all) of one's friends are White.[64] Further, men who more frequently visited dating platforms were more likely to think sexual racism was acceptable, suggesting that users are disciplined by explicit racial sorting practices built into many online dating platforms.[65]

Rather than highlighting the voices of those who have long held power, we should privilege the experiences of those who are most marginalized and harmed by dating companies' choice to allow sexual racism to exist on their platforms.[66] Outcomes of sexual racism, like many other facets of racism, can have negative impacts on users' mental and physical health, a conversation I return to in Chapter 4. Many social scientists have documented the negative mental health outcomes users experience when confronted with sexual racism. Khoa Phan Howard found that Asian men experience an overwhelming amount of sexual racism in the gay dating arena, both online and offline. He and several other scholars argue that these experiences lead to lower life satisfaction and lower self-esteem for Asian men.[67] Likewise, sociologists Lawrence Stacey and TehQuin Forbes report that Black men feel dehumanized when they are fetishized in online dating communities.[68] Men in their study also reported that racial fetishization prevented them from entering into genuine connections with other users and that they were unable to escape racial stereotypes.[69]

Scholars across the social sciences report that repeated experiences of sexual racism increase psychological distress, characterized by increased presence of mood or anxiety disorders, reported substance abuse issues, and unhealthy eating behaviors and/or excessive exercising.[70] Perhaps the most concerning impact of sexual racism is that repeated encounters may influence individuals to be more sexually risky to mitigate perceived disadvantage of being a person of color.[71] Risky sexual behavior includes unprotected intercourse and unsafe physical meeting locations.[72] These practices of negotiated risk were associated with daters of color across gender and sexual orientation. If these practices cause so much cross-cutting harm, why then does society continue to treat sexual racism as though it is a harmless matter of sexual choice?

My response is that color-blind narratives that guide much of racial discussion in the United States also shape our ideas about sexual racism. Sociologist Eduardo Bonilla-Silva writes in *Racism Without Racists* that over time, racist beliefs and actions have become less overt, and explicit mechanisms of racial social control have become less societally accepted.[73] Yet, individuals still manage to hold these beliefs—and convey them to others using coded language or, in Bonilla-Silva's framing, language of color-blind racism. The social forces that prescribe White beauty ideals can no longer advise Black women to bleach their skin, as newspaper ads did in the 1950s and 60s. Today, Black women have mastered "laying their edges," a practice that involves flattening naturally kinky, curly hair that frames the face so that it appears to be wavy—inching them ever so slightly closer to White beauty and desirability standards. While sexual racism seems to be the last stronghold of acceptable racialized discourse, even these practices can be masked on digital dating platforms and in the larger societal conversation about interracial dating.[74] When individuals quietly explain racialized beliefs to partners and close friends, they use a color-blind ethos to perform acceptably racist language.

For example, instead of outright racism of the past, such as antimiscegenation laws, people indicate that their preference for White partners and friends is "just the way things are."[75] This belief, that there is some natural order that compels daters to stay inside racial lines, is one of four frames outlined by Bonilla-Silva. Abstract liberalism, naturalization, cultural racism, and minimization of racism are all strategies that are used to indirectly talk about race and provide seemingly race-neutral reasoning. Abstract liberalism involves using ideas associated with political liberalism (myths of meritocracy and equal opportunity) in an abstract way to explain racial matters. For example, one respondent told my research assistant Rachel, "I don't know, I just feel like Black people just don't work as hard," when she was asked why she was not comfortable dating Black men. Implied is the idea that Black people are lazy and that if they worked harder, they could get ahead. Of course, this reasoning does not take into account the many social structures that inhibit equity for Black men. Instead, this statement relies on the myth of meritocracy to drive the narrative that if anyone works hard enough, the person can achieve society's measures of success.

The next frame, naturalization, allows White people to explain away racial phenomena by suggesting that division is a natural occurrence. For example, another respondent shared: "My parents never said I couldn't date anyone of a particular race, I just always saw people matched up . . . like it makes sense if you think about it. Like attracts like." Hidden here is the belief that, logically, one would only choose those who are like oneself racially. Another frame, cultural racism, relies on culturally based arguments to explain the standing of minorities in society; one such example is the idea of Black women having too many children, which forces them to become dependent on food stamps. Implied here is that Black women have uncontrolled sexual appetites—a long-held and often repeated stereotype that frames Black women as welfare queens.[76]

Lastly, the minimization of racism frame suggests discrimination is no longer a central factor that impacts minoritized people's lifetime outcomes or standing in society. This includes sentiments like "Slavery was so long ago" and "White people living today shouldn't have to pay for what our ancestors did" and "Black people living today aren't slaves, so who cares?"[77] Slavery, in many forms, still exists today and deeply impacts communities of color.[78] Further, the U.S. American slave trade ended relatively recently—officially in 1865, but as many historians document, its unofficial end can be dated well into the early 1900s.[79] Some find that peonage, a form of entrapped labor based on falsified labor contracts needed to pay off debt outlawed in 1867, can be documented as recently as 1963.[80] It is simply untrue that slavery ended so long ago as to have no repercussions for U.S. society. In reality, the United States was built and developed by slave labor but largely excluded Black descendants of enslaved people from fully experiencing the benefits of freedom (voting 1965; admission to desegregated schools and universities 1954; and interracial marriage 1967) until relatively recently. The language of color-blind racism conceals inconvenient truths about the origins of many race-based social inequities and repackages them as nominal slights against people of color that should be disregarded.

Though my focus is not on using the frames of color-blind racism to analyze my interviewees' responses, I find them useful for contextualizing how sexual racism exists just below the surface in the interactions described by my respondents. At times, individuals I interviewed communicated that they felt an interaction was racist though the person they were involved with did not explicitly use racist language. All of these frames can be observed throughout responses from those I interviewed across racial groups. Even folks of color have internalized some of these color-blind racist frames and use them to explain why they are not comfortable dating other people of color.

I want to linger for a moment on the naturalization frame because this rhetoric is so commonplace; it deeply pervades all levels of society but especially tech culture, which, of course, influences those who write code for the digital dating platforms we use. As Bonilla-Silva explains, naturalization allows individuals to reason that racial divides are just the natural, biological order of the universe.[81] In fact, racialized distinctions were invented by the White ruling class to justify slavery, colonization, and imperialism. With this myth being so deeply engrained globally—that differences in race are natural—it is not an aberration that programmers and computer scientists would write code with these beliefs in mind.[82] In what appears to be contradictory logic, White people use racial myths to justify the idea of nonracialism: if the differences between races were always present and biologically drive us to seek out those like us, then it cannot be racist to lean into racist preferences in our intimate lives. For example, many data and network scientists (who often implement code for dating companies) rely heavily on the idea of homophily.

When sociologists Paul Lazarsfeld and Robert Merton first introduced the idea of homophily in social science, they described a social process whereby individuals aligned along similarities in social life—such as political views, religious beliefs, and economic status— and in marriage, mating, and dating.[83] In the 1950s, this was probably truer than it is now as technology has greatly expanded our capability to seek out and learn from individuals who differ from us.

But the explanatory power of homophily has become a favorite tool under naturalization framing. In their book, *The Dating Divide: Race and Desire in the Era of Online Romance*, Celeste Curington, Jennifer Lundquist and Ken-Hou Lin provide ample evidence countering the naturalization argument that homophily drives sexual racism in dating. According to their data, Whiteness is the key indicator of the number of matches a person using an online dating platform will receive—not the principle of like attracts like:

> Instead of being disregarded by minority daters, we find that Whiteness provides men great advantage in the world of online dating. The pervasiveness of White desire also shows us that racial preference in sexual marketplaces is not merely personal. These "preferences" largely reflect the history of racial oppression and separation . . . underscoring how the legacy of state inference in intimacy continues to uphold White dominance. White masculinity and femininity are seen as right, attractive, and good, while non-White, regardless of gender, is constructed as unattractive.[84]

These findings—that Whiteness is the main desired category in dating— are not unique to their rigorous study of a large mainstream online dating platform. Other minoritized daters generally stuck to the rule of homophily, preferring those of their own racial or ethnic group, with one exception: minoritized daters preferred White matches over their own racial or ethnic group.[85] Another group of studies additionally demonstrates that, at times, minoritized daters prefer Whiteness (expressed through colorism) within their own racial or ethnic groups. Across racial and gender groups and sexual orientation, internalized sexual racism has disciplined daters to desire Whiteness above all else.[86]

~~Digital~~ Sexual Racism

Digital sociologists, those who study how society works in light of digital technologies and culture, largely hold the view that social media, the internet, and digital technologies extend our social lives. Some scholars have adopted the perspective that the advent of online dating platforms has birthed a new kind of sexual racism—*digital* sexual racism.[87] Sociologists Curington, Lundquist, and Lin rightfully argue that "online dating allows people to express sexual preferences for Whites or Asians or Blacks without public judgement, leading to a new form of digital-sexual racism."[88] Yet, I reject the recent inclination to attach the term "digital" to existing sociological phenomenon to explain how the rise of digital life and culture have influenced longstanding social forces. Digital technologies do not fundamentally change the processes of socialization: how we come to know implicit norms or values; how explicit beliefs are passed down within families, churches, and communities; or how individuals come to understand their own conception of self or other aspects of their identity. However, digital technologies afford greater access to a wealth of socializing stimuli much more quickly.

To explain further, sociologists within a particular school of thought, symbolic interactionism, think of other members of society as a mirror that reflects back to us our notion of the self. Our "selves" and our identities change all the time. The self is not static because we are always taking in and processing bits of information that we then act on. Digital life means that we have a much larger mirror, and we get input about our beliefs and values from a much larger group of people, allowing the agents that socialize us to be a much larger group of people in society. When it comes to sexual racism and online dating, I maintain that online dating platforms and apps do not create a new type of digital sexual racism; they simply extend the reach of sexual racism and make it easier to enact through processes of automation.

Where Curington and colleagues see this practice as new, I frame it as the same old practice of sexual racism rooted in the matrix of domination that has worked to disenfranchise people of color throughout U.S. history.[89] While our framings of the "digital" nature of sexual racism may diverge, our observations about the processes of sexual racism in online dating platforms have much overlap. They contend that:

> The contemporary context of neoliberalism, consumerism, *and* the rise of new digital technologies give rise to a unique form of digital-sexual racism—one that disguises enduring racial discrimination in intimate life as nothing more than idiosyncratic individual preference. These "individual preferences," in the meantime, massively and systematically segregate cyberspace, reinforce categorical thinking, and police digital self-presentation, all without the need of in-person avoidance and confrontation. . . . [T]his new racism allows users to filter or ignore entire groups of people on the basis of those markers, yet it remains invisible from the public eye. At the same time, the anonymity fosters aggressive forms of sexual racism that rarely occur in face-to-face courtship markets. We call this "digital-sexual racism" a distinct form of new racism mediated through the impersonal and anonymous context of online dating.[90]

I do not refer to "digital" sexual racism throughout this work because I see the root of sexual racism to be driven by the same social forces that gave birth to it; it is a tool of intersectional subordination used to maintain the status quo of White racial purity (though this may not be an explicit line of reasoning for every user), desirability, and racialized gendered politics. Simply put, this is not a new kind of racism (sexual or otherwise). In my view, the value of studying sexual racism in online dating platforms lies within the structural and disciplinary domains of power. Sexual racism exists within each of us. Each of us has the capacity to act on sexual racism or to decide to question and reject those impulses. I argue that dating platforms make processes of sexual racism more covert through automation, therefore affording widespread consumption of sexual racism on digital dating platforms. Dating apps quietly select through either assumed or observed racial biases of users and segregate available matches accordingly. They do this without the knowledge of the user, allowing the user to swipe blissfully in what I call the *myth of neutrality of choice*. This myth of neutrality implies that matches received on a dating platform are based solely on user inputs. This artful myth conceals the darker truth that dating platforms play matchmaker with a faulty set of White supremacist assumptions about attraction and desirability, informed by what are considered to be acceptable arrangements of race, gender, femininity, and masculinity. These assumptions are then exerted onto users, without their knowledge, at times guiding them to encounter sexual racism. Hence, if a user already holds beliefs rooted in sexual racism, digital dating tools help normalize and routinize these beliefs.

A last consideration for the emerging concept of digital sexual racism: I reject the idea that overt forms of racial aggression rarely happen in face-to-face dating markets and that these elements of racial harassment are unique to digital sexual racism. Previous comparative work that includes daters in offline and online settings demonstrates that individuals encounter sexual racism in all facets of social life. These kinds of terrible incidents of gendered, racial harassment have been happening for centuries. Overall, sexual racism is, at the core, a systemic and personal issue. Yet, we cannot ignore the processes of automation built into dating apps that normalize and conceal sexual racism. In the next chapter I explore how dating companies use algorithmic scoring and ranking systems to automate sexual racism. As users and consumers of these technologies, we have the right to demand transparency about how intimacy platforms collect and use our data to generate potential matches. To do this, we, the users, need to know when (and how) sexual racism drives results that are presented to us.

TWO

Automating Sexual Racism

When I first began thinking about the ideas that would become this book, nearly six years ago, I was almost certain that dating platforms considered race as a factor for algorithmically scoring desirability and attractiveness. But over the years, I have routinely encountered the black box problem—online dating platforms do not like to share their data and processes. After that conference plenary in which Christian Rudder, the cofounder of Ok-Cupid (now part of Match Group), laughingly exclaimed, "If your matches are ugly, it is probably because you're ugly," I became obsessed with uncovering the secret of how the algorithms determine who is ugly. When I found out, I wished I didn't know the truth.

Austin Carr, a journalist at *Fast Company*, was shown his "desirability" score during a visit to Tinder's offices while gathering information for a story on the company's then-CEO Sean Rad. He also wished he hadn't bothered to ask when he was told that his score of 946 put him at "the upper end of average." As Carr discovered, Tinder uses an Elo (or ELO) scoring algorithm, which is traditionally used to assess the skill level of players relative to other players where there must be an ordered hierarchy. In other words, one may achieve a better ranking if one skillfully plays the game. During Carr's visit,

Tinder's vice president of product compared the ranking system with playing *Warcraft*:

> "whenever you play somebody with a really high score, you end up gain-ing more points than if you played someone with a lower score. . . . It's a way of essentially matching people and ranking them more quickly and accurately based on who they are being matched up against."[1]

Tinder thinks of users as players in a game where the goal is to achieve the highest-ranked attractiveness score. A data analyst at Tinder further contex-tualizes, adding that the algorithm should be viewed as a "vast voting system": "Every swipe is in a way casting a vote: I find this person more desirable than this other person, whatever motivated you to swipe right. It may be because of attractiveness, or it might be because they had a really good profile."[2]

Social life is never that simple though, even when we try to make it seem easily quantifiable with science. Our ideas about whom we think is desirable and attractive are largely contextual. And if your context is centuries of de jure and de facto racial segregation and discrimination, that context will cer-tainly inform your beliefs about attractiveness and desirability. The Tinder data analyst who disclosed this information is simply a mouthpiece for the cadre of data scientists and computer engineers at Tinder, OkCupid, and other online dating companies who believe that attraction and desirability can be neatly quantified, that swipe logic simplifies the process, and that "hot or not" ranking algorithms would be the preferred choice of all users.

Although each dating company has gimmicks that attempt to separate their platform from the rest of the pack, most use forms of the same propri-etary algorithms. This is especially true for companies within Match Group that, according to its "Privacy" page, shares systems within the dating com-pany conglomerate.[3] The rights for those outside Match Group to use par-ticular sorting and matching algorithms has been difficult to establish. In what has turned into a drawn-out legal battle (2018–2020), Match Group filed a lawsuit against Bumble for patent and trademark infringement based primarily on the claim that Tinder's swipe logic and the stacking of profiles waiting for user interaction are patented. Bumble responded by filing a coun-terclaim, asserting that Match Group obtained trade secrets from Bumble under false pretenses of acquisition negotiations. One of Bumble's central claims is that the swipe logic and other features built into Tinder should not be patentable in that they do not meet the threshold of a patentable invention. Tinder, of course, maintains that the swipe logic and underlying algorithms revolutionized the online dating space.

Regardless of which company you're rooting for—Bumble or Tinder/Match Group—the larger issue is that the structure of mobile dating interfaces is incredibly similar across platforms. The underlying logics and sorting algorithms are widely used across the online dating industry, whether you access platforms via your home computer or a mobile phone. One thing that Bumble and Tinder/Match Group can agree on is a commitment to maintaining the security of trade secrets. This shared interest is where the monopolization of ideas, tools, and structures ultimately harms users. We cannot know with absolute certainty how dating platforms use our data to produce the playful experience we have come to enjoy or perhaps love-hate but use out of apparent necessity.

In this chapter, I examine the patent that's likely at the center of the Bumble versus Tinder litigation to assess algorithm-based matching and sorting systems. Whether in mobile dating apps or on online questionnaire-style dating sites, these systems are ill-conceived at best and full on nefarious at worst. At first glance, the algorithmic systems outlined seem to meet the intended goal of simplifying the experience of dating for individuals. But in an effort to simplify, rationalize, and increase efficiency, online dating engineers have flattened elements of human sociability that should not be disregarded. By sharing my close reading of Match Group's filed patent, I hope to highlight how racialized assumptions in programming translate to users of color experiencing bias.[4] I also aim to demonstrate how sorting mechanisms explicitly operationalize race, gender, body size, weight, and other factors to determine desirability and attractiveness. Lastly, before we dive in, I offer a note on interpreting patents. Though an item or idea appears in a patent, it does not mean that a company is acting on the ideas in the patent. That being said, most users who are familiar with Tinder, Match.com, OkCupid, and many other online dating platforms will likely readily recognize their user experience within the structures I cover here. Patent applications can represent a certain aspirational logic—an intention or something a company might be moving towards, even if the ideas described within are not currently implemented. So, let's get into it.

The (White Heteronormative) Love Machine

U.S. patent number 10,203,854, "Matching Process System and Method," was issued on February 12, 2019, to Match Group on behalf of inventors Sean Rad, Todd M. Carrico, Kenneth B. Hoskins, James C. Stone, and Jonathan Badeen. This patent was filed as a continuation of previous iterations dating back to 2008. Because this patent was submitted by Match Group, we can reasonably assume that the presented algorithms (coded in the patent as "systems," "machines," and "embodiments") may be used across the companies in the conglomerate, though with varying implementations and iterations. Several matching and sorting systems are covered, and we can reasonably deduce which algorithmic systems are likely implemented in swipe-based systems (think Tinder) versus questionnaire-based dating platforms (such as Match .com and OkCupid).

Because a central goal of mine in producing this work is to encourage Match Group and all dating platforms to adopt greater transparency about how their systems operationalize race, gender, and other identity categories to assign matches, I present several excerpts from the patent, modified only slightly for grammatical clarity. I use brackets to indicate where I have edited jargon for readability. At times, I cut extraneous information (indicated by ellipses). I encourage readers to view the full patent description by searching for patent number 10,203,854 on patents.google.com.

Match Group defines their algorithmic sorting system as:

A method for profile matching . . . [where] each user profile comprise[s] traits of a respective user. The method includes receiving a preference indication for a first user profile of the plurality of user profiles . . . Depending on the specific features implemented [e.g., variations in platforms], particular [platforms] may exhibit some, none, or all of the following technological advantages. Various [platforms] may be capable of dynamically updating match search results based on user activity. . . . In addition, some [platforms] may provide the ability to evaluate the

attractiveness of potential matches. . . . Some [platforms] may be capable
of generating the pool of users based on both explicit and implicit criteria derived from other social networking systems.[5]

If the language seems intentionally obtuse, that is because it is. As my colleagues with expertise in patent law at Harvard University's Cyberlaw Clinic
tell me, patents are written in a way that protects the invention and interests
of the company, by being broad enough to cover a variety of implementations
and abstract enough so it is hard to replicate the invention or product in
question.

By doing a close reading of the language used in the patent, it becomes
clear that these systems of automation are not created in a vacuum devoid of
societal values, norms, and beliefs. Independent of whether Match.com or its
subsidiaries (child companies) implement the systems in the ways described,
the patent reveals the fundamental orientation of those involved in the development of these systems in resolving so-called issues in matchmaking. The
language surrounding the motivation or need for this particular technological innovation reveals that there is socially contextualized reasoning devoted
to thinking about how systems ought to automate social processes.

In the following section, the patent uses language of homophily, "people
having similar and/or compatible character traits and values should be
matched," to explain why a matching and sorting algorithm is needed.[6] Homophily is the belief that like attracts like, not only where social categories
are concerned by also where racial preference is concerned. This covert messaging about how people relate to one another is just of many unnamed
positionalities, on the part of those writing the patent (likely patent lawyers)
that influence the tenor of the overall patent application.[7] This unacknowl-
edged positioning of being an entirely male and majority White leadership
team (probably those who wrote the patent and those in leadership positions
within the company) certainly comes through in the perceived advantages of
automated matchmaking systems:

> While some believe that on-line dating is simply a matter of matching
> supply and demands, there is statistical and empirical evidence to sug-
> gest that successful online dating entails far more. For example, people
> having similar and/or compatible character traits and values should

be matched together. However, effectively linking two participants to-gether can prove to be a challenging endeavor. Coordinating a relation-ship between two like-minded individuals can be a significant chore, as there are a number of obstacles and barriers that must be overcome. . . . Another problem is that search results of these services contain many irrelevant entities to the searcher. This costs the user of the service time and may deter them from continuing through all of the search results. Another problem is that large numbers of unwanted communication re-quests can become a nuisance to the user. Too many nuisance requests may deter the user from further use of the system. Users with the most attractive profiles are oftentimes the ones that receive the most un-wanted attention. If the users with the most attractive profiles cease to use the system, the quality of the user pool deteriorates.[8]

It is clear that Match Group has formulated an imagined user who is highly attractive and would prefer to only be shown other highly attractive users. Further, this excerpt conveys a belief in a predetermined measurable quality of peak attractiveness, demonstrated by their use of ELO, a single axis ranking algorithm to order users' level of attractiveness. In this case, skill may be demonstrated by acquisition of a high number of other highly attractive matches, frequent usage of the platform, and editing or manipu-lation of photos that are used in profiles. Match Group claims to have em-pirical evidence supporting their belief that this ELO attractiveness ranking drives the online dating marketplace. Please note, however, there is little in-dication about where this evidence comes from. The reader is supposed to take at face value that it exists and to trust that this empirical evidence was collected in a way that limits bias.

Social scientists debate the existence of an immutable measurable stan-dard of attractiveness or beauty. Those who purport to have a science about peak attraction are almost always talking about quantifiable measures of beauty rooted in a European aesthetic such as ideal symmetry, a Roman nose, and strong jawline. Beauty, desirability, and attractiveness are socially constructed and differ greatly by context.[9] Even within U.S. culture, there are many different subcultures that ascribe to very different norms about beauty aesthetics. As a Black woman in the United States who has seen a lot of mainstream movies, Bradley Cooper and Ryan Gosling do absolutely nothing for me—even though they've both appeared on hottest lists in popular magazines numerous times. Hence, the writers of this patent set out to solve the problem of being too conventionally (un)attractive according to White European beauty standards. But by doing this, they neglected to consider an age-old belief: that beauty is in the eye of the beholder.

This excerpt also reveals the main motivation for perpetuating hierarchical beauty standards (that are also intertwined with conventional beliefs about how one performs gender): highly conventionally attractive users generate profit for the platform. The online dating industry thrives on keeping highly rated users on platforms and guards those users from being bombarded by individuals deemed less attractive: "Too many nuisance requests may deter the user from further use of the system."[10] Platforms prioritize the user experience of highly conventionally attractive users because, "If the users with the most attractive profiles cease to use the system, the quality of the user pool deteriorates."[11] In short, they believe users are coming to the platform looking for the most attractive individuals (even if the goal of attaining said users is merely a gamified aspirational pursuit).[12]

Tinder notoriously provides economic incentivization to access the most popular users. When a user with a free account swipes right (to indicate interest) on a highly popular user, Tinder at one time prompted them with "You've just swiped on a popular user. Send a super like to increase your chances of matching." "Super likes" boost a user to the top of highly popular users' result match decks, and they are highlighted with a neon blue outline and a star. At the time of writing, users are allotted five free super likes, then they must pay via monthly subscription to continue to use the feature. In this way, Tinder monetizes highly attractive users, underscoring their emphasis on keeping these users happy by filtering out "nuisance requests" from users who are categorized as less attractive. They've also been known to charge more or less depending on geographic region, LGBTQIA+ status, and age (though they've promised to review these pricing strategies).[13]

Most dating platforms can be subcategorized as either questionnaire-based (e.g., OkCupid) or swipe-based (e.g., Tinder), regardless of whether they are accessed via a desktop or a mobile phone application. Match Group outlines several different "embodiments" or online dating platforms. I've included a diagram from the patent (Figure 2.1) to show how the corporation

FIGURE 2.1 Diagram from the Match Group patent. The part labeled "FIG. 1A" demonstrates how users interact with automated matchmaking systems.

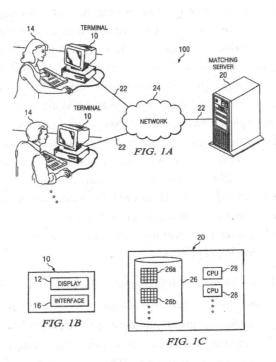

U.S. Patent   Feb. 12, 2019   Sheet 1 of 11   US 10,203,854 B2

FIG. 1A

FIG. 1B

FIG. 1C

Source: U.S. Patent 10,203,854.

conceptualizes how a user might differently interact with various "embodiments." (All images presented in this chapter are copied directly from the patent and have not been modified.) The user interface may differ slightly on mobile- and web-based platforms, but the algorithms that govern them operate in largely the same manner.

In one embodiment, [the algorithm] for profile matching comprises receiving a plurality of user profiles. . . . Matching server **20** may include software and/or algorithms to achieve the operations for processing, communicating, delivering, gathering, uploading, maintaining, and/or generally managing data, as described herein.

As an example only, consider a case where user 14 [Kate or Will] is interested in participating in an on-line dating scenario. [Kate or Will] can access the Internet via terminal 10 [a laptop or computer—a non-smart phone application], travel to a web site managed by matching server 20 and begin the registration process. As part of the registration process, [the matching sever] may ask [Kate or Will] a series of questions which identifies characteristics about [Kate or Will]. Thus, [the matching server] may ask [Kate or Will] a series of questions which identifies [user characteristics]. Thus, [the matching server] may ask about height, weight, age, location, and ethnicity of [Kate or Will]. It may also ask about the birth place, parents, eating habits, activities, and goals of [Kate or Will]. [The matching server] may further use the registration process to discover what user [Kate or Will] may be looking for in a match, such as age, weight, height, location, ethnicity, diet, education etc. Further, [the matching server] may ask [Kate or Will] to indicate how important certain factors are when looking for a match. . . . This same process may be repeated by several different users 14, causing [the matching server] to contain a plurality of profiles.[14]

Most users who are familiar with OkCupid or Match.com will recognize the seemingly unending questions needed to sign up for an account as described above. Though I caution users about framing their preferences around the desired traits mentioned, it is at least transparent that companies use this information to assess potential matches. When a user signs up for a comprehensive matching service, it is to be expected that the algorithm will respond to user input.

Alternatively, another described "embodiment" appears to outline the algorithms that govern swipe-based platforms such as Tinder and Hinge, which seemingly infer the same kind of inclusion and exclusion criteria, though via less transparent means:

Matching server 20 is operable to compare geographic positions associated with the plurality of user profiles in user profile [pool] with a geographic position associated with [a user]. Explicit signals may be imported from a social networking [platform], such as the number of shared entities in a social graph of user[s] either within system 100 *or other social networking [platforms]*.

In some embodiments, [the matching server] may further be configured, as part of the user registration process, to link to users' existing profile within [a social networking platform]. [The matching server] may be configured to parse the profiles of the users in [a set] e.g., collecting data and applying algorithms. For example, [the matching server] may use explicit signals from [a social networking platform] such as common friends, common interests, common network, location, gender, sexuality, or age to evaluate potential matches between [users]. [The matching server] may also use implicit signals such as for whom [a user] expresses approval and disapproval. Implicit signals may also include facial recognition algorithms.[15]

Many online dating platforms prompt users to sign up or log in via a social network (typically Facebook, Instagram, or Google) and then use this relationship to collect user data and infer common interests and aesthetic choices in partner preference. Note that in Figure 2.1, user activity is depicted as being contained within system 100 (which is the entire matching system, algorithms, and shared technologies across dating platforms). Yet, Match Group readily acknowledges that some implicit signals about preferences are collected outside of system 100. It is one thing for Tinder to look at a set of users' shared presence in Facebook groups or shared taste in music, as various iterations of the platform have disclosed this information to users. It is another entirely different thing to use such information gathered about everyday use patterns to ascertain an individual's taste profile in other humans in the manner described. Apparently, daily interactions, such as liking a friend's picture or sliding into someone's DMs on Instagram, may be used to generate data about the kind of people one might be attracted to. Further, it is not enough to hide this information in a lengthy, jargon-filled terms of use agreement. Such practices should be provided to users in an accessible manner, an issue I return to in Chapter 5.

The idea of social network data-informed matching becomes even more alarming when we consider that Instagram and Facebook (both part of Meta) were accused in two separate lawsuits of watching users' faces while they scrolled.[16] In one lawsuit, where Facebook (now Meta) was accused of illegally sourcing more than 100 million Instagram followers, the company offered to settle for $650 million, adding that the data were inadvertantly collected due to a "bug."[17] This kind of facial recognition data can be used to predict emotions such as joy, desire, and disgust, albeit with limited accuracy.

To imagine further, think about your daily Instagram scrolling. In one sitting you may encounter political messaging, models, diet and exercise influencers, and posts from religious or spirituality groups. For everything that you encounter, Meta may have been watching to see how you'd respond to that voluptuous model, the dad bod pics your friend from college posted, or that Black Lives Matter post. However you respond, Meta may interpret your response through time spent on photos, click data, or, potentially, facial recognition software. And that information is used to determine how you might respond to curvy women, dad bods, or users with #BLM in their dating profile. This is not what users of social networking sites or dating platforms signed up for, and it is a grave trespass of trust on the part of all companies involved.

Face Mapping Matches

The dangers of facial recognition software extend beyond collecting users' responses while scrolling. Facial recognition algorithms consistently fail to properly detect and categorize the faces of women and darker-skinned individuals.[18] In 2015, Google incorrectly tagged Black people as gorillas—that was a facial recognition algorithm.[19] In Detroit, where police are encouraged to used facial recognition software in routine policing, the chief of police claims that the software fails to correctly identify subjects 96 percent of the time. The American Civil Liberties Union (ACLU) has documented many ongoing cases in which individuals were arrested under false pretenses due to faulty facial recognition software. Because of these failures, facial recognition software was provisionally banned in policing in several cities including Boston and San Francisco.[20]

Though there are several widely used algorithms for facial detection, few have been trained on racially and ethnically diverse data sets, meaning they are ill-equipped to deal with the full variety of human diversity. In a review of racially biased facial detection algorithms, a group of data scientists found that in a widely used data set of approximately 1,000 individuals, only 20 were Black.[21] Further complicating the issue, many images of the same person are needed to conduct solid analysis, and most training data sets that have numerous photos of the same individual are composed of celebrities or well-known political figures (i.e., those we idealize as having the most symmetrical and most attractive faces). Facial detection algorithms are trained on the most ideal faces, mathematically speaking; most humans do not naturally have ideally symmetrical faces without surgical intervention. Yet facial detection algorithms work with over 90 percent accuracy on White men—the same group that built and trained them.[22] For the rest of us, algorithms consistently fail to recognize and appropriately categorize us—especially women, Black individuals, and people between eighteen and thirty (which is, coincidentally, the target age of many dating platforms).[23]

Most sets of training data provide limited diversity and are not labeled for race or ethnicity, leading to low accuracy, high rates of false matches, and low reliability in faces with higher levels of melanin.[24] The high presence of melanin or darker skin tones, rather than race per se, appears to be the most salient factor in accuracy of facial recognition. In tests of leading commercially used facial recognition algorithms, facial skin reflectance (the ability to reflect light off the skin) most readily predicted inaccuracy. Those with darker skin have lower reflectance, and those with lighter skin have higher reflectance. In a study conducted by Cynthia Cook and colleagues, lower reflectance resulted in lower matching scores and longer algorithmic processing times. Skin reflectance is the statistically superior method for predicting error rates in algorithmic facial recognition rather than self-identified racial or ethnic labels, indicating that if facial detection algorithms were calibrated for darker skin, they may work more effectively.[25] Computer scientists have also found that the nation of origin of algorithm designers can influence the racial stereotypes that introduce bias into racial classification systems.[26]

The algorithmic process for facial recognition and subsequent racial classification systems involve many algorithms at various steps of a lengthy procedure of classifying images (e.g., the support vector classifier algorithm: SVC), categorizing (e.g., the K-nearest neighbors algorithm: KNN), and structuring images (e.g., decision trees).[27] The process typically involves face segmentation, facial features detection, face alignment, embedding, and classification. Key features are used to determine facial structure, such as nose, lips, eyes, and eyebrows.[28] Images are broken down into small patches, then into pixels where the pixels are assigned a numeric value and broken down into shades.[29] The numeric value of pixels is used to determine shape and texture of the face using the local binary patterns (LBP) method (among others).[30] Figure 2.2 depicts how facial recognition mapping centers objects on the face and how the whole face is divided into regions for aligning computer vision.[31]

It is very difficult for humans to accurately categorize people by race based on phenotypical appearances such as eye shape, nose width, hair texture, and skin tone. If humans, with all of the cultural context that we've developed over the entirety of our existence, cannot properly, with 100 percent certainty, categorize individuals based on appearances alone, why would a computer equipped with a sophisticated mathematical equation be able to accomplish such a task? Even if it could, race and ethnicity are not static categories. They are always changing and are contextually decoded. Here in the United States, I am readily perceived as Black. In many locales around the globe, due to my lighter skin tone, I have been told that I am White. It

FIGURE 2.2   Facial recognition technology maps and segments the face for computer vision.

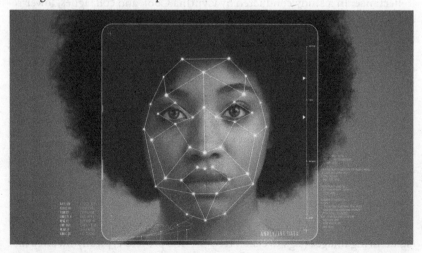

Source: Fractal Pictures/Shutterstock.com.

should make users uncomfortable that a system programmed by an industry that is overwhelmingly male and White would presume to be able to accurately categorize individuals by race and then apply those same categorizing conditions to users globally. Match Group reports that Tinder has 75 million active monthly users worldwide, and yet their patent suggests they use facial recognition algorithms in a manner that relies on a Western framing of the phenotypical expression of genes as they relate to race.

> In some embodiments, matching server 20 may be configured to apply a relevance algorithm which determines the content and order in which [the matching server] displays potential matches to [a user]. A relevance algorithm may be based on both explicit and implicit signals from [a user]. Explicit signals include information entered by [users as part of their profile], such as heigh, weight, age, location, income, and ethnicity. *Explicit signals may also include information about the characteristics of [users] seeking a match such as gender, hair color, eye color, or occupation. . . . Explicit signals may be imported from [a social networking platform]*, such as the number of shared entities in a social graph of [a user]. Implicit signals may be based on the behavior of [users] either within system 100 [the online dating website] or other social networking platforms.
>
> . . . For example, [the matching server] may use explicit signals from [a social networking platform] such as common friends, common interests, common network, location, gender, sexuality, or age to evaluate potential matches between [users]. [The matching server] may also use implicit signals such as for whom a user expresses approval and disapproval. *Implicit signals may also include facial recognition algorithms to detect ethnicity, hair color, eye color, etc. of profiles that [users have] expressed interest in.*[32]

A relevance algorithm "may" include facial recognition algorithms that detect ethnicity, hair color, eye color, and so on of profiles users have expressed interest in. That means when you upload your photos to a dating platform, an algorithm categorizes your relative attractiveness based on your eye color, your hair color, and your race based on these features. As discussed above, it may also already know this information about you before you upload a single thing if you've linked your profile to a social networking site such as Facebook or Instagram. The relevance algorithm asseses the content of a potential match's profile, including their "race," and then orders the appearance of potential matches in the stack before you swipe through them.

Automating Eugenics?

Race is socially constructed and contextually specific, but because we treat it as though it is a real, biological unchanging truth, it has real social implications—especially where processes of racial categorization are concerned.[33] Many systems have attempted to fully capture the multitude of ethnic and racial categories (yes, the Black/White binary classification system we focus on in the United States is one of many possible systems!). Where some see racial categorization as a neutral process necessary for recordkeeping and the tracking of human migration, most social scientists argue that this procedure is far from neutral. Contemporary systems of racial categorizing, including facial recognition software, cannot escape the history of previous failed systems. Given Match Group's explicit inclusion of race, hair color, and eye color as sorting mechanism to which facial recognition algorithms are applied, it is worth noting how similar this process is to another racialized system of categorization—eugenics.

Eugenics is the science of selective breeding for the general "improvement" of humankind. Eugenics is also known as race biology. Taken together these meanings of eugenics suggest that the root of this pseudoscientific movement is deeply tied to justifying the elimination of non-White racial groups.[34]

Some scientists and medical practitioners ascribe to the idea of positive versus negative eugenics—meaning that eugenics can be used positively to "opt out" of certain genes that indicate for cancer or other health maladies. Negative eugenics is what we traditionally associate with the Nazi purification campaign and White supremacists' desire to see the White race maintain racial purity by discouraging the reproduction of those who are deemed unfit. Unfitness includes existing in a non-White body, occupying a lower class, existing with economic instability, a propensity to commit crime, and a tendency to over-reproduce. Just as race is socially constructed, sociologists understand that these other traits of unfitness are also not naturally occurring but are largely products of a capitalist society—where survival of the fittest is an implicit value in the marketplace. In the United States, where capitalism is king, reduced social safety nets and severely limited reproductive education foster a proclivity toward crime, economic instability, and so on because individuals do not have the financial security needed to thrive.

Positive eugenicists argue for the ability to greatly improve the quality of human life overall. But at what cost and who will primarily reap the benefits? The cost is testing on Black, Brown, and Indigenous people who are still routinely forced into processes of eugenics such as sterilization or unknowing participation in medical trials.[35] Those who will primarily reap the benefits are wealthy White people—perpetuating a racial imbalance. The unfortunate truth is that this is the way medicine has worked historically, with much of our medical knowledge coming from Nazi science or testing of "medical advancements" on enslaved or marginalized populations in the United States.[36] For example, the well-known Tuskegee syphilis trial, where Black men with late stage syphilis were denied treatment for "scientific" study, demonstrates how the general population benefited from the exploitation of a marginalized group.[37]

We often talk about the racial and ethnic discrimination associated with Nazi eugenics, but their approaches were also ableist. So too are U.S. studies that appear helpful but are actually grounded in ableist eugenics practices. For instance, in the 1990s, scientists at a U.S. research university recruited young Black boys for a medical trial designed to assess whether race could be linked to the (in)ability to moderate "aggressive behavior." Financially insecure parents were coerced to enroll their children into the study by the promise of big payouts. During the trial, the boys stayed in a facility overnight without their parents, routine medicines and water were withheld, and they were subjected to hourly blood draws and forcefully administered a serotonin boosting drug.[38] These doctors believed that an ability to regulate emotions might be linked to race and thought these conditions ideal for studying their hypothesis. I'd be aggressive too if I was drugged, scared, and thirsty. Yet, the scientists likely believed that the scientific knowledge gained from conducting the study would outweigh the harms and ethical violations they committed.

Hence, the framing of eugenics, on the whole, is an ableist and racist pursuit—one that primarily benefits wealthy White people, whether we call it positive or not. Sure, we want to be aware if we have traits that indicate the presence of genes that foster the development of cancer or Parkinson disease. But when we start dabbling in selecting out traits for Down syndrome or autism, we communicate that those individuals have lower value in society or no place in the world—which is simply untrue. Instead, medical gene notation should probably stay away from the framing of "positive eugenics," and we should be thinking about equity in accessibility throughout society, which my colleague Sasha Constanza-Chock writes about at length in *Design Justice*. Beyond equity,

> design justice requires full inclusion of, accountability to, and ultimately control by people with direct lived experience of the conditions the design team is trying to change. Not only is community leadership ethical, but also, the tacit and experiential knowledge of community members is sure to produce ideas, approaches and innovations that no one else would be able to create.[39]

Match Group's patent reveals that the company's design ethics are far from just. Rather, eugenicist ethics map very closely to Nazi ethos:

> In some embodiments, [the matching server] may analyze factors such as, but not limited to average number of words per sentence, total number of words with greater than three syllables, and total number of words in the profile. . . . From these statistics, matching server 20 may also be configured to generate a readability score by, in one embodiment, taking the average of the Flesch Kincaid Reading Ease test, the Flesch Kincaid Grade Level test, and the Gunning Fog score. Other embodiments may utilize any other combination of these or other tests to determine a readability score. *In some embodiments, analysis may be used to determine the IQ of an entity, the grade level of the writing, or how nervous the entity generally is.* An advantage of this embodiment may be that the *system provides [users] with a metric for determining approximate intelligence of other users.* The readability score may be used, for example, in the matching process to identify potential matches.[40]

Intelligence should not be reduced to a numeric standard because it is also culturally contextual. Intelligence in one context may not translate to another cultural context. Intelligence tests simply predict measures of achievement within an unbalanced system of social oppression. Yet Nazi eugenicists "preached that persons with 'mental retardation' were 'useless eaters,' undeserving consumers of precious, finite resources, and polluters of the Aryan gene pool."[41] Following the same eugenics logics, state surveillance of individuals with "low intelligence" led to the forced sterilization of several thousand poor and working class White, Black, and Indigenous people in the United States in the 1930s.[42] My point is, although we associate eugenics practices most closely with the Nazi massacre of Jewish people, the prevailing "scientific" thought of the time pervaded Western countries as well. Sterilization of "lower intelligence" individuals was documented in the United States, Canada, Sweden, Denmark, and the UK, among others.

Though some may draw a distinction between mass murder of "low intelligence" individuals on the part of Nazis and forced sterilization campaigns in other countries, all of these practices are disgusting and inhumane. I raise the point to interrogate the use of science in the pursuit of betterment. When we unquestioningly adopt scientific practices because they are en vogue, we risk the widespread proliferation of bad science. If it is the case that dating platforms look for patterns demonstrating lower intelligence and categorize individuals accordingly, then they further eugenicist pursuits covertly. Additionally, the methods claimed to assess intelligence (e.g., the Gunning Fog Index, the Kincaid Reading Ease test, and the Flesch Kincaid Grade Level test) are not actually measures of intelligence. Instead, these tests measure syntax, vocabulary development, and language proficiency. Those who use these measures in educational settings note that motivation and interest influence how individuals score.[43] They are not reliable measures for capturing intelligence in a dating profile. Anyone who has spent time on dating platforms knows that some individuals just are not interested in filling out a profile so they add the bare minimum to meet the text requirement of the platform. This does not mean they are not smart; on the contrary, many that I interviewed conveyed a desire to share common interests upon the first in-person meeting with potential match, saving details in hopes of generating an interesting conversation, which is, in my view, a smart strategy.

In addition to measures of intelligence, dating websites' algorithms that use facial recognition software look for the phenotypical expression of certain desired genes in a face. This means that individuals who do not exhibit a normative beauty aesthetic are evaluated as less attractive by algorithmic systems. Then user profiles are sorted by whether they fit this ideal beauty standard. Those closest to the ideal standard are more highly rated by the scoring algorithm. Those furthest from the standard are likely awarded the lowest attractiveness scores. This sounds eerily similar to early eugenics practice, supported by the science of the times, which has since been demonstrated to be faulty (due to lack of repeatability and validity); these practices involved measuring individuals' head shape and size to support the claim of the biological superiority of the White race.[44] Parsing out attractiveness with facial recognition software—coupled with the automated pairing of those with the highest attractiveness scores (likely those closest to Whiteness)—automate sexual racism and uphold the hierarchy of supposed White racial superiority. This is especially troublesome considering the numerous studies that find that Whiteness appears to be the most desired trait in online dating environments.[45]

If the scoring algorithm is an assessment of beauty where beauty is a racialized aesthetic, then only those within that frame will receive the highest score. Remember, according to the cofounder of OkCupid, Christian Rudder, if your matches are ugly, then you're ugly. Absent from this statement, though, is the contrapositive: if your matches are beautiful, then you're beautiful. By this logic, we can see how a certain standard of beauty is evaluated, reinforced, and maintained through dating platforms that use facial recognition software as part of a process to evaluate desirability and attraction.

However, the algorithms that sort matches also consider user feedback. Hence my claim here is not that facial recognition algorithms are solely to blame for automating sexual racism. Online daters "cast votes" or provide feedback about who is hot or not, which also impacts a user's score. Eugenics is embedded in a profile-sorting process whereby: individuals' baseline attractiveness is measured by facial recognition algorithms that detect their eye shape, eye color, nose width, skin tone, lip thickness, and other phenotypical expressions of certain genes; individuals are compared with other highly popular users in the pool (which means they have been rated as highly attractive by input from others on dating platforms); the algorithm determines how much an individual has in common with the user who is swiping;

and, lastly, the algorithm learns the users' preferences based on their swiping behavior. Sexual racism is automated throughout the entire process, but users have the power to reify sexual racism through swiping behavior that is an expression of their own internalized belief systems.

Still, the danger in automating sexual racism lies in users' unawareness of these processes. Most believe they are seeing a neutral stack of potential matches ordered by geographical closeness, but the Match Group patent reveals that, at least in theory, the rule of physical proximity is sometimes overruled if there is enough "commonality" between users:

> In yet another embodiment, matching server **20** may be configured to score the location comparison in light of other factors; as an example, matching system **20** may be configured to return a score consistent with a 10 mile difference in location even though there is a 50 mile difference [between users if they] have the same income, education, and age.[46]

Hence, commonality or relevance seems to be the key driver of how available profiles are presented to users (Figure 2.3). This commonality score can

FIGURE 2.3   This image from the patent (labeled FIG. 5), conveys how algorithms manage users' profiles.

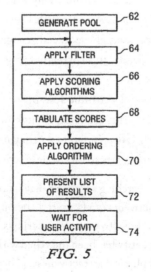

FIG. 5

Source: U.S. Patent 10,203,845.

include income, age, education, and race/ethnicity—all of which, as argued in the previous chapter, inform the presentation of a gendered desirability construct in accordance with gender role scripts. Dating platforms' attractiveness scoring and sorting appear to follow eugenicist logic in that they pair those with phenotypical expressions of "fit" genes together, encouraging the mating of those who most exemplify a White racial aesthetic.

To clarify, I offer the following scenario as an example of the implications of algorithmic dating platforms' use of racialized sorting processes. According to Match Group's outline of the relevance algorithm, individuals are sorted based on what they perceive to be desirable to a user. If you are a relatively attractive White man, you will probably see many blue-eyed, blonde women in your swipe deck because Match Group believes this is what you *should* desire based on your social location as a White man. If you are a relatively attractive Black man, you too will probably see many blue-eyed, blonde women in your swipe deck because Match Group likely believes this is what you *should desire to attain* (following the logic of Whiteness as the most desirable aesthetic). However, as a Black man, depending on how your own attractiveness is evaluated, you may be presented with blue-eyed blonde women who are a 3 while your White friend is presented with blue-eyed blonde women who are an 8, even if you are sitting next to each other while swiping. This is because the algorithm likely undervalues attractiveness of Black, Brown, Indigenous, and Asian people—especially if they are darker skinned, because, as discussed above, facial recognition algorithms consistently fail to accurately detect and correctly categorize non-White faces in routine tests.

I certainly do not trust algorithmic systems to appreciate the full beauty of melanin in all its forms. This scenario, though fictive, is based directly on my reading of the Match Group's patent as they explain how the relevance scoring algorithm interacts with attractiveness scores:

> In some [platforms], matching server 20 may be configured to impute a level of physical attractiveness to [a user]. [The matching server] may be configured to monitor how [frequently a user] has been viewed as well as how many times that entity has been [matched with other users] in order to impute the level of physical attractiveness. [The matching server] may

further be configured to generate a score based on this data. Further, in some embodiments, [the matching server] may impute physical attractiveness to an entity based on the imputed physical attractiveness scores of other entities. [The matching server] may compute an average of the imputed physical attractiveness scores of the other [users] and the present [user]. Empirical data indicates that people are more likely to match with people of similar attractiveness. Thus, in many embodiments, a user may obtain an advantage in that they are able to be presented with potential matches that, according to one measurement, are as attractive as the user.

... Another example of how [the matching server] may use this data involves making it more likely that an entity will appear in a user's result list if the entity and that user have a similar attractiveness rating. *So, if a user has an average rating of 6, then an entity with an average rating of 5 may be more likely to appear in the user's result list than an entity with an average rating of 2.*

As another example, a commonality score may be generated based on the comparison between each entity and the seed. *In some embodiments, this commonality score can be a measure of how physically similar the users are to each other.* This score may be generated based on the number of users that have expressed a positive preference for both the seed and the entity being compared. This score may also be generated based on whether the seed and entity have been viewed together in one session. Further, the more times the seed and entity have been viewed together, the larger the commonality score. The law of large numbers may allow for a vast amount of such commonalities to be established over a few days.[47]

To further explain how ranking algorithms sort users, I provide an example in which the patent authors use Harry and Sally, evoking a 1989 romantic comedy in which the couple meet continuously over the course of twelve years, but their timing is always off. Finally they realize their romantic love for each other. This film reference makes an interesting and likely deliberate choice by the algorithm inventors that highlights the need for an online dating platform.

As example only, consider a registered user, Sally, whose profile was created by matching server 20 in January. Since that time, [the matching server] has recorded the number of times Sally's profile has appeared in any user's [list of matches]; assume that this has occurred 10 times. Further, [the matching server] has also recorded the number of times a user has viewed Sally's profile by clicking the view button [that is] associated with Sally's profile; assume that this has happened 5 times. In this manner, [the matching server] has constructed a ratio that represents the imputed physical attractiveness of Sally's profile. Still further, assume that Harry, a registered user, now submits a query. [The matching server] has evaluated the imputed physical attractiveness ratio of Harry's profile. When evaluating Sally's profile for inclusion in [the match stack that is awaiting user action from] Harry, [the matching server] will compare the imputed physical attractiveness of Sally's profile and Harry's profile. The more similar the ratios associated with Harry and Sally's profiles are to each other, the more likely it is that Sally's profile will be selected by [the matching server] to be in Harry's result list.

In another example, assume that Sally's profile has not been registered long enough to generate a meaningful imputed physical attractiveness ratio. [The matching server] may then generate an imputed physical attractiveness score based on entities that Sally does have commonality scores with. This computed average may be weighted by the strength of the commonality score between Sally and each entity with whom she has a commonality score. Continuing the example, assume that Sally has a commonality score of 5 with Lucy and 10 with Julia. When [the matching server] computes Sally's average, it will give twice as much weight to Julia's imputed physical attractiveness score than to Lucy's.[48]

I'll continue using the names from the example the patent has laid out. For the sake of clarifying how scoring and ranking systems can be racially biased, let's decide that Sally and Julia are both White while Lucy is Black. Because Sally is a new user, and Julia and Lucy are both established users, the patent indicates that Lucy's and Julia's physical features will be compared with Sally's physical features to determine commonality, likely through facial recognition algorithms. We can reasonably believe that the algorithmic system will note higher similarity between Sally and Julia, the two White users, giving this pair a commonality score of 10. Because Lucy is less similar in appearance, due to her being someone with features that are associated with being Black, she will be marked as having a lower commonality score of 5, with Sally. The system determines a baseline for Sally's attractiveness based on her commonality with Julia, the conventionally attractive, established White user.

Following the logic of the relevance algorithm as outlined by Match Group, when the algorithm assigns an attractiveness ranking, Sally may be ranked higher than Lucy even though Sally is a new user without a lengthy history of feedback from other users because of their disparate commonality scores. It could be the case that even though Lucy is an established user with a longer history and thus more feedback (via swipes) from other users, Sally may still appear in Harry's match stack before Lucy because "Sally Ideal" is more physically similar to Julia, and the system has determined that women like Sally and Julia are Harry's type (Figure 2.4). Lucy may eventually appear in Harry's stack but likely after Harry is fatigued. Users tend to swipe in seven-minute sessions with less attention to detail devoted to each passing profile as time goes on.[49] Remember, in the previous example, Sally was deemed hot enough to land Harry, an example the patent illustrations seem to drive home. To be clear, the patent does not racialize the characters in the

FIGURE 2.4   An illustration from the Match Group patent showing the user interface of a swipe-based dating platform. "It's a match!"

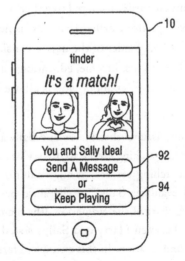

Source: U.S. Patent 10,203,845.

examples, but if we are to apply real world parameters, it is surely the case that people of color are compared against popular and "highly attractive" White users—in short, Match Group likely believes we all need to be having what Sally's having!

Because racialized users are phenotypically dissimilar to White users, it is almost guaranteed that they will be given a lower score. When the technological error of facial recognition algorithms is paired with faulty social beliefs about how those in racialized bodies perform masculinity and femininity scripts, a hierarchical racialized system of attraction and desirability is produced within online dating ecosystems.

Misogyny in the Machine

Sexual racism is a convergence of beliefs about acceptable performance of masculinity and femininity scripts at the intersection of gender and race. Hence, my examination of Match Group's patent also notes where power differentials converge at this intersection.

> Matching server 20 may be configured to weight the demographic similarities and differences based on the sex of [the user]. The demographic data may include, but is not limited to, age, education, ethnicity, income, and location.[50]

Gender and race/ethnicity are considered together when estimating degrees of similarity. This excerpt also clarifies that "sex" is not solely considered in generating a match; rather, gender of the user is considered in light of other social categories such as status, income, educational attainment, and age— all of which have gendered rules about who is allowed to occupy space and power therein.

> As an example only, assume that Harry and Sally are registered users who have profiles in matching server 20. Harry has submitted a search request to [the matching server]. While fulfilling this request, [the matching server] evaluates Sally's profile since her profile is in [the matching pool]. As part of the evaluation, [the matching server] looks at the differences between Harry and Sally's stated age, income, education, ethnicity, and location. In this example, Harry is 10 years older than Sally, makes $10,000 more per year, and has a Master's degree while

Sally has a bachelor's degree. Even with these disparities, [the matching server] will give Sally's profile a high score which makes it more likely that Sally's profile will appear in Harry's result list. However, if it was Sally who submitted the search, and [the matching server] was evaluating Harry's profile, a different score is possible. So if it were Sally who was 10 years older, made $10,000 more per year, and had a Master's degree while Harry had a Bachelor's degree, [the matching server] would give a low score to Harry's profile, making it less likely that his profile would appear in Sally's result list. [The matching server] may be configured this way because empirical data has shown that these demographic differences do not have an equivalent effect on the choices men and women make regarding matches.[51]

Throughout the patent, it is clear that the scoring and ranking system is rooted in social ideologies about gender and acceptable performances of masculinity and femininity. Sadly, Harry and Sally are beholden to heteronormative gender scripts governing relational power, proxied by income and educational attainment. From this example we can see that it is acceptable for Harry to be a bit older and make $10,000 more than Sally. But it is unacceptable for Sally to be a bit older and make more money than Harry— meaning that if Sally falls outside the age range of what is considered the peak of age desirability for men corresponding to her age group, she will likely receive a lower score. There are too many examples of computations concerning gender and age throughout the Match Group patent to reproduce here, indicating a core belief in hegemonic gender ideologies, on the part of the company, and likely within the broader online dating industry.

Curating Control

Who is considered ugly, attractive, beautiful, cute, or otherwise desirable by dating platforms is not as informed by user choice as online daters think it is (or should be). Yes, user choice is seemingly considered as part of a feedback loop that informs "votes," but those decisions cast through swipes and clicks are only given value in the dating platform infrastructure. Dating platforms have created a system where interaction is currency that better positions players. The more you interact with a platform, the more you provide the system with information by which it determines your match recommendations. The industry needs you to keep playing to boost their profit so dating platforms curate your experience as they learn more about you. As we think about how algorithms automate sexual racism, we must also consider the artful design guiding us through a curated experience in which users are led to believe that they have autonomy of choice about their potential matches. In reality, dating platforms perform what I call the *myth of neutrality of choice.* The myth relies on tricking your senses through a tactile, sensory-loaded experience. Not only do users look with their eyes, taking in visual cues about others, on swiped-based apps, but users have to physically express a choice through the swipe gesture, calling users into a playful experience—one that exists outside of the usual clicking and scrolling associated with other kinds of information-seeking processes with digital technologies.

Social scientists and technologists use the term "affordance" to think about how the design of online platforms allow or hinder user experience and interaction with each other.[52] An affordance can refer to real or perceived accessibility of a technology. In online dating, a platform such as Tinder or Bumble affords a gamified dating experience. Sociologists Jenny Davis and James Chouinard describe technological affordances as both the functions attached to a technological platform and the ideas perceived by users of that platform.[53] Digital technologies can afford or allow movement and agency on platforms, but they can also constrain in other ways. For example, if we were to compare Tinder and Match.com, the affordances are markedly different, neither having inherently positive or negative value over the other. Tinder allows for a relatively structured experience. A user uploads their photos to the platform and is then asked to input their phone number for verification purposes, persuaded to grant the platform to access their location, encouraged to specify how far they'd like to search for potential matches, and told to indicate a preferred age range and preferred gender options. Once a match deck (stacked list of potential suitors) is produced, users can swipe right to indicate interest in a person through a "like," or left, to indicate "nope," not interested. These affordances are relatively limited in terms of how users may choose to engage. Both users must swipe right to match. Only then can they talk to each other.

Conversely, other platforms under the Match Group umbrella, such as OkCupid or Match.com, afford a different kind of interaction, even though they are all online dating platforms. On Match.com or OkCupid, users are prompted to answer several questions about themselves and their ideal match. The platform guides them through questions about preferred height, weight, income bracket, education level, political beliefs, and so on. Users can set filters or indicate which (if any) of the preferences are deal breakers. They are required to fill out a profile about themselves, and that profile undergoes a mysterious internal review process (to ensure users are not violating community guidelines), whereas on Tinder, profiles could, at one point, be left blank. Another affordance of questionnaire-based platforms is that users may peruse a panel of potential matches, viewing multiple individuals on a screen, rather than swiping through one user at a time. Lastly, questionnaire-based platforms often allow users to reach out to each other to encourage a match. Individuals might send a message indicating interest that may cause someone to give them a second look, leading to a match. On swipe-based platforms, there is no second look (though users can pay to "undo" a swipe, but it is only applicable to the immediately preceding swipe).

Theories of technological affordances speak directly to the gamification of online dating and how platforms structure our interactions with each other. Davis argues that technologies request, demand, encourage, discourage, and refuse user action through user interfaces and cultural conceptions of those interfaces.[54] I'll use the same terms to describe how dating platforms afford various user experiences.

Requests recommend action from users, but there may be workarounds. For example, Bumble suggests users upload six profile photos for a complete profile. Users can still use the platform without doing so, but Bumble will prompt users every time they review their profile by indicating a percentage of completeness. This prompt serves as a reminder that the platform is designed to be used in a particular way and creates a notification that some may find annoying enough to cause them to finally complete their profile. A dating platform demands a course of action when its use is predicated on stated guidelines. Tinder demands that users input a phone number to continue using the app. This demand is outlined in the terms of use, and users cannot proceed without receiving and entering a code texted to their phone number. Tinder does this to verify human activity as opposed to a bot account or fake profile. This means that without a phone number and mobile device, some would-be users are excluded from Tinder and platforms that utilize mobile phone text verification. Davis and Chouinard note that users may rebuff demands but with great intentionality.[55]

Dating platforms encourage users when they foster or emphasize a preferred course of action, while stifling or suppressing others.[56] On Tinder, users are encouraged to "super like" highly popular users to "stand out from the crowd." When a person swipes on an average user, there is no prompt to "super like" though the option always exists. What is not clearly stated to users is that they are only allowed five super likes per day before they are prompted to purchase more by upgrading to a paid subscription with unlimited super likes. This structure in the platform encourages users to aim for those who may be just out of their league (to use the logic of the platform). Occasionally, one matches with a highly popular user by sending a super like, boosting the user's ego and encouraging the person to continue using the platform. Those who do not wish to super like highly popular users must overcome the psychological hurdle of realizing they probably won't get a response from this person unless they super like them, and Tinder makes users decline the prompt.

Dating platforms discourage actions when exercising a choice involves concerted effort to overcome built-in barriers.[57] For example, at the time of writing this book, on Bumble, if a user wishes to report another user's behavior to the company, the person must go through four steps. First, the user must navigate to the messages section, click on the profile in question, click the three vertical dots in the top right corner of the app, then choose from "voice call," "unmatch," or "report." It is no accident that "report" is listed last among a set of actions because reporting users causes more effort for platforms. I return to a detailed discussion of safety and reporting mechanisms in Chapter 5.

Lastly, dating platforms refuse actions when they are unavailable to users. For example, users on Tinder and Bumble have no way of following up with someone who does not match with them, whereas other dating platforms allow users to send messages to those with whom they have not matched or where there has not been mutually indicated interest. In some cases, users get around platform refusals by leaving the app altogether and contact users on Instagram or Facebook, a move that is commonly referred to as "sliding into DMs (direct messages)."

Affordances shape how we interact with platforms as well as how we interact with each other. As noted in Match Group's patent abstract, online dating companies believe that affordances of their platforms are helping users find a match more efficiently. Social theorist George Ritzer has written for decades about the tradeoffs of capitalist power and technological efficiency. In what he terms the McDonaldization of society, he details how the principles of optimization of the fast-food industry have come to dominate other sectors, including technology. In Ritzer's view, the following technological dimensions are linked to developed, hyperrational, postmodern societies:

- *Efficiency*: the optimum method from getting from one point to another

- *Calculability*: or the emphasis on quantifying human elements

- *Predictability*: an assurance that all outcomes will be similar

- *Control*: the way that technologies exert power over others

Ritzer argues that we have fallen into a trap of hypermodernity where our efforts to streamline processes have led to irrationality.[58] For instance, dating platforms aim to connect individuals, yet they demonstrate irrationality by filtering users according to a racialized hierarchy of desirability. While some individuals certainly appreciate a racialized experience, others, like most people interviewed for this book, would prefer greater diversity in their match deck. Ultimately, it may be more rational where profit is concerned to allow users access to the full breadth of users, regardless of their attractiveness rank. Instead, users are siloed according to their perceived level of attractiveness as a mechanism of control.

Many have written about the gamified experience of dating platforms as a method of social control.[59] Elisabeth Timmermans and Ellen De Caluwé suggest that this control is exerted to coerce users into a gamified system where appearance dominates game outcomes.[60] On the whole, the gameplay design of dating platforms guides users into the commodification of a White Western beauty aesthetic and racialized desirability, further contributing to automated sexual racism.

Sexual Racism in the New Jim Code

Sociologist Ruha Benjamin frames the New Jim Code as "the employment of new technologies that reflect and reproduce existing inequities but that are promoted and perceived as more objective or progressive than the discriminatory systems of a previous era."[61] She goes on to say that racial codes and computer codes that include race are a mechanism of social control just as Jim Crow laws exerted social control in the past. Jim Crow laws emerged after the dissolution of slavery and took the place of other forms of racial control. Legalized segregation under Jim Crow lasted in the United States until the late 1950s. Jim Crow connotes a set of principles that dictated separation of racial groups in public (and sometimes private) spaces, which rendered "colored folks" as second-class citizens. It was not until *Brown v. Board of Education* (1954) that the Supreme Court ruled that segregation was fundamentally unjust. Benjamin's argument suggests that the same types of racial segregation result from biased code and racist implementation of algorithmic technologies. For example, Safiya Noble documented how searches for "Black girls" generated pornographic images of young Black women while a search for "White girls" resulted in images of young White children at play.[62] While Google appears to be a neutral technology of efficiency, it generates irrational, racially segregated results.

Further technological efforts toward efficiency, such as Match Group's goal to simplify the matching process by presenting users with the highest commonality scores where race is a key indicator, often deepen and hide discrimination while "appearing neutral or benevolent when compared to the racism of a previous era."[63] This discriminatory design replicates and extends the power of racialized social hierarchies. Although sorting systems and facial recognition algorithms often claim objectivity, Match Group's patent demonstrates a belief in fundamentally racist and eugenicist views about dating, and moreover, about people.

Just as sexual racism was tied up in Jim Crow rules of the past through laws limiting interracial marriage, it appears that the New Jim Code also relies on the structural legacy of a gendered and racialized power dynamic. As early as 1691 and as late as 1967, there was federal and state-level legislation that attempted to define and demarcate boundaries of acceptable racialized sexual attraction. Algorithms that automate sexual racism present a new system by which companies can define the boundaries of acceptable racialized interaction. And because users are not aware that this shapes their experience, they may buy into the presented racialized hierarchy of attraction. Yet, this racialized system of categorizing and sorting has been patented, demonstrating how legal processes continue to support and protect institutions' ability to enact a New Jim Code while marginalized users carry the weight of the consequences.

THREE

I'm Just Not Comfortable with Them

The Myth of Neutral Personal Preference

rac·ist | rā-sist

noun

a person who is racist: someone who holds the belief that race is a
fundamental determinant of human traits and capacities and that racial
differences produce an inherent superiority of a particular race
***MERRIAM WEBSTER:** HTTPS://WWW.MERRIAM*
-WEBSTER.COM/DICTIONARY/RACIST

Yeah, so when I—So, I—okay, hmm, this sounds bad but I, I had dated
someone that was a different race than me in the past and it was totally
uncomfortable. And I don't know why but it was just uncomfortable for
me. So, you know, I wouldn't date someone that was a different race
than me going forward. Not because I'm racist, but because I was
uncomfortable, and I don't want to be uncomfortable anymore.
REAGAN, INTERVIEWED IN FEBRUARY 2020

Most people, relying upon dictionary definitions of racism, think that if they do not personally have racist thoughts and do not intentionally commit racist acts, then they are not racist, and therefore, are absolved of race problems in America.[1] Even if this were true (and it's not true for many reasons), this line of thought seems to stop short when we are talking about sexual racism.[2] As the interviews with twenty-seven White individuals demonstrate, sexual racism is the last social arena where it is acceptable to hold racist views and still consider yourself "not racist." This chapter makes the connection among systemic racism, so-called neutral racial partner preferences, and sexual racism in online dating excruciatingly clear. I also cover how the narratives and logics of White daters' personal sexual racism contribute to, and are privileged by, automated sexual racism.

George Lipsitz, professor of Black Studies, argues that there is a deep investment in maintaining Whiteness as the nonracial social standard.[3] This implies that White people do not think about their choices as being about race because Whiteness is the assumed natural social order. Yet, by operating within the frame that their choices are meaningless and raceless, they uphold subtle cultural agreements about what Whiteness is and who explicitly constitutes "the other."[4] Through fashion, music, film, television, and other aspects of popular culture, the boundaries of White culture and "other" culture are determined. Hence by operating with the mindset that dating choices are personal and neutral, when they are very much a product of racialized social thought, society upholds the idea that there is a natural social order pushing people to reject non-Whiteness in their intimate lives.

Individuals' seemingly personal, "natural," neutral choices about racially unacceptable partners collide with the Whitening machine that is Silicon Valley to produce automated sexual racism. Because the tech world sees itself as the post-racial utopia that the future promised, it operates within this myth that simple choices made in and about code are done without regard to race and have little implications regarding race in the social world. For example, some computing systems use a "master–slave" filing system.[5] The tech world would have you believe that this is just what processes are called—as if this terminology magically appeared. But Yarden Katz, scholar of American culture, argues that the history of computing and the internet are deeply tied to eugenics and racialized science.[6] It follows then that "slave databases" that receive and answer queries from the "master database" originate from racial framing and thinking.

How the tech world operates is important because it has totalizing power with regard to social life. In *Race After Technology: Abolitionist Tools for the New Jim Code*, Ruha Benjamin argues that because tech companies are largely unregulated in the United States, they often act with impunity in ways that other sectors cannot. They are able to make technology that operates with racist logics, like faulty facial recognition systems, ranking algorithms, and matching algorithms that are then used in other industries, like credit scoring, policing, insurance valuation, healthcare, and so forth.[7] This means that seemingly race-neutral solutions to social problems, which actually code and sort on race, ripple into other industries, causing a culture-wide reorientation to using racist tech that masquerades as being race-neutral. Due to their omnipresent power, the tech industry's decisions influence other industries and most, if not all, areas of our social lives.

The issue is that though there is growing awareness, most do not know that technology is embedded with coded racial bias. In the context of online dating companies, the obfuscation of racialized and gendered ranking and sorting systems helps support the idea of neutral personal preference. Users come to dating platforms hoping to explore the possibility of connecting with those geographically near them. But, as demonstrated in the previous chapter, those that appear in a match deck, waiting for a swipe of (dis)approval, have been ordered and ranked by a system that considers race, gender, and possibly IQ. For White daters, this means that their stack of matches, shaped by commonality scores, might appear to be more racially homogeneous than the actual diversity that is present in their geographical location. The lack of disclosure about these processes leads users to believe that the online dating experience is a reflection of the kinds of people one might encounter walking into a bar or club. In reality, dating platforms provide a racially curated sexual marketplace wherein individuals are presented with a racially segregated dating experience whether they'd consciously choose it for themselves or not.

This artful ruse supports the idea that like attracts like by pushing together those with greatest commonality (racial and otherwise). Daters are led to believe that they simply match more often with one type of person because "that's just the way things are," but in actuality, dating companies use algorithms to manipulate users—creating a feeling of serendipity similar to what daters might find when meeting someone offline by chance. For example, the Match Group patent states that the matching server can be configured to make users' results more appealing by

> pointing out coincidences in the profile data that give [users] a sense of fate. . . . [The matching server] may be configured to search for similar initials, birthplaces, birth dates, birth month, birth year, university, first names, last names, user handles, parental occupations, and keywords to identify users who may give another user a sense of fate. In other embodiments, [the matching server] may use the fate characteristic as a metric in the matching process.[8]

This manufactured fate hides the work of the racially curated sexual marketplace by supporting the belief that users just stumble upon a dating experience that is racially segregated.

The catch, though, is that there is a cyclical element with regard to social networks and dating. Dating companies' algorithms likely draw inferences about one's preferences based on demonstrated user behavior. The system might infer that a user prefers racial commonality based on user activity across linked social sites, meaning that online dating systems create racialized experiences because users demonstrate that's what they want in some way or another. Dating companies are not solely responsible for bias in online dating. Individuals have personal beliefs that are rooted in sexual racism. Dating platforms automate sexual racism and conceal the work of that automation, leading users to believe that their sexual racism is innate, natural, and reasonable.

To demonstrate the cyclical nature of automated sexual racism, I conducted a qualitative analysis of twenty-seven interviews with White respondents. For some brief context, I did not conduct these interviews myself because best practices in qualitative research dictate that one should try to avoid interviewer effects when talking about sensitive subjects such as race and racism. In lay terms, White people aren't as likely to tell Black researchers how they truly feel about racial issues. Instead, my empathetic and kind research assistant Rachel Keynton, who is White, conducted all of the interviews with White respondents, expertly drawing out the most salacious perspectives on interracial dating and online dating platform use.

To set the stage for the rest of the chapter, I share some of Rachel's conversation with Reagan, who is a thirty-six-year-old self-identified heterosexual Caucasian woman from Indiana:

> Rachel: Are there any preferences you've found in somebody that you did date in the past? You know, drawing from experiences with previous partners, like something that you really liked about them? Just anything that you consider when you're making choices, like if you're swiping through these apps, things that—[*interrupted by respondent*]
>
> Reagan: Oh okay, gotcha. Yeah, so when I—So, I—okay, hmm, this sounds bad but I—I had dated someone that was a different race than me in the past and was *totally* uncomfortable. And I don't know why but it was just uncomfortable for me. So, you know, I wouldn't date someone that was a different race than me going forward. Not because I'm racist but because I was uncomfortable, and I don't want to be uncomfortable anymore. Um—
>
> Rachel: Of course. Can you tell me a little bit more about that person and, um, you know, what was their racial identity and what things you kind of didn't see eye-to-eye on?
>
> Reagan: Yeah, he was, uh, African American. We didn't meet online. We were volunteering together and went to school together. Um, and, yeah, it was just—And it wasn't anything like—It was his personality really that made me uncomfortable, but I think there was like something in me that couldn't connect with him because of race too. So, I don't—I just don't wanna have to—I don't know. I wouldn't—*If*, say, I was on a dating app right now, if African American men came up, I would probably say no. Like swipe whatever way or whatever. Just because I've been through that and I'm like, I'm not gonna waste my time, and I don't want to waste their time. It's probably not gonna be a comfortable situation so I don't wanna do that.
>
> Rachel: Um, have you ever talked to friends or family about dating somebody of a different race? And, you know, how do you think they would feel if you for example—or your kids—if you brought home somebody of a different race?

Reagan: Yeah. I never talked to my kids about it. Um, so my cousins and I always, uh, talk about it. And they too have dated, um, men outside of our race. And we've all had different experiences. One of my cousins—I mean, her, like, soulmate was a guy of a different race, and he was murdered, and she has to go on living without him. It's kind of—it kinda stinks. So we've got everything from that—to me who's like "no!" and everything in between. So, um, yeah.

Rachel: So you said if you were swiping through and you encountered an African American man, you would probably swipe left? Would you think differently if you met an Asian man or a Latino man?

Reagan: Yeah. So an Asian man probably—I don't know, it's hard to say and it sounds so shallow, but I know for me it's more like I don't wanna be uncomfortable and I don't wanna waste someone's time basically. Um, everything comes down to time for me, because I'm a single working mom so I have zero of it. [laughs] In fact, then, I was a single working mom that was also in school. Back when I was using these dating apps.

So I really had no time to waste. But yeah, a Latino man, I don't know. I might consider that. [laughs] Um, just because I love Hispanic music. I love Hispanic food. I love the culture—so my son, um, one of his best friends when he was growing up was Hispanic and they, you know, the family of like twelve lived together and they threw huge parties for like every—I mean, somebody like sneezed, "Oh let's have a party!" Like, it's a huge party all the time. So I love the culture. I love how family is so important a lot of times in Hispanic culture. And I do feel comfortable around Hispanic people. Just never met one that I would want to date. But I don't—I don't think I would necessarily say no to all Hispanic people. Um, an Asian person, I don't *know*. It's hard—I mean, at Notre Dame you see Asian, um, people but [*laughing*] not in the real world around South Bend, there's just not that many of them. So I guess I never thought of it before, but I don't know, that's a tough one. I don't know what I would do. I don't know.

Rachel: You seem to have pinpointed some cultural differences between racial groups that you think makes a difference—[*interrupted*]

Reagan: Yeah. It just all goes back to comfort. It's not necessarily that like, you know, all Black people—a Black person will come up [on a dating app] and I'm like, "Oh I'm definitely not gonna be comfortable with him," but it's just, I don't know, I've had the past experiences and I don't—I guess I'm just judging by their picture, like "Oh yeah, that particular Black person is like other Black people I've known" and I'm just not comfortable with them so I don't wanna do it.

I suspect the discomfort Reagan experienced in the relationship was her own racism:[9] "I think there was like something in me that couldn't connect with him because of race too." White people are often uncomfortable acknowledging, talking about, and dealing with their racism and racist thoughts. Sociologist Robin DiAngelo calls this fear of being confronted by one's own racism "White fragility."[10]

More than just fear of being racist, White fragility includes defensiveness, argumentativeness, resistance, anger, and guilt. When White people are confronted with negative feelings about their racism, they often react with silence and withdrawal.[11] Reagan reacted to her racial discomfort by completely withdrawing from dating situations that might lead her back into the vague uncomfortableness. Reagan's interview also demonstrates what sociologist, Eduardo Bonilla-Silva refers to as "color-blind racism."[12] White individuals often proclaim that an issue is not about race, taking a color-blind stance while simultaneously referring to race and upholding racial stereotypes in defense of their raceless worldview. In Reagan's case, she is "not racist"; the Black man she dated just had a *personality* that made her uncomfortable, and she just doesn't want to be uncomfortable for some unstated reason. She never explicitly tells us exactly where the discomfort is rooted. Yet she relies on stereotypes about Hispanic people to explain why they don't make her uncomfortable. They love to party, have good food, and play great music. Asian people she only sees on her local university campus—not out in the real world, so she is uncomfortable with them. Reagan's explanation about her discomfort conveys that it is, in fact, about race, when she uses racial and ethnic stereotypes to justify what she does like about some ethnic people and cultures. Reagan recognizes that race plays a very explicit role in her approach to finding a match, yet she does not recognize this thinking as racist. This is sexual racism at work. Reagan knows it is bad to feel the way she does about having racial preferences in partners ("this sounds bad") but is unwilling to concede that the guilt she feels is connected to her own racism. Why are White people so unwilling to confront their own racism?

There's an entire field dedicated to understanding and answering this question. Whiteness Studies, aptly titled, spans disciplines and includes philosophers, sociologists, psychologists, and other scholars who examine how White people think about and make sense of race.[13] These scholars often conceptualize Whiteness as pathological, meaning that social actions of Whiteness are both deeply ingrained and automatic.[14] White pathology is described as a social-psychological process of internalizing ideology about what it means to be White in highly racialized societies—especially when White individuals are atop the power hierarchy in those societies. As sociologist Jessie Daniels explains, White pathology does not simply reside in the minds of White individuals; it is also a way of being in the world, a manner of navigating society, and a system that functions to reinforce domination and social inequity.[15]

White pathology pervades representations of U.S. popular culture through an imposed worldview.[16] Sociologist Joe Feagin refers to this worldview as the "White racial frame." Feagin suggests that White people have controlled racial narratives in the United States for four centuries. In that time, they have shaped the way all of us think and talk about race and racism.[17] My answer to the question about why White people seem to be unwilling to acknowledge their own racism is grounded in the work of the White racial frame. The White racial frame and Whiteness are both tools created to aid in convincing both outsiders (non-Whites) and insiders (White people) of White racial superiority and domination. Even "not-racist" White people are subtly reminded that Whiteness sits atop the power hierarchy through everyday interactions, and especially through the technologies we use. The normalizing power of the White racial frame is so omnipresent that we hardly notice it unless we look for it. For White individuals to acknowledge their own racism, they would have to recognize that they have bought into the narrative that value-laden distinctions in racial groups have significant social meaning. To do so would clash with another set of White American values: civility, niceness, and rightness. In the contemporary era of color-blind racism, liberals, moderates, and conservatives alike recognize that civility and decency are guiding principles. This is why dog whistle politics gained such popularity. After the civil rights movement, if politicians wanted to express racism, they had to use words and discourse that were racist adjacent. It was no longer socially acceptable to be explicitly racist. The hollow sense of "niceness" has become a guiding principle in civility.[18]

Another guiding principle embedded in contemporary Whiteness is the ability to live free of racial tension. White people, especially those occupying middle- to upper-class status, are typically afforded the privilege of comfort and safety. They are so unfamiliar with discomfort that they will go to great lengths to maintain the feeling of comfort, especially when talking about race. DiAngelo argues that the socialization of White individuals in the United States does a disservice, making White individuals racially illiterate.[19] Most White folks believe that if they are good people, they cannot be racist. Measuring one's ability to be racist by dictionary definitions is not enough because those definitions do not explain how racial hierarchies are reproduced through everyday interactions, casual ideologies, and systematic racial inequity. The exchanges that occur in the minutia of life—the way we talk about our dates among friends, or the way our parents subtly (or not so subtly) communicate whom we can and should not bring home—all combine to shape our thinking about racial groups in society. The thing is, our everyday actions are political.

Bonilla-Silva's framing of color-blind racism helps clarify how seemingly neutral personal actions actually have social and political consequences.[20] Several others that were interviewed for this chapter echoed Reagan's discourse of neutral personal preference couched in color-blind racism. I'll quickly summarize relevant frames of color-blind racism to demonstrate how White individuals reason their way through sexual racism without thinking about themselves as racist. Naturalization, cultural racism, and minimization of racism are discursive mechanisms that are used to indirectly talk about race and provide seemingly race-neutral reasoning.

The *naturalization frame* allows individuals to reason that racial divides are just the natural, biological order of the universe. In fact, racialized distinctions were invented by the White ruling class to justify slavery, colonization, and imperialism and have since been internalized under the White racial frame. These racial distinctions result in material social divides such as integrated segregation, in which neighborhoods, parks, and schools are no longer legally segregated, but they are still primarily racially divided because of local and national politics and systemic racism.[21] With a compounding effect, the results of housing discrimination and other racialized barriers to wealth and resources add to the appearance that races just naturally don't seem to mix. Another frame, *cultural racism*, relies on culturally faulty arguments, such as dark-skinned Black women are always "ghetto" and thus unsuitable for marriage. This is used to explain why it is acceptable to summarily exclude dark-skinned Black women from one's dating pool. Lastly, the *minimization of racism* frame suggests discrimination no longer impacts the life chances of people of color—meaning that it's okay to have a personally held racial bias because these individual decisions do not add to the overall negative outcomes for people of color as they experience racism.

Brandon, age twenty-four, who self-identified as a straight White male, first explains that he is pretty flexible in terms of his partner's religious, political, and educational background. He then uses the naturalization frame to explain why he seems to primarily end up with "White girls":

Rachel: Do you believe that your ideal partner should share the same political beliefs and ideologies as you?

Brandon: No, not at all. Just be tactful about or be mature about it, I guess. The girl I dated the longest was more or less the exact opposite of me in every political thing, but like, we got along because, I don't know. I don't know that that should necessarily be a binary thing in my opinion.

Rachel: Uh huh. What about education? Do you believe that your ideal partner should have the same level of education as you?

Brandon: No, not, not at all. As long as she's, you know, able to hold a conversation and is not like obviously a complete moron. It doesn't really matter to me what level of education she achieved.

Rachel: Okay, and in terms of religion or religiousness, do you believe that they should share your same religious beliefs?

Brandon: No. Again, that one's sort of like politics where you can be religious and you can be whatever religion you want, just don't necessarily browbeat me about it or make it this whole thing, I guess.

Rachel: Mhm. And do you believe that your ideal partner should share the same racial identity as yourself? And why or why not?

Brandon: Um, yeah I normally date White girls. So that's just a personal preference, I guess. I don't know that it's necessarily something I've talked about. It's just what I tend to find attractive, I guess.

Rachel: Can you tell me a little bit more about that? About that attraction or lack of attraction?

Brandon: Umm.

Rachel: Is it physical or is it something else?

Brandon: I don't know. I mean I grew up in a town that was basically entirely White, in an all-White family, so some of that may have just been lack of exposure until I went to college. I don't really know. I can't comment intelligently on it.

Brandon conveys that he is flexible about his partner's religious views, political perspectives, and level of education, all of which have been shown through research to be relationship deal-breakers for many.[22] Ironically, the only area that he is inflexible about is something that people cannot change about themselves: their race or ethnicity. He says that his preference for White women is probably due to a lack of exposure because he grew up and went to school with White individuals. He can't comment intelligently on his all-White existence because he's never had to think about it. This is the normalizing work of the White racial frame. White people are a global minority. Yet, in the United States, many White children grow up never meaningfully engaging with non-White people, as if that's a natural occurrence rather than the successful design of racist social systems. If by chance, a child growing up in these racially segregated conditions manages to develop a worldview that appreciates the beauty of diversity, the person might still internalize the values of Whiteness because it is the social default.

Scholars from the field of social psychology, informed by their position as practicing therapists and their academic backgrounds, Arianne Miller and Lawrence Josephs conducted a study on White daters' racialized reasoning in mate selection. These psychoanalysts insist that White people who are not openly racist may still ascribe to "mass fantasies" or racial narratives about individuals of color.[23] Hence, it is socially acceptable to live near, go to church with, and even maintain close personal friendships with people of color—all the while experiencing racist thoughts towards them.

This antipathy is probably not exhibited toward people of color who are considered neighbors or friends, but it is directed at others who look like them and probably share life experiences with them. Miller and Josephs find that some White liberals, who may be willing to act as allies, and even champion fair treatment for people of color, will not cross the race line in physical intimacy or in romantic relationships—especially where Black individuals are concerned. This racial taboo, as explained in earlier chapters, in has existed since before the founding of the United States, yet it is still deeply pervasive. Miller and Josephs suggest that this conflicting obsession and revulsion of Black sexual bodies may stem from a classic Freudian Madonna–whore complex or racialized "oedipal splitting."[24] Oedipal splitting asserts division and hierarchy between pure love and acceptable forms of lust over devalued forms of love and lust.

Racialized oedipal splitting occurs culturally when Whiteness and romance between White couples represents the purest, idealized form of love, sex, lust, and intimacy. The White racial frame positions Blackness and interracial sexual or romantic relationships as devalued forms of love and partnership. By relegating Black people to the position of societal loser, White individuals remain able to see themselves as societal winners. Miller and Josephs suggest that growing up in U.S. society that is intensely competitive and motivated by materialism and individual success leaves people obsessed with status, even—or especially—where intimacy is concerned. Hence, their professional experience of working with White patients and scholarly expertise inform the opinion that White individuals exhibit pathological narcissism. This kind of racialized narcissism includes both extreme grandiosity and vulnerability with regard to race and racial issues. Because it is less and less acceptable to outwardly behave or express thoughts of that nature, sexual racism allows for a last arena where White individuals can assure themselves of their superiority. But when their private racism is uncovered by friends, potential mates, or in Reagan's case, an interview about online dating, this extreme vulnerability kicks in, ushering in White guilt. According to these practitioners and scholars, when Black people are always positioned by society as the oedipal losers, White individuals can rest assured that they are sexually aggressive, powerful, and superior. White discomfort may be triggered by the implicit pathological need for assurance of racial superiority. At times, this discomfort may be at odds with White fragility because there is a tension between wanting to view the self as a good person who is not racist and the deep need for that racial superiority to be validated.[25]

Philosopher and psychiatrist Frantz Fanon contends that a primary goal of Whiteness is to perpetuate racial dialogue in private and public spheres.[26] In other words, White people are invested in making sure that race continues to matter, that race continues to be seen as biologically real and significant. Sociologists Jennifer Mueller and DyAnna Washington contend that White people are deeply familiar with the benefits of racism, which is why they continue to show allegiance to the racial status quo.[27] White individuals understand that their current lifestyle and standing in society can only be maintained through the subordination of non-Whites, yet they feel a moral responsibility not to enjoy it. This tension allows them to enjoy White privilege while maintaining the belief that they are good people.[28]

Updating Fanon for the twenty-first century, Zeus Leonardo and Michalinos Zembylas add that the ability to always construct the racist as someone else, a problem of some other White person, is a hallmark of the current era of feigned post-racialism.[29] Because many White people do not want to be racist and have embarked on some (un)learning, there is a tendency to say "I used to be racist" or "I used to think this way," conveying that there is a separation of a former "bad Whiteness" and a present "good Whiteness" in the same White person.[30] Yet where dating is concerned, this separation seems to matter far less.

As I've written this book and discussed it with colleagues, particularly more senior colleagues, I have often gotten the question, "But, isn't it okay to just have a choice about preferences in a partner—these are just natural, right?" These well-meaning White people who teach classes about oppression and racism fail to see how they are, in that moment, an embodiment of the technology that is race.[31] Just as the White racial frame continues to produce narratives that substantiate the cultural claims and hierarchies of Whiteness, sexual racism continues to masquerade as a neutral, raceless rationale about partners because it is a convenience in service of White comfort. This myth of neutral personal preference allows White individuals to evade the discomfort of their own quiet, concealed sexual racism. Though the rest of this book was written primarily for people of color, this chapter was written for White people because the racist is, at times, you. The data in this chapter will not allow me to conclude otherwise.

Intergenerational Lessons on Sexual Racism

Gina Castle Bell and Sally O. Hastings, two social psychologists who study interracial relationships, find that parental approval can greatly influence the outcomes of relationships.[32] Individuals perceive social support (or lack thereof) through parental validation of those they are dating. In the study of relationship support, individuals experience parental advice as three different forms of communication: emotional (concern and care), informational (novel information), or instrumental (acts of service).[33] Parental views can also communicate ideas about society's expectations. When a parent expresses negative racial views, or explicitly racist views about potential partners, individuals internalize this information and make decisions about partner choice, either to fulfill social expectations or simply to ease relational tension within families. Alternatively, they may internalize racist views and choose not to date non-White partners.

Rachel's interview with Logan, age thirty-one, who self-identified as a straight White male, demonstrates how parental views on interracial relationships may be internalized by their children and influence relationship and dating choices:

> Rachel: How do you think your parents or your close family would feel about you bringing home a person of a different race?
>
> Logan: [laughs] Not good. My folks are pretty racist. That would be complicated.
>
> Rachel: Have you ever talked to them about this explicitly?
>
> Logan: [laughing] No, definitely not! But we don't talk about stuff, so it's not, like, particularly out of bounds.
>
> Rachel: Sure. And similarly, how do you think they would feel about you having a child with somebody of a different race? Does that change the equation at all?
>
> Logan: I have no idea. They wouldn't like it. I also don't really care that much, like about how they feel about it. But, yeah, I don't—my mom

would, like, be fine about it. But my dad is very racist. And I care less about what he thinks accordingly.

Even though Logan says that he does not take his father's racist views into account, his responses earlier in the interview suggest that his father's racism shaped his worldview. This is especially apparent as he uses the naturalization frame of color-blind racism to explain why he seems to only be attracted to women who look like him:

Rachel: Do you believe that your ideal partner should share the same racial identity as yourself? And why or why not?

Logan: I don't believe that that should be the case. It has always been the case. Ah, not always. Uh, I think it's just easier to be attracted to somebody who looks pretty much like you. And given the universe of people to date, you're just—I've just always ended up with White women. Just because I don't meet as many not-White women.

Rachel: Can you tell me a little bit why you think it is easier to date somebody who looks more like you?

Logan: Uh, no, I couldn't. I think that's probably a bad thing. I don't know why.

Perhaps years of exposure to his father's racism influences why Logan always seems to find himself with women who look like him. Bell and Hastings find that emotional responses from one or both parents about the prospect of dating non-White partners can be particularly jarring and formative.[34] Individuals internalize the White racial frame from parents early on, and these lessons are reinforced in light of partner choice. In fact, lessons about Whiteness, including how to maintain Whiteness, are particularly important in the context of mate selection. For White families, perpetuating Whiteness through familial marriage ties is a direct investment in Whiteness.[35] Many scholars of the law have argued that Whiteness is a legal property, made a commoditized asset. Legal systems have historically been invested in maintaining Whiteness. The First Congress (1789–1791) established that individuals seeking citizenship must be "free Whites of good character with two years' residence in the United States." Though the parameters for citizenship expanded over time, racial requirements were not entirely eliminated until 1952.[36] The Expatriation Act of 1907 stripped U.S.-born women of their citizenship if they married non-citizen immigrant men; this law was abolished in 1922, unless a woman married an Asian immigrant or non-citizen who was ineligible for citizenship. This exception for marriage to Asian immigrant men did not end until 1931. The U.S. government and, in particular, White men were so invested in marking the boundaries of Whiteness through marriage, reproduction, and citizenship that they tried to legally control whom women could marry. It wasn't until women were able to vote in 1920 that serious movements to change these regulations began.

White men still seem to be deeply invested in maintaining Whiteness through marriage and mating. Many of the individuals interviewed for this chapter conveyed that it was their fathers, rather than their mothers, who would express disapproval for dating outside their race. Patriarchy is inherent to Whiteness, especially in the United States where women were not allowed to officially participate in politics for more than a century.[37] Women were seen as the property of their husbands and, as such, instruments of maintaining Whiteness through childbearing.

Due to this kind of oppression, it is generally established by political scientists that White women are less conservative than White men concerning racial issues.[38] White men are more prone to buying into a bootstrap mythology that denies racism's systemic effects on upward mobility and overall life chances. Likewise, generally, White women are more likely than White men to support affirmative action on the basis of their belief in structural discrimination. Yet, White women are less likely to engage in interracial relationships themselves and less likely to form close personal relationships with those outside their race than White men. But they are more likely to express approval of others' interracial relationships than White men.[39] Hence it follows that respondents' mothers are more relaxed about whom their children might date compared to their fathers. White women might internalize ideas about appropriateness of interracial relationships but choose not to force their beliefs on their children. White men are more vocal about whom their children date, especially their daughters, because the tradition of patriarchy dictates that men historically presided over how their daughters dated.

Perhaps mothers do not feel the need to compound negative judgments about their child's partner choice because fathers already do so loudly.

Hannah, a twenty-six-year-old, self-identified heterosexual Caucasian woman living in South Carolina, spoke about her father's general anger toward Black folks and racial issues:

> Rachel: How do you think your parents would feel about you bringing home a person of another race?
>
> Hannah: Um, my mom would be super welcoming to anyone. My dad definitely has conservative, and I would say, at a lot of points, racist views, which is very unfortunate. And so I think he would adjust eventually. And I don't think that he would express any anger towards me, or that person like up front, because he wants to, like, hide that part of himself. But I think that it would bother him a lot. Maybe forever.
>
> Rachel: Is that something that you've ever discussed with either of your parents?
>
> Hannah: My dad knew about my ex-boyfriend who was Black. They never met. In his discussions—well, I would never call them discussions, more so arguments—and the argument was never within the context of my relationship. But more so just him making comments, in general, like that I would consider racist and offensive. And you know, pulling back up this example of myself being in an intimate relationship with someone, like with a Black man, you know. And that it's—he's not really a discussion type of man, so, no.

It is noteworthy that Hannah refers to her dad's views as conservative *and* racist as though they are almost synonymous. Social scientists have demonstrated that conservative political beliefs are often associated with resistance to new ideas, hold more traditional beliefs about marriage, and have negative racial attitudes.[40] Several studies demonstrate that White individuals with politically conservative views are less likely to show openness for interracial dating specifically between Black and White individuals.[41] Sociologists reason that this opposition to Black and White intermingling is due to a desire to uphold the racial hierarchy, which is difficult to do when people are blurring racial lines by procreating mixed-race offspring.[42]

Because some conservatives hold to ideas of a racial hierarchy, for them it is acceptable to date some people of color but not others. This is a recurring theme among the interviews conducted for this chapter as another excerpt from Brandon's interview demonstrates:

> Rachel: I'm gonna ask you a series of questions. Have you ever dated anybody who was not White?
>
> Brandon: Yeah, I've gone out with several Hispanic, Latino, whatever you want to say, women.
>
> Rachel: And how would you characterize those relationships? Did you have any apprehensions about being with them because their race was different than yours?
>
> Brandon: No, it was fine. It was good. Went about as far as a lot of my other relationships with White girls so like, it was—It doesn't really play a huge role for me. It just seems to be that's what I sort of trend towards, but it was fine going out with the Hispanic women.

It is acceptable to date Latinx or Hispanic individuals because they are viewed as being adjacent to Whiteness.[43] Though anti-Latinx immigration sentiment is certainly at an all-time high, particularly for darker-skinned and working-class individuals, most U.S.-born Latinx, especially if they are light-skinned, are considered White passing or White presenting. That explains, in part, why Reagan and Brandon would be comfortable dating Latinx individuals but not any other people of color. Scholars who study immigration write about the Whitening effect in Latinx communities.[44] As the United States experiences increasing waves of immigration from Mexico and South and Central America, racial lines will be increasingly blurred along the White–Latinx divide. Documented immigrants or U.S.-born Latinx are considered non-threatening to Whiteness, especially because many Latinx communities, like Cuban populations in Florida, ascribe to conservative views themselves.[45] This attempt at assimilation assures White individuals that some Latinx do not present a threat to Whiteness or White ideals of hierarchy because they themselves are trying to become White.[46]

This dynamic, of course, causes internalized racism and colorism, which I discuss at length in the next chapter. But I touch on it briefly here because it demonstrates how familial pressure operates to maintain Whiteness, even in Latinx families. Mariel, thirty-three, who identifies as Hispanic White, shared her frustration with navigating pressure from her grandmother to have children with a White person:

Rachel: How do you think your parents, or your close family, would feel if you brought home a person of another race?

Mariel: [laughter] My mom doesn't care, but my grandmother is very, very old fashioned. You know, I'm a first generation, you know, American. And so, my grandmother is very, um, I don't want to say racist, but she just doesn't like Black people. And it's not just Black people, it's anybody with like a dark complexion. Because she's like that towards dark Mexicans.

And I remember one time I told her, there was, you know, some guy from a baseball team, from—I think he was Dominican or whatever, and he was Black. And I was like, oh, I was telling her about it. And she's like, "Think of your babies." Like, think of the babies. Like, how they're going to be judged later in life and how—And I'm like, "Grandma, do you know what times we're in? Like, people have mixed babies all the time. And they're pretty cute." I was like, "I don't really think people care about that anymore." And she just—couldn't, like, get through it.

I mean, I've always traveled to Mexico with her, like deeper into Mexico. . . . And one of the guys who came in to deliver the sodas and the chips for the stores and stuff like that was, you know, a light-eyed—like, he had colored eyes, he was light-skinned, and she was like trying to like push me to talk to this guy. And I'm like, "What?!" Like, are we talking to the same—like, are you the same person? Because you get mad at me for talking to anybody—But you know what I mean? That's how I know, like, that's who she likes.

Like, she likes these very White-looking guys, I guess. And so I'm just like, "What?" But she doesn't like Black guys. She's like always, like, fearful of how hard it's gonna be for the kids when they grow up, or as they're growing up. And I'm like, "Uhh, I don't live in Mexico." Like, we're pretty much all diverse here. But she doesn't get it. And I get it. She's older, she grew up in a different time.

The White racial frame has made White supremacy so normative that even those who are harmed by it have bought into its logics, perhaps in part because assimilative strategies are protective. In the case of Mariel's grandmother, she was afraid her great-grandchildren might endure racial prejudice in Mexico and/or in the United States. This attitude is a well-researched concern with extended family members expressing concern about biracial children being socially excluded.[47] At other times, it might just seem easier to go along with the pressures of Whiteness and receive the White privilege that comes along with it. Ultimately, this hierarchy of desirability intersects with political and religious ideologies about rightness. Whiteness is not just hegemonically desirable: it is positioned as morally right.

Swiping in Racially Curated Sexual Marketplaces

The hierarchy in acceptability politics around interracial dating generates some questions. Why is it acceptable to date Latinx and Asian folks but not Black people? Data from OkCupid and other dating platforms also demonstrate that this hierarchy of desirability is tied to White beauty ideals and perceptions of racialized desirability.[48] Dating platforms capitalize on this racialized desirability hierarchy by allowing individuals to sort by race and then automating the process. Several dating platforms allow individuals to filter by race or ethnicity along with other categories such as religion, political affiliation, and education level. Some of these filters do offer a protective affordance for marginalized users. For example, it may be helpful for daters of color to filter out White individuals if they are afraid of routinely encountering unsolicited racial fetishization or casual racism.[49] Alternatively, those from a different point on the power continuum might be enacting sexual racism when they use race or ethnicity filters to either target specific groups for racialized sexual experiences or filter out an entire racial group because they are uncomfortable with them. What's worse, dating platforms know that individuals will pay a higher price for this capability, so this sorting feature is often hidden behind a paywall. This means that those with economic resources can participate in *racially curated sexual marketplaces.*

The racially curated sexual marketplace is a digital space where Black, Brown, Asian, Indigenous, and other people of color are commoditized as sexual objects. All people can shop for particular racialized, sexual experiences. But this automated racially curated sexual marketplace most often benefits White individuals who will pay to play. Though sometimes hidden behind a paywall, racial filters on dating platforms incentivize either racial exclusion or targeted racial fetishization. Though dating apps are used at times for excitement, for an ego boost, or to explore kinks, that is an entirely different experience than seeking out individuals based on the belief that they might be more sexually liberal *because* of their race.

Many respondents spoke about being more likely to use apps if they allowed users to search for specific qualifications and to filter (un)desired races. For instance, David, a thirty-four-year-old self-identified White cisgender Jewish man, told Rachel that he stopped using Tinder because it was "low-class" compared to other dating platforms that afforded easy access to a racially curated sexual marketplace:

> Rachel: You like Hinge because it allowed you to kind of—[*interrupted*]
> David: So Tinder is very like, here's everyone. Here's Blacks and Whites and Chinese and all this stuff. And I'm like, I'm not into like half of them. So most of it was just like swiping just to like spend time. And so that's why Tinder kind of like got thrown out. Hinge was just that much better because it just seemed like a little upper class. Just, it was like a Lexus to a Toyota, I guess.

What's interesting about David's desire to filter out Black and Chinese women is that he also mentioned that he had race-based sexual fantasies in his private sexual life. With partners who might play a role in his *public-facing* life, he was seeking the ideal type within the White racial frame of desirability. This distinction is important because it highlights that the racially curated sexual marketplace is designed for play and private experiential consumption, rather than for seeking public-facing, long-term dating relationships:

> David: So even with my specifications, it's still almost like on the upper scale of impossible to find someone who's for me. . . . The girl I'm

seeing—She's not like, you know, the hot bimbo that like—she's a cute girl and I kind of was like, "Oh yeah, when I swipe I'm always looking for like a big boobed, blonde, brunette, like just like someone fit," you know. And she's like, "So why would you have swiped me?" I'm like, "I don't know if I would've swiped ya." You know, like, but I'm dating you.

So like, what [dating apps] did for me was it actually like, took away something—I can't remember the word I'm trying to use but like, it took away from people because I was looking at girls as inanimate objects at that one point, and I was like, I'm not even looking at their profiles, I'm looking at their face. And then I was like, "Okay, this is re*****d"[50] because, like I said, the girl I'm seeing—if she heard me say this, it's like the worst thing ever—but she's not like the most gorgeous girl in the entire world. But I like her so much because she has everything else put together.

David conveys that dating apps caused him to view women as inanimate objects. While the structure of swipe-based dating apps are known to afford objectification of people, especially women and femmes,[51] David seems to be in a perpetual state of objectifying women. Even the woman he was seeing at the time of the interview was, according to his own inner dialogue, an object that checked—or not—boxes of what his desired mate should be. David's checklist consists of almost every marker of Western, European aesthetics of desirability: "big boobs," blonde hair, and fitness. Even though the woman he was dating failed to check all the boxes, she was still desirable because she is "put together," which, in the context of the rest of his interview, I take to mean that she has a good job, is reasonably attractive, and can converse well with others—something that David mentioned was very important to him. David is looking for a trophy wife, someone he can show off because how the world evaluates his partner signals affirmative cues about his adherence to Western heteropatriarchal masculinity scripts.

Ultimately, "Black and Chinese women" fall outside of what David believes to be socially acceptable frames of desirability, yet at another point in the interview he relays that he had hooked up with "other races." Again, the naturalization frame of color-blind racism is used to explain why race plays a role in his decision making about partners: "As a White man, I think you're just taught to stick with your own. So I never really like ventured out to find others but I've definitely hooked up with, you know, other races, so it's not like I'm against it." David is not against hooking up with women of other racial backgrounds, and the racially curated sexual marketplace offered on dating platforms has served this end well. But his dream trophy wife is a White, blonde woman. He uses different dating platforms depending on the kind of experience he's seeking at the moment—looking for a wife or looking for a racially exotic hookup.

To get a clearer view of how racially curated sexual marketplaces afford racial fetishization, I (or Rachel) asked all 100 participants directly if they ever had race-based sexual fantasies. Only four respondents reported that they had, and they were all non-Hispanic White. Though four may seem like a relatively small number, it is important to keep in context the proportion of interview respondents. Out of the entire interview sample, twenty-six were Black, twenty-two were Latinx, and twenty-five were Asian. The thought of race-based sexual fantasies had never occurred to most of them. Yet four individuals—two White men and two White women, roughly 16 percent of White respondents compared to 0 percent of respondents in other racial/ ethnic categories—said they had racial fantasies but had never talked about them with perspective partners. To respect privacy and ensure comfort of respondents, we did not ask for details about these fantasies.

The next few interviews are from respondents who said they did have race-based sexual fantasies, and they highlight how these daters commod- itize, dehumanize, and stereotype matches of color. Linda, a fifty-two-year- old self-identified straight White woman, conveyed that she did not have strong preferences for a partner that shared her racial identity, but she did mention that dating platforms offered greater opportunities to try out all the racial "flavors." "And there's a few flavors I haven't had yet that I'm willing to have. Okay?!" In order to better understand how Linda approached dating non-White partners, Rachel asked the same set of direct questions around dating people of color that all participants were asked. Their conversation emphasizes the dimensional nature of sexual racism. Individuals are othered by sexual racism based on their non-Whiteness. At the same time, they are idolized for their "exoticism" and treated as though they are simply an expe- rience to try:

Rachel: So I have a few specific questions about these flavors that you're talking about.

Linda: Okay.

Rachel: We have four broad racial categories that we are thinking about. So first of all, have you ever dated or been involved with an Asian man?

Linda: No! I have not! I mean, I want to be though. I want to try.

Joshua, age thirty-two, is another respondent who said he had race-based sexual fantasies. He self-identified as a White straight male and talked about using dating apps for racialized sexual tourism. Joshua also identified as a Christian and said he would not be interested in dating someone who was not a spiritual or religious person. The first hints of Joshua's proclivities toward exoticizing women of color emerged when he told Rachel about his ex-girlfriend:

Joshua: So she was like really, really dark. She was like the Pocahontas type kinda. You know, she is extremely, extremely dark, and she had like this Caribbean vibe I guess because like she'd wear like these flowery shirts and dresses and stuff. And I would wear a polo and jeans. I mean like we were opposite, but it was good. It was a good thing. Um, I mean, but if I were to meet somebody that was, you know, Hispanic, Latin, you know, African American, and if we got along and we were connected, then I have no issues with it.

Rachel: Okay. So I'm gonna ask you about whether you've dated or been involved with somebody. And that just means in any capacity like whether it's a casual date or hookup or a long-term relationship. Um, so have you ever dated or been involved with an Asian person?

Joshua: There's an inside joke there. No and I wish.

Rachel: Can you tell me more about that?

Joshua: I love Asians. I am highly attracted to Asians. I have never been out with an Asian.

Rachel: Can you tell me more about your attraction to Asian women?

Joshua: Uh, I guess, dark skin, um, is different, you know? I guess, if I had to—you said earlier about like your ideal mate and stuff [unintelligible]. The ideal mate is not I guess plain Jane, you know, something more, I guess exotic. Like you know, if I bring home a girl that we went to school together years ago, I mean, cool but it'd be much more fun to bring someone that's completely different from the different side of the world. As long as she spoke English. [*laughs*] So we can actually communicate.

Despite the recording disruptions, it is clear that racial fetishization factors into Joshua's attraction to women of color. He mentions dark skin when referring to his ex-girlfriend who was Black and again when he explains what he likes about Asian women. Then, he explicitly says that it would be much more fun to bring home someone who is exotic and different, rather than a "plain Jane." The need to communicate with his ideal mate is only an afterthought. A later portion of the interview confirms that Joshua equates racial and ethnic differences with non-White, outside the box, boundary-pushing sexuality:

> Rachel: Sure. For this next question, I'm just looking for a yes or no answer. You don't have to elaborate at all. But do you have any race-based sexual fantasies?
>
> Joshua: Yes.
>
> Rachel: Okay, um, have you ever expressed them to any potential partners?
>
> Joshua: No. No, not really.
>
> Rachel: Have you ever sought out these experiences with casual partners?
>
> Joshua: Like different fantasies?
>
> Rachel: Mhm.
>
> Joshua: Yes.
>
> Rachel: And what has been the response to that?
>
> Joshua: Um, just a shot in the wind. I was going, uh—It was a girl that I met on one of the dating apps, uh, around this time last year. Asking her about, like, group play, like group sex and whatnot. I mean she was from, uh, the Dominican Republic or something and I was thinking like, "Hey you know she's not from here. Maybe she has like some kind of—maybe she thinks outside the box." And I just asked her. We were having drinks and I just asked her. I was either gonna get a slap in the

face, her cuss me out, or give me an honest answer and she gave me an honest answer.

Joshua knew that what he was proposing could be potentially upsetting to his date. But he thought it would be acceptable to ask her about his race-based sexual fantasies because of what he perceived as her otherness and exoticism. White men are allowed to act this way because they are seldom held responsible for their actions. Because of their position atop the power hierarchy, cis White straight men feel as though they have access to women's sexuality even in nonsexual contexts. As I described in the Introduction, I have had a personal experience with this kind of man. Although our conversation was not sexual—or even private for that matter, as we were on a Face-Time call with my friend—the random Tinder White dude tried to force his private racialized fantasies on me without my consent. This interaction highlights the danger of automated racially curated sexual marketplaces: they collapse the context of casual sexual and nonsexual interactions where many women of color use Tinder to find legitimate dates and seek partners for long-term relationships (despite its reputation as a hookup app). At the same time, others are seeking out racially fetishized interactions. This context collapse normalizes sexual racism.[52] Some users may be drawn to online dating platforms to explore racial taboos because they cannot find partners with whom to explore these ideas offline. If that's the case, they should seek out platforms specifically made for fetishes where individuals can engage with consensual race play.[53]

How to Be Anti-Racist While Dating

I hope to have demonstrated in this chapter that racial personal preference in dating is not neutral. Rather, this myth of neutrality conceals underlying racist logics of desirability hierarchies. The seemingly private choices that we make on dating platforms actually shape how algorithms interpret users' desires. If daters continue to feed sorting and ranking systems sexual racism, online dating platforms will continue to racially curate sexual marketplaces because algorithmic dating systems are designed to meet and *increase* user demand. If users continue to treat sexual racism as a benign private choice without social consequences, racist actions on dating platforms will continue to demonstrate demand for algorithms that automate sexual racism. Put simply, if there is a demand for automated sexual racism, the designers, coders, and leadership at dating companies are happy to oblige as demonstrated by the Match Group patent.

Perhaps you've made it to this point and, after processing possibly new information, you may be asking yourself if it's possible to not be racist while dating. For starters, I suggest you read *How to Be an Antiracist* by Ibram X. Kendi.[54] Dealing with racism is part of life, and the burden for undoing its harms primarily falls on White people. That means that before dating, individuals should do the work of unlearning all of the implicit lessons that situate Whiteness as the normative standard of desire and acceptability. It also means that being in healthy interracial relationships will involve a lot of deep emotional work, analyzing perspectives, and taking on the burden of protecting your partner from the racists in your family. Several of the White women interviewed by Rachel, from relatively different backgrounds, shared how they've navigated dating partners of color over their lifetime, the lessons they've learned, and how they use that knowledge for their own personal growth and to increase the awareness of others.

Brynn, twenty-five, who self-identifies as a White straight woman, talked about navigating the hierarchy of racialized desirability and shared how a Black partner's previous experiences with racial fetishization came up in their relationship:

> Rachel: You said you've dated a few Black men. And was race ever something that came up in the context of those relationships?
>
> Brynn: Every time. Every single time. It's the first thing Black men usually ask me that's serious—"Have you ever dated a Black man?" Um, it's usually about, um—I don't—It's hard to describe, but they're worried that they would be too much for a White girl [*laughing*], I guess. Their jokes, their friends, their family, their whole lifestyle. They're worried that a White girl's culture wouldn't mesh well with their culture, which I totally understand. I was raised in a whole different world, um, never dealing with any kind of racial discrimination. So dating Black men

was kind of a new thing for me. And whenever you're with a Black man, there are people that kind of—There are other people that are against interracial relationships, and it seems like you only have that problem when it's a White person with a Black person. Nobody really says anything if you're with, like you said, a Latino or an Asian, but for some reason with Black and White, it's a big deal. So it is an adjustment, whenever you grew up in a world where you didn't have to think about race, and then you date somebody of color and you have to understand their side, and you have to understand why it's frustrating. It is definitely eye-opening. But it's worth it to me.

Penelope, age twenty-eight, self-identified as a White straight cis woman, was at the time of the interview working on her doctorate in anthropology. She had similar life lessons as Brynn and explained them through her position as a social scientist:

Penelope: Yeah, I mean, I guess I don't, in my mind, like, have an ideal. You know, there's no like, racial hierarchy in my mind, in terms of what I find attractive or what I feel like I would want in a partner. Also just, again, like, being an anthropologist, race is not a biological reality. It's socially constructed. So for different people of different ethnic and racial identities, they're going—even within those categories, there's so much variation and difference and diversity. So for me, I don't see it as something that has, you know, clear discrete borders. I see it more as, you know, something that makes up a person's identity and makes them who they are. And then, if I'm attracted to that person, you know, their racial identity is tied to that but, for me it's so much more important for me just to have an individual and see myself as a partner of that individual, than really looking to their racial or ethnic identity as like one of the top things that I would want or check off a list or something like that.

Lastly, Erin, twenty-six, who self-identified as a White bisexual cisgender woman, embodies how the personal is political. In her everyday life, she advocates for others in her family to take on anti-racist ethos and refuses to date anyone, including people of color, who are colorist or have internalized sexual racism:

Rachel: Do you believe that your ideal partner or partners should share your same racial identity? And why or why not?

Erin: No. I mean, they can, but I—No. No preferences. I just think—I will say that I don't want to date men of color that wouldn't date women of their same race. Like, if a Black man who's like, "Ugh, I can't with Black woman. Like, they're blah, blah, blah, blah, blah." I'm like, "Uh, I'm out." Um, but that's the only thing where it comes to race, of like—And then I wouldn't want to date a White guy, even though I'm White, if he only wanted to date White people.

Rachel: Can you tell me a little bit more about that?

Erin: Like, that's just weird and creepy and racist and I'm not gonna help him unlearn that shit. Like, I—You know, I think both of those stem from like, I mean, I—You know, I think both of those stem from like, I mean, racism, and then also sexism in the way that it intersects. So, I don't want to engage with that in my personal life.

Rachel: Okay. So how do you think that your parents would feel if you brought home a person of another race?

Erin: They'd be fine with it. My mom really liked my last boyfriend who was Asian.

Rachel: Have you talked about this explicitly with your parents or your family?

Erin: No, because my mom is super cool, and I don't talk to my dad. So, yeah. Because—yeah, with my mom, it doesn't need to be said. We've already had all of our conversations about race outside of the dating realm. Um, like, I got—you know, I got her to believe Black Lives Matter and a lot of other important things, so you know, I don't—I think she's walking the walk in terms of genuinely believing what she says she believes.

For many folks of color, especially Black people, not-being-racist is the bare minimum asked of White people in our lives. In truth, we'd prefer that you be anti-racist. Being anti-racist means that you'll have to acknowledge your complicity in upholding systemic racism and admit to yourself (and others) that you've benefited from White privilege. It means that you'll have to embrace discomfort in those moments when you're reminded of your own racism—by a partner, friend, or colleague.[55] To be anti-racist means that you are committed to distorting the White racial frame and disrupting the power it seeks to maintain.[56]

Beyond reading Kendi's *How to Be an Antiracist*, you must become an advocate, ally, and accomplice, meaning that you offer emotional and moral support as well as being willing to risk your livelihood and safety, just as many people of color do walking down the street in America.[57] It also means that you participate in social movements and that you vote for candidates who dismantle systemic racism and racial disenfranchisement.[58] You must also cultivate what DiAngelo terms "psycho-social stamina" with regard to discussing race, meaning that White people must not be so quick to give up or become fatigued when discussing issues of race and racism, especially in their dating lives.[59] Lastly, have a plan for calling your friends to account. How will you challenge your close friend who regularly espouses sexual racism myths? As the next chapter reveals in grave detail, providing comfort in these uncomfortable moments is complicity.

FOUR

I've Always Wanted to Fuck a Black or Asian Woman

Being Racially Curated in the Sexual Marketplace

Though dating apps automate the process, sexual racism existed long before dating platforms operationalized, scaled, and commoditized it. Individuals and society created sexual racism, as detailed previously. Yet automated sexual racism helps to normalize personal racialized preferences. Personal actions on dating platforms create a feedback loop telling dating companies that certain programming logics are acceptable or even preferred. With every swipe, match, and message sent, users tell dating companies what and who they want to see. By sending messages laced with racial fetishization and sexual racism, users commend dating platforms for creating a thriving racially curated sexual marketplace.

Sexual racism is exasperating for many folks of color because it seems there's no way to win. We are at once fetishized and demonized. We are both desirable and reprehensible. Women of color, especially, are burdened with the labor of care and plagued by the Madonna–whore complex in which they are expected to take on the nurturing or motherly role while also being rejected for being seen as hypersexual. We are shaping trends in beauty industry aesthetics, and yet we are not suitable to bring home to mama. For every trait of fetishized racial beauty or aesthetic of desirability, there is an equally impactful, less socially acceptable negative expression of sexual racism. This is why it is so important to recognize sexual racism as racism.

Though it can seem as though expressions of sexual preference on dating platforms are neutral, they have real and lasting consequences for those on the receiving end. The weight of frequently encountering sexual racism, racial fetishization included, is so burdensome that many choose not to use online dating platforms. This experience is so universal to daters of color that it seems almost normal. For example, when I asked seventy-three respondents of color about encountering racial harassment or fetishization, approximately 20 percent, across racial and ethnic categories, reported that they routinely received messages that directly used language of racial fetishization. I found that these self-reported measures were based on those who understood and could verbalize their experiences as being rooted in race-based harassment and, specifically, racial fetishization. When I holistically assessed interviews with respondents, with attention directed toward experiences described with other daters, the number of those who experienced sexual racism was much higher, closer to 60 percent. The discrepancy between self-reported negative experiences and my own estimation is likely due to the fact that many have accepted sexual racism as an everyday aspect of online dating. It has become so routine that it is not noteworthy.

There are two compounding and interacting forms of racial sorting and sexual racism at work in online dating. The first is the automated sorting, ranking, and matching systems that use race as a data point, working in the background of online dating systems without user knowledge. But this automated sexual racism also converges with individual sexual racism to produce an experience that is overly burdensome for people of color in online dating communities. Early results from a study on Black women's online dating experiences suggest that Black users are keenly aware of both the racism in dating culture and automated sexual racism on dating platforms. The study from the student-led research group—consisting of graduate students Jasmine Banks, Mel Monier, Miranda Reynaga, and myself (in the role of advisor)—demonstrate that Black women, in particular, feel the effects of automated sexual racism.[1]

Our team asked Black women how they thought dating sites work to understand if users have any perception of algorithmic sorting. Several respondents discussed algorithmic effects and race. Grace shared that she felt the algorithms on dating apps were biased: "I feel like when I first jump on there—it was like very much like they did try to connect [me] to race—like people who look like me, like the physicalities." Yolanda, another respondent in this study, suggested that dating platforms are using feedback from daters to strengthen algorithms' racial sorting capabilities:

> So they definitely ask for feedback quite often on the app. Like when you match somebody . . . when you "unmatch" with somebody, they ask if you met somebody. So I think, looking at that and then I have seen that they have like "star" matches that they think you would match best with. I definitely see that they think that I like Black men who are pretty tall and oddly have a similar body type.

These brief excerpts suggest that some users of color perceive that algorithms include race as part of sorting logics, and these two women explicitly expressed discomfort about online dating platforms using racial sorting. When asked if she thought online dating algorithms are equitable, Mary summarized succinctly, "I don't think they're equitable because it's just so many like things—just like being a Black woman, I feel like we're not given shit."

Accordingly, this chapter centers daters of color and explores how sexual racism is internalized and experienced on dating platforms. The previous chapter explored how White individuals normalize sexual racism by focusing on interviews with White individuals. These chapters are siblings in that they are distinctly qualitative, meaning that they are rooted in interview data rather than other data sources because it is important for readers to see how their individual choices about personal racialized preference are not neutral matters of choice. Rather, the choices are impactful and continue to normalize the belief that sexual racism is a harmless expression of personal taste. The obfuscation of racial algorithmic sorting perpetuates the belief that swiping through racially curated sexual marketplaces is an expression of taste. This chapter centers and uplifts the voices of those in the margins, centering them as experts on sexual racism.

To that end, I make every effort to protect and honor interview respondents by using pseudonyms that are true to ethnic, racial, and national origins. The interview excerpts I share here are short glimpses into the lives of seventy-three individuals who graciously gave their time to me—a gift for all of us to help understand the social consequences of our actions. The reality is that we (myself and you the reader) only get to see the impact of sexual racism on these respondents' lives from the vantage point of the thirty to forty-five minutes they were able to share with me.

Think about the habitual nature of using dating apps. We often log in after a long day to swipe for a dopamine boost or open the app when we're sitting around with friends. Imagine for a moment the weight of receiving a message full of racial hate at one of those times, demeaning to the core, and realizing that people hate aspects of you that you cannot change. Or, in another scenario, someone might decide that your chocolate skin would make an incredible snack. You can be a snack without having your soul devoured. One might think that such messages would be flattering but to receive them repeatedly might leave one wondering if others are only interested in them because of their "exotic" features. Routinely encountering racial fetishization and sexual racism can result in negative health outcomes, including increased anxiety and psychological distress, disordered eating, and substance abuse issues.[2]

Dating from the Sunken Place

Jordan Peele introduced viewers to the Sunken Place in his film *Get Out*. The Sunken Place refers to "a helpless state of consciousness where [bodily] agency and autonomy are subjugated by a well-to-do white suburban family" and serves as a metaphor for contemporary race relations in the United States.[3] In the film, Black individuals' bodies were unknowingly selected, based on visual aesthetic, intelligence, and physical prowess, to play host to White consciousness. In a style intentionally similar to auctions of enslaved people in the 1700s, White bidders would try to win Black bodies, which they would then hypnotize into taking a back seat to their own bodily functions. White brains were surgically implanted into Black craniums, giving them near-total control over the body's consciousness. But the Black person was still conscious in the Sunken Place, trapped inside, knowing that they had lost complete control over their life and body while a White consciousness dictated their every move.[4] White individuals paid a high price to experience this bodily tourism—the chance to experience life in a Black body that they fetishized for all of the stereotypical reasons: smooth Black skin and athleticism to name a few. These White antagonists fetishized Blackness so much that they wanted to fully experience Blackness but only on White terms.

The Sunken Place has become cultural shorthand for the Black experience in White America. We can see that so much is out of our control yet in social settings we are often forced to adhere to White heteropatriarchal standards. Where online dating is concerned, the Sunken Place metaphor is almost too perfect for Black daters because individuals often want to try out what it's like to be with a Black person, to be *inside* a Black body. This explicit positioning as a sexual experience, like an amusement park ride, is exactly the kind of bodily takeover that is represented by those in the Sunken Place and those who wish to subjugate and own Black bodies for their amusement and sexual gratification.

Racial fetishization divorces humans from their humanness by reducing them to parts—their skin, their lips, their hair, their behind, and so on. On a fundamental level, fetishization takes a nonsexual object or social idea (in the case of race) and treats it as a purely sexual object. Racial fetishization divorces whole humans from their features, such as eye color, eye shape, nose size/width, skin tone, hair texture, penis size, and hip measurements. Of course, some of these individual parts are sexy, no matter whom they belong to. But when they are sexy or desirable because of a racial marker, fetishized sexual attraction becomes sexual racism. I'm not here to kink shame anyone. Fetishes, in general, are not necessarily unhealthy, and some Black women have created thriving businesses making money off of race play and racial fetishization (e.g., Mollena Williams who is an expert in race play).[5] But here we are talking about nonconsensual racial fetishization that is rooted in stereotypes about unchangeable, skin-deep phenotypic features. If someone's skin is only sexy because you think of it as chocolate or caramel, that's a problem (for many reasons). I assure you that folks of color who are into race play will explicitly let you know. If you are seeking them out, I encourage you to do some deep self-inventory to assess where these racialized desires come from. Until then, you can assume the rest of us are not interested unless stated.

Jamaal, a self-identified straight Black man who used a variety of online dating platforms, shared about a budding relationship that failed when he realized his new partner was trying to keep him in the Sunken Place: "I went to her place for Thanksgiving, and then there was just—I was trying to see if the relationship would work out, and at some point she made me feel like she was exploring some sexual jungle, some dark man or stuff like that, or maybe she was just with me because I was Black, you know?" Jamaal decided that she was *too* into his Blackness and that they could never have a healthy relationship together.

Jewel, thirty-six, a self-identified straight African American woman, told me about her online dating experience, which also calls up imagery of the Sunken Place, and in some instances, explicit master–slave role play:

Jewel: Yeah, like I get a lot of couples who are looking for unicorns—I didn't know what the heck a unicorn was, but I get a lot of those messages, and I'm African American and they generally come from White couples looking for their Black unicorn. I guess they want some type of spice added into their marriage or their relationship, and I seem to attract that kind of group because on Tinder that's pretty much who messaged me like all of the time. I also get a lot of just fetish people who have fetishes where they like, you know, Black girl fetish or bondage fetish. I had one guy who wanted me to like act like his slave master and tie him up and put him in bondage. It was just really weird, offbeat people that would kind of hit me up.

Apryl: So he wanted you to tie *him* up, not the other way around?

Jewel: Yes, like I was going to be the slaveholder and he was going to be the slave. He wanted me to put him in bondage. And he elaborated on how he'd show me, literally, how to tie the knots, and tie him up. I guess it's one of those kind of S&M type of things, bondage things, I don't know, I'm not into that. I don't judge anybody who is, but he specifically wanted me to be the slaveholder and him the slave.

Apryl: So do you feel like this was a regular BDSM fetish or did you feel this was racially fetishizing?

Jewel: I *know* it was racially geared. I mean, come on, he wanted me to be
the slaveholder, and he wanted to be the slave . . . just fetishized, like
where because I'm Black it's fetishized.

Apryl: Is that the only time you've experience racial fetishization?

Jewel: No, so this one guy messaged me in my DMs [direct messages]
on Instagram, and he was a complete stranger, don't know him, and
he messaged me and seemed to be cool at first, just talking, and then
the comments started. Some of the comments he was making, I could
already tell we were going down that fetish route. Like he would just
always draw attention to my skin color, and it comes off as compliments
of course, because he's fetishizing it, like oh, your beautiful chocolate
skin, your deep skin tone, your melanin—like, everything always cir-
cled back to my skin color. Like it didn't seem like it was ever about
anything else; it was simply just—I don't even know the word to use,
but completely in love with the color of my skin, but in a very weird
way. And eventually, I don't think I gave him any type of notice. I just
blocked him completely from my Instagram, because it was just weird
to me.

Apryl: That's really, really interesting. So would you say that your experience is similar to other Black women, or do you think that your experience is somehow unique from the experience of other Black women?

Jewel: I think my experience is the same as other Black women, because
the people that I have asked about their online dating experience were
my Black female friends, and they typically—it's maybe not the exact
same experiences as me, but they had little to no success or they find
out that the people that they're attracting are not necessarily the people
they want to attract.

By Jewel's account, these experiences are commonplace for her and her
friends. Black women are barraged with these types of exploitative experiences and bodily tourism—so much so that it interferes with finding meaningful, fruitful relationships. Two Black women I interviewed encountered
racial fetishization so frequently that they began saving screenshots of offensive commentary to share and vent about with their friends.

Hazel, a biracial Black woman with lighter skin, encountered the idolization aspect of racial fetishization. Under the cultural narrative of European beauty standards, lighter skin is to be desired, and darker skin is positioned as undesirable. In fact, there is an entire subculture predicated on the production of biracial babies because they are "the best of both worlds" and according to popular Instagram discourse, the cutest of all children. Accordingly, biracial children often have lighter skin tones than their parents of color but maintain desirable traits of capitalistic exoticism, such as curly hair and "tan" skin. Hazel, who was familiar with this cultural narrative, shared screen captures of a conversation with Manuel, who expressed his attraction to Hazel because of her skin tone (Figure 4.1). Hazel attempted to curtail the interaction as soon as she realized what was happening by asking what was meant by "not too dark."

FIGURE 4.1   A screen capture of a conversation between a participant, Hazel, and a match on Bumble.

Source: Williams's interview with Hazel. Participant granted permission to include this photo.

As sociologist Shantel Buggs observed, biracial and multiracial women are particularly on guard for displays of racism during the age of Black Lives Matter.[6] Hazel knew what was being implied. She simply wanted to see it spelled out in Black and White (pun very much intended). Manuel replied, "I love light skin women. Not too into the dark look. Like seal [referencing Seal, the dark-skinned Black musician] complexion." When Hazel did not respond, Manuel added, "I got a type. Everyone should have one. Haha." Manuel's directive—that everyone should have a type, even one that is implicitly grounded in aesthetic racial choice—is the prevailing, unquestioned social norm.[7] Our implicit beliefs about desirability and attractiveness are inherently racialized because we live in a society where race holds deep and significant social meaning. Though the idea of having a type is widely taken for granted as a harmless personal choice, Manuel's contextualization makes exceedingly clear that the bounds of his personal choice are in fact an aspect of sexual racism because they are demarcated by his rejection of darker skin tones as a desirable dating aesthetic—not too dark.

Alternatively, Deja, a Black woman with a self-described medium skin tone, regularly experienced another facet of racial fetishization: sexual tourism. The screen captures from her conversation with Kyle exemplify the online inhibition effect otherwise known as hiding behind a keyboard (Figure 4.2). Kyle's opening statement, "since we've never met, and I don't know [y]ou," implies that he feels free to express opinions he might not if he were in an in-person, face-to-face context. Kyle shares that he is both "intimidated and also enamored" at the thought of being with a Black "girl." Deja doesn't care because she's heard this too many times. She ends her interaction with Kyle by educating him, to hopefully help out the next Black woman he matches with.

Deja shared another Sunken Place dating exchange in which she called out racial fetishization in a conversation with James, a White man (Figure 4.3). On the heterosexual side of Bumble dating (as opposed to Bumble Bizz or Bumble BBF), women send the first message to allow men to start chatting with them. Deja opened with a casual starter: "Hey what's up! :)" For James, the message he sent probably felt just as casual: "Oh you know just looking for that good ebony queen." In some circles, this kind of message may have been appropriate and acceptable if it had come from a Black man. Here James is appropriating the insider colloquialism "queen" used in Black

FIGURE 4.2   A screen capture of a conversation between a participant, Deja, and a match.

Source: Williams's interview with Deja. Participant granted permission to include this photo.

communities to address Black women. Further, as Deja points out, "ebony" is a category on most major porn sites. In fact, in 2014, Pornhub, arguably the most popular pornography platform, encouraged consumers to solely use the ebony category in honor of Martin Luther King Day.[8] Rest assured, that's not the kind of racial equality the reverend dreamed of!

Though the problems with racial fetishization are many, the most pressing is that many—like Manuel, James, and Kyle—view these kinds of race-based idolizations as positive or even sweet expressions of personal preference. But racial fetishization has negative outcomes, both practical and psychological, for those who regularly experience it in online dating. Dating

FIGURE 4.3   A screen capture of a conversation between
a participant, Deja, and a match on Bumble.

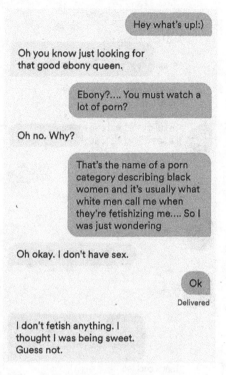

Source: Williams's interview with Deja. Participant
granted permission to include this photo.

from the Sunken Place means that Black women, nonbinary folx, and men
report feeling as though they only exist to fulfill experiences of sexual tourism or exoticism, objectification by potential matches, and difficulty initi-
ating and maintaining interracial relationships. These feelings are a valid,
internal safety mechanism that protects marginalized folx from the dangers
of unmitigated hate that may turn violent.

While some of these interactions occurred outside of dating platforms
(either on other text-based messaging apps such as WhatsApp or out in the
physical world), these individuals were first encountered on dating platforms.
All of these real-life accounts—shared by Jewel, Jamaal, Hazel, and Deja—
highlight that dating from the Sunken Place requires enhanced vigilance to

protect oneself from bodily and emotional harms of sexual racism. This is especially true in light of the big gap in safety measures for sexual harm experienced by women and femme-identified folx of color on dating platforms and in dating culture.[9] This gap in safety for women of color, especially Black women, is not new. The pattern is well established throughout history as Black women are seen as legitimate victims of sexual harm because society views them as hypersexual deviant temptresses.[10] One respondent told me about the weight of dealing with this stereotype:

> I know that there's this history of the hypersexuality of the Black woman, and it just makes you feel uncomfortable or it makes *me* feel uncomfortable. . . . It's just very problematic to me, and I don't exactly understand why people still hold those views.

This harmful cultural trope positions Black women as legitimate and appropriate victims of sexual harm in society. Because this narrative is widely believed, its prominence seeps into our criminal justice system, redoubling existing inequity in those systems. The belief that Black women are hypersexual and animalistic has resulted in higher rates of rape and sexual assault of Black women in the United States, while those who commit sexual crimes against Black women receive lighter sentencing than those who sexually assault and rape White women.[11] Scholars of the law argue that these discrepancies in protection have established legal patterns that allow for inferior treatment of Black women concerning sexual harm. As discussed earlier in this book, enslaved Black women and men were routinely raped with no legal ramifications. This legacy of open access to Black sexuality and Black bodies remains and is evidenced by disproportionate protection under the law and disproportionate protection from sexual racism on dating platforms.

"Yellow Fever" Is Sexual Racism

This idea—that people of color are somehow innately more sexual—was a theme that emerged in interviews with individuals across racial and ethnic backgrounds. According to most of the women of color with whom I spoke, White individuals appear to be the demographic most likely to commit unsolicited racial fetishization. When I asked Audrey if she had ever experienced racial fetishization from matches on a dating platform, she remarked, "I would say a handful of times, and the people that it's come from—the only race that I've experienced that type of fetish from, is White men." Tai, a twenty-four-year-old self-identified bisexual Asian woman, shared that she gave up on dating White men altogether because they were too racist even when they thought they weren't. She indicated that it was specifically "White dudes" who expressed the most sexual racism towards her: "Let's just say there's a reason why I'm dating a person of color now. I dated pretty much three White boys, in my entire life. The first one—our first time meeting, he already told me he had 'yellow fever.'"

Tai told me that she learned a lot about herself from that relationship and had since done more exploring. She also indicated that campus life at a small Christian college in California, where she was one of very few Asian students, limited her dating options. Hence her relationship with one of her previous White male partners was one in which she was constantly countering his racism and trying to educate him:

Yeah, he was like, "I have yellow fever" . . . the first thing he told me was, "I'm into Asians, I have yellow fever." And he's the kind of guy that's into baseball, cars, and imported models—I can list it on one hand. Oh, and soccer. But pretty much really stereotypical White dude. Like, as stereotypical as you can get. And I had to teach him why—and his roommates would make racist jokes against me, and they were super conservative. . . . And we were very obviously a bad fit for each other, but he was a sweet dude and not bad looking. The dick wasn't bad, it wasn't terrible, and I was in college, so I was like, eh, one dick for now. . . . And eventually we broke things off, because I was like—I have no feelings for you.

. . . [Now] he's dating someone who's the complete opposite of me, and was pretty much everything he asked for in the perfect Asian girl-friend. She's half-Filipina half-White, so she's Asian enough to pass but still White enough to fit his standards. She's way shorter than me, and she's super quiet and doesn't cuss. And doesn't have tattoos—like I have hella tattoos. She's like the complete package [for him].

My interpretation of Tai's reflection (given the full context of my interview with her) is that the ex-boyfriend found someone who would tolerate his racism and racial fetishization.

Interestingly, his new partner is biracial and in accordance with Tai's analysis, White-adjacent. She is Asian but is likely able to conform to White, Christian heteropatriarchal standards of desirability: she's quiet (the biblical New Testament speaks at length about desirable women having a meek and quiet spirit); short, in a Western society where Asian women are expected to be small and diminutive; and doesn't have tattoos, which is akin to the all-American, girl-next-door aesthetic. Tai's insights are important because they convey the deep connection between sexual racism and what are considered socially acceptable and desirable dating qualifications.[12]

The trope or biblical characteristic (depending on your religious views) of a meek, quiet, and submissive wife is something that Asian women frequently encounter. Coupled with the "cute" Asian ideal—wherein cuteness is a racialized aspirational quality of being small, with feminine features, less defined muscle tone, and large childlike eyes—Asian women face a specific brand of sexual racism. They are expected to look like children and be sexually compliant in and outside the bedroom (Figure 4.4).

FIGURE 4.4   Graph depicting relative prevalence of attractiveness language across racial and ethnic groups.

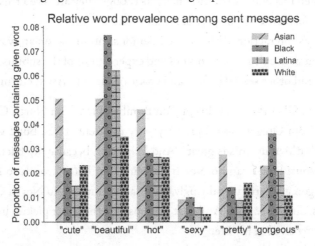

Source: Hanyu Chwe, Apryl Williams, and Ronald Robertson, "Testing Racial and Gender Toxicity on Tinder: A Mixed Methods Approach." Proceedings of the 56th Hawaii International Conference on System Sciences, January 2023. https://hdl.handle.net/10125/102886. Reprinted with permission.

In another study I conducted with colleagues Hanyu Chwe and Ronald Robertson, who were, at the time, both graduate students at the Northeastern Network Science Institute, we found that Asian women were told that they were cute more often than any other racial group.[13] In our study, we used eight fictive Tinder profiles consisting of two Asian models, two Black models, two Latina models, and two White models. We wanted to see if there were any differences in the way Tinder users responded to women who presented clear racial or ethnic distinctions. The results confirmed previous research showing that White women elicited the highest number of matches and received the most messages.[14] Hence we were not surprised to find data supporting the stories I'd been hearing from many of the women I interviewed. The kind of attention received and the words used to interact with women does differ along racial lines—meaning that men who talk to women on Tinder may adjust their language to follow racialized scripts when talking to women of different backgrounds. It is no coincidence that the words most frequently used to describe Asian women are "cute," "beautiful," and "hot" where other groups are referred to as cute remarkably less often. In U.S. American culture, Asian women are depicted as being all of these things at once, and they are expected to be submissive in the bedroom. When they are not, men respond with entitlement, as though they are owed this kind of bodily performance on the part of Asian women.

Sydney's interaction with a match demonstrates how Asian women are confronted with cultural stereotypes and expectations of the submissive cute aesthetic and other sexual racism and erotica related to Asian culture:

Sydney: Okay, so I met this guy on Bumble. He's from North Carolina, I'm from Oregon, so they're very, very different states, but I was like, "He's different, this is great." And I thought, because my friend had a Missouri boy, I can do North Carolina, but his approach to me was: Oregon girls are typically ugly, especially compared to North Carolina girls, but you're cute. And that was possibly the worst pickup line I had ever received in my life.

Apryl: Yeah, why start with that?

Sydney: It was strange. But three days after that, since we exchanged Instagram accounts, he wanted to FaceTime me and I was kind of scared. . . . And when we FaceTimed, he asked how I sounded "White," whether I knew how to use chopsticks, and if I was into tentacle porn—it was very odd.

Apryl: Oh no! What is tentacle porn?

Sydney: I wasn't quite sure at the time—but I assume it's like a fetish that some people have where tentacles enter a woman's body?

Apryl: Oh no, no, no—Okay, I was not ready for that.

Sydney: I know! And then we talked about politics, and he was a very hardcore Trump supporter, and I was like, okay, that's fine. He thought that I would immediately end the call because I'm from a blue state, but I said "no, I'm very open to different opinions." He went on to say, "I'm a redneck, but I've lived in LA for a bit—I feel like if I lived on the West Coast, I'd have an Asian friend. By the way, are you submissive?" And that took me back—"I was like, what?" It was very strange. Because he said he had an ex-girlfriend who was Filipino, and she was submissive. That made me really uncomfortable, so I kind of just nervously laughed it off.

Apryl: Okay is there anything else you wanted to say or that you wanted me to know about this experience?

Sydney: Yeah, that was during winter break. And I'd stopped talking to him for a little bit because I had gotten back to school and was focusing on the adjustment back from winter break, and he wrote me a whole paragraph about how I would be wasting his time because we hadn't talked as much, and I was like—"I have to go."

While the cute aesthetic originated in Japan, globalization of Japanese culture and global flows of racialized tropes about Asian masculinity and femininity without context mean that Western cultures, especially U.S. audiences, tend to conflate Japanese, Korean, Cambodian, Filipina/o, Vietnamese, and Chinese cultures into one big racist pot. There is a long history of Japanese art and erotica that is contested in Japanese culture. The internet has exported this aspect of Japanese culture without the contested context, with English-speaking audiences dubbing tentacle porn with language of sexual harm and rape. In any context, women in the tentacle porn genre are often depicted as being raped by humans with tentacle extremities or, worse, by octopuses or squid that have been personified. The twisted allure of tentacle porn is that a woman is having animalistic sexual interaction with a nonhuman entity, often by force, against her will. This imagery of Asian women, or "race-less" women in hentai cartoon porn (which is associated with Asianness), makes connections in popular consumer culture that Asian women are up for any kind of animalistic sex in which they are meek, quiet, subdued, and often overpowered.[15]

Similarly, culturally inaccurate stereotypes are ascribed to Asian men—namely that they are feminine, less muscular, and less masculine, regardless of ethnic or national origin.[16] Kevin, a twenty-five-year-old self-identified Asian man, conveyed that he has a hard time dealing with racial fetishization and Asian stereotyping on dating platforms:

> A lot of people conflate being Asian with like, K-pop artists, and I'm not even Korean. I'm actually Chinese myself, so it's kind of weird because it's like usually the attention is [audio unclear], but every time it's like, they're not trying to get to know me as a person, it's just like, oh, you're Asian, you must like this Asian thing.

When I asked Ashley and Ren, two Asian women, if they had ever experienced racial fetishization, they immediately recalled two frequently encountered phrases: "Oh, shit, you're Asian, you must have tight pussy" and "Is your pussy sideways?" I heard this same stereotype, rooted in sexual racism, that Asian women have "slanted pussies" from five additional Asian women that I interviewed. Tai too reported hearing this phrase often and retorted, "No, bitch! I don't know where the fuck that comes from, but no! I have the same ass vagina as everybody else—well obviously we're all different, but not *that* different." Another woman reported that she'd been told "your pussy must be sideways and tighter" so many times that she'd lost count; especially at the onset of the pandemic, she felt that people were emboldened to verbalize their racist thoughts about Asian women. When I asked Tai if she thought these kinds of comments were simply bad jokes (like the color-blind media culture would lead you to believe) or were overt acts of racism, she responded:

> I think both. It was definitely like a bad joke—I was just like, what the fuck?? But I've definitely heard that stereotype before. [deep breath] I've

heard a lot of dudes talking about this, and they're like, oh, I love to date Asian women because like, their pussy's tighter—fuck if I knew. I stopped listening after that comment, but I was just like . . . dude. Can you like, not? Yes, I'm Asian, I speak Cantonese, I speak Mandarin, but I'm still Asian American. I grew up here, I am just as American as you are, there's no reason to like, fetishize me. I also don't understand why guys are like—"Hey, is your pussy slanted?"—like, I [*trails off*] I don't see how that would encourage me to want to sleep with you, because I don't want that dick inside of me. And I don't get that from women—like, women, when I get hit on, or when I hit on women, it's more of like, hey, I love your tattoos, tell me more about them, or dude, I love your earrings, or like, damn, girl, you look hot—it's just way more wholesome.

Consuming Latinx Culture

The Latinx folks who were interviewed for this project reported experiencing sexual racism less often than other groups. The relative infrequency of self-reported exposure to sexual racism may be due to the fact that in my sample of interviewees, there are several Latinos/Latinas who pass for White or identify as White—meaning that they do not outwardly demonstrate the physical or linguistic markers that others would decode as Latina/Latino or Hispanic.

For Latinx-identified daters, the kinds of sexual racism they experienced was often more covert and more likely to surface during sustained relationships with individuals. Gabriel, a self-identified gay Latino, shared that dating White men is more difficult because bringing them to family functions involved more labor than joy. "It's kind of like—it's not really fun if you're explaining everything to them, like an event that's amusing for them—it's a different feeling." Gabriel indicated that bringing White partners to family functions felt like a type of touristic or voyeuristic event. They were not respectfully taking part in their date's familial culture. They were having a cultural experience that was markedly different than their regular White life. Similarly, many Latina women with whom I spoke said they simply did not feel comfortable dating outside of their local ethnic communities because of growing anti-immigrant sentiment in the United States, especially from populations that are demonized in the media such as Mexican, Ecuadoran, Honduran, and Guatemalan immigrants as well as others from Central and South America.

Previous work by sociologists Cynthia Feliciano and Jessica Kizer suggest that those whose primary identification is Latinx or Afro-Latina/o were more likely to shy away from dating White people, probably because their identity is shaped by experiences of anti-Blackness and anti-Latinx immigrant sentiment.[17] It may feel safer to date those whom family and friends can vouch for instead of taking the risk of going on a date that has the potential to become unsafe or that may present the threat of deportation for those who hold liminal status or are undocumented.[18] After listening to interviews conducted with White respondents, about their fetishistic preferences for Latinx or Hispanic culture (which I covered in Chapter 3), this is probably a wise approach to take.

Internalized Sexual Racism and Colorism

Sexual racism impacts us all, especially people of color—and not just because we experience its effects. All of the stories I've shared in this chapter so far are about how sexual racism from White individuals (or those who are White presenting) harms daters of color. Unfortunately, people of color also internalize the ethos of sexual racism, including the stereotypes and cultural biases it produces, contributing to the automating of sexual racism. This can cause racial or ethnic conflict between non-White daters.

Many have bought into the cultural narrative that European beauty aesthetics are most desirable because of widespread anti-Blackness across the globe. In Asia, and in some Black communities, this belief manifests as skin bleaching to maintain paler skin tones, while in Middle Eastern cultures it manifests as nose jobs intended straighten or slim broad noses, to achieve social capital granted to those who are able to achieve and perform a European aesthetic. What this means within communities of color is that lightness of skin tone is a privileged, desired, and negotiated commodity.[19] Families with lighter skin tones across Asian, Latinx, Indigenous, and Black communities often try to reproduce light skin tones through selective matching with others of lighter skin tones.[20]

This myth, that lighter skin is more desirable, is directly linked to the ideas and status that come with it. Having a lighter skin tone implies that one's bloodline is intermingled with European ancestry and that those with darker skin are less civilized and truer to their "colored" roots. Lighter skin is viewed as a desirable trait because it comes with social privilege. Lighter skin implies European ancestry in earlier phases of immigration (in the cases of Asian and Latinx families), meaning that those long-established interracial families likely had more economic resources to immigrate or have had a longer time to amass wealth in the United States.[21] Those who are lighter skinned are perceived as having greater commonality with White people and are thus afforded the status and privilege associated with Whiteness.[22] Sociologists have found that multiracial daters who primarily identify as White are more likely to participate in racial status hierarchies and colorism.[23] For many, this is a strategy of assimilation to avoid racial/ethnic harassment or prejudice, but others simply reproduce racist beliefs and racial meaning making because it is socially beneficial to perform Whiteness.

Colorism and internalized sexual racism plague us all, even as we work to resist settler colonialism and the White racial superiority of Western beauty ideals. Cheyenne, a twenty-six-year-old self-identified Indigenous Latina woman, shared her journey to understand her family's colorism:

> I find that my family has, some relatives more than others, some internalized racism that I think they need to address. Meaning that, if I—not my parents—but definitely some of my aunts, if I brought in a White person, that would be highly lauded, like celebrated, as in "You're doing something good for the race." There's some whitening going on there, and I definitely have some aunts, like whenever I have over some of my friends who are White women, they just kind of crowd around them, like they're thirsting for Whiteness, and if I would have a White guy, they'd be like, oh, he's so beautiful, he's so attractive, your babies are going to be so White and beautiful. Like it sounds very strange to say it in English, but in Spanish, whenever there's a baby, like a good compliment you can give a baby is, "Que linda tu bebe, esa guera," like, how pretty is your baby, they're White, they're very light.
>
> So I think if I had a White partner, then it would be seen as a good thing. I think if I brought in someone who was of our background, like

Indigenous or Latinx, then it would be taken okay— my family's from Guatemala, so from Latin America, so someone who's Latinx or Indigenous of Latin America, then it's something familiar. They might speak Spanish, and for my parents, that's okay. Where my parents would— well, not my parents, but some—my grandmothers, definitely, they have a lot of anti-Blackness that they need to work through. Kind of like how they, my grandmas, or some of my aunts, have more of a celebration for Whiteness, it's the opposite for Blackness. And I've seen it with some of my cousins who have dated or are dating, currently, Black men, and how upset their parents are, or I've seen it with one of my cousins who was dating a Black woman, and how his mother got really upset at him, and he had to defend why he wanted her to be his girlfriend, like why he loved her so much. And I find there would be much more of this legwork to do, and I guess much more of this anti-racist work to happen with certain family members to address their internalized racism towards Whiteness and Blackness. I guess with folks of Asian backgrounds, I think I can't imagine any—

I don't know, I guess I think my parents for some reason wouldn't push back, or from some of my others, I think if anything, the racism that they deal with is they have this tendency to just call anyone of Asian background "Chinos," so just categorizing them all as Chinese, and I guess it would be much more educational on their behalf, of that there's a lot of countries that are also Asian, just like Latin America. I think there'd be a lot of that, of addressing stereotypes or some of the racist language that might be used.

These familial dynamics cause stress for daters who are concerned about their potential partners' well-being. Nathan also shared that he is more cautious about bringing Black or Latina women home to meet his mother because he'd "have to gauge whether or not the person would be interested in trying to deal with my parents' expectations around what they want in a potential romantic partner, so that's part of what factors into my decision making around meeting someone." In any relationship, partners have to choose how they will navigate family input about their relationship, but potential racism from family is clearly an additional burden.

Asian daters with whom I spoke, in particular, grappled with the effects of internalized sexual racism and anti-Blackness in their communities. They had a heightened sense of how their ethnicity or nationality impacted their chances for finding success using dating platforms.[24] At the end of the interview, when I asked Bryan, a twenty-two-year-old Chinese and Vietnamese man, if there was anything else he wanted me to know about his dating experience that we'd missed in other parts of the interview, he remarked:

> As far as online dating goes, at least in my perspective—I don't know, I have other Asian friends who might've been more successful, but I find it, I don't want to say odd, but I guess you could put that term 'cause he's Sri Lankan; he's Brown, and there's often stereotypes of a person with that skin color, and he tends to have more results than I have—it's not by a large margin, but he has had more results than I have. I'm not sure if it's the setting of him living in California near LA or is it because he's out there more often, he's more active, doing other stuff, and I'm just going to the gym and going home. But he seems to be a lot more successful in his search than I have been.

Bryan's hunch—that cultural distinctions in residential areas may be responsible for differences in dating success—is supported by sociological research. Studies suggest that openness to Asian interracial dating varies by geographical location.[25] He also conveyed that his kind of Asianness was less desirable than that of his friend who was Sri Lankan. In the United States, Vietnamese individuals are sometimes depicted as "jungle Asians" as opposed to "fancy Asians" who often speak British forms of English due to the history of colonization of India and Sri Lanka.[26] These subtle respectability politics are noticed by those who suffer from their deployment. Even though Bryan felt the sting of prejudice, that experience did not always cause him to reflect on his own views on dating outside of his race:

> Growing up in Vegas and my representation growing up and seeing "Black women" is that they're very ratchet, very ghetto, in terms of representation, and so that's not the highest view I see them. My good friend in Arizona, he's Black, and I've talked to him about these things, and he said if you're ever interested in getting with a Black woman, you should probably go for a light-skinned one, those are the ones who are better, and I've heard that same thing echoed by older African American friends I hang out with.

Even the Black men in Bryan's life perpetuate the belief that only light-skinned Black women are suitable for long-term dating or courtship. This is unsurprising given studies showing that colorism is gendered in Black communities, with Black men being more likely to buy into colorism.[27] Though Bryan's friends seem to be primarily responsible for his present outlook on dating Black women, his early opinions, like most of us, were formed by his family. Our parents are our first and most regular communicators of social norms, beliefs, and ideologies. Because familial logics are communicated to us explicitly and implicitly, it takes a lot of unlearning and relearning to move away from a lifetime of social indoctrination, especially when these cues come from older, revered members of our families and social networks.

Family matriarchs and patriarchs may wish to protect their kin from society's prejudices by maintaining lighter skin tones through assimilation.[28] Sociologists Richard Alba and Victor Nee suggest that marrying into Whiteness can be an attempt to integrate into mainstream American White culture.[29] Accordingly, half of U.S.-born Asian Americans marry White partners.[30] This attempt at assimilation also reinforces racial sexual desirability politics. Tai again remarked on her parents' desires to see her marry someone within her ethnic group. I asked if she'd ever dated Black and Latinx folks, and if she'd had any apprehension about dating outside her race. Her response highlights the emotions associated with navigating family members' views on race in dating:

> Yes and no. So, my parents are really traditional, so anybody—and they've lowered their standards now, but they used to be like, you have to marry a Chinese from the mainland! And now they're like—he's [her current partner] Korean, that's good enough. But my parents disapproved of anyone who was Black, anyone who was Latinx—even Filipinos; it was weird. But yeah, they—I mean, I brought [those previous partners of color] along anyway, 'cause I don't give a fuck! I was like, "That Black shit?" I don't give a fuck, imma bring up whoever. So all of my boyfriends have like come through, and mom has not been rude—whether or not she approves, I don't really give a fuck. Yeah. They did not like that, did not like—even my [current] boyfriend, they're like, "Ugh, fine, he's Asian. She seems set on him, this is her longest relationship."

Daniel, a twenty-eight-year-old Asian man, also shared his family's views on dating outside the race:

> If I can be honest, my parents actually—they haven't said much about who I should date except my dad who said explicitly not to date Black people.... They were also against Hispanics. They never asked me about it when they knew I was dating her. Pretty much they just wanted another Asian girl or White chick, and I did not really like that view, but that's just their view and doesn't influence who I choose to see.

Beyond colorism, some individuals of color with whom I spoke reported on their family's outright racism. Bryan told me about Chinese parents in general and their views on dating Black women:

> Again, I'm not trying to be rude here, but I don't know why Chinese parents will joke around, oh, he's going to bring home a Black girl, and then here comes the racism, she'll bring him fried chicken and watermelon all the time. That's pretty racist, and that's not how it works at all.

Asian anti-Blackness is well documented throughout social science research, but the convergence of the COVID-19 pandemic and the resurgence of the Black Lives Matter movement recently brought it to the fore of news media discussion and national consciousness in the United States. There is an often-overlooked intersection between anti-Black and anti-Asian sentiment rooted in beliefs that both groups are dirty and untrustworthy.[31] Yet anti-Blackness deeply pervades Asian cultures in the United States and abroad. Historically, Asian countries have made explicit efforts to prevent Black individuals from immigrating to their countries.[32] The same can be said for Asian enclaves in otherwise Black neighborhoods in the United States.

Anti-Blackness in Dating Culture

A prevailing thread in Black philosophy argues that society was built upon worldwide systems of chattel slavery.[33] Because Black enslavement is a central building block to our current capitalist systems that circulate globally, all future iterations of society that emerge from this foundation will intrinsically manifest inequity for Black individuals. This will remain true until we rectify and make reparations for the inhumane basis of the modern capital-ist systems from which we, in the Global North, all benefit (to varying and disparate degrees). Further, continued success of social life as we know it is predicated on maintaining and regulating Blackness, whether through rules that dictate law and order, extractive popular culture that relies on appropri-ating and White-washing Black culture, or the mass production of African fashions and so on.[34]

Ironically, we are told that this version of anti-Blackness is not about race. Yet, as philosophers contend, due to our capitalist systems being rooted in racial colonization, society as it exists today is deeply tied to race. Therefore, the commoditization of dating markets is also predicated on anti-Blackness. Historically, throughout the world, dating or matchmaking was tied to the exchange of commodities.[35] One family traded a woman for land or re-sources. Conceptualizations of dating that invoke imagery of love are a much more modern occurrence. This is not to say that love did not exist before. Love has always existed. But dating and courtship have also always been part of exchange relations. Hence the modern commoditization of dating is also part of a capitalist anti-Black system.

If dating is thought of as an exchange of commodities, social capital is also a commodity. Under our capitalist system—which denies Blackness, and specifically the enslavement of Black people, as well as appropriation of Blackness, as the reason for its success—dating markets seek to avoid the truth that all continents share a lineage. Though biologically speaking there are no pure races, scientists generally agree that modern humans originated in Africa and spread to various continents, meaning that racial differences are truly just skin deep; we all share a great deal of genetic material.[36] Yet social capital dictates that White racial aesthetics are more desirable and valuable than others.[37] To talk about our shared ancestral lineage as rooted in Africa would upend social systems that are predicated on the belief that racial dif-ferences offer valuable sites for social commodity exchange. To ignore this shared history is anti-Blackness in action. Those in power maintain the myth of White racial superiority. People in societies who have been colonized by those with the mindset of White racial superiority grow to accept these stan-dards. All people of color must understand that their oppression is tied to anti-Black racism and colonialism.[38]

Sexual racism is also tied to anti-Black capitalism, especially in the United States. As discussed in Chapter 1, sexual racism emerged because White owners of enslaved people wanted to control how enslaved peoples reproduced. They also wanted to discourage White women from having sexual relationships with Black and Native people. When we refer to sexual racism as simply an expression of neutral personal preference, we ignore the inherent anti-Blackness in it. By cultivating racial logics in dating, users encourage dating platforms to automate racially curated sexual marketplaces. Hence openly acknowledging sexual racism would force users to recognize their own anti-Blackness, anti-Asianness, and anti-immigrant biases, allowing us to move toward creating safer spaces for everyone.

FIVE

Safety Thirst

Who Gets to Be Safe While Dating Online?

When researchers talk about safety in online dating, or lack of safety, they are primarily referring to the safety of White cisgender women. But even this relatively privileged group of users is not completely safe. Though safety cannot ever be fully guaranteed in any social situation, the outlook on safety while using dating platforms is bleak, and some researchers are concerned that the online dating space is growing increasingly unsafe for everyone.

ProPublica reported increasingly high rates of registered sex offenders using Tinder.[1] Elena Cama found that digital violence and sexual harm is most often experienced by women and girls on dating platforms (as compared to men and boys using online dating platforms).[2] Another study found that there is an increased risk of cyber stalking as individuals are less aware of how their dating platforms are connected to other digital media and/or leave digital traces about their personal information.[3] Social scientists are also devoting increasing attention to "cyber dating abuse," which involves controlling behavior, jealousy, hostility, and direct aggression with matches on dating platforms.[4] Further, news outlets across the globe and research experts warn that digital dating apps are linked to an increase in rape culture and sexual harm including unsolicited sexual images, sexual assault, and re-venge porn.[5] One article from *Slate* explains "dating apps are rape culture" where rape culture is described as elements of culture that support rape as an excused or minimized social infraction.[6]

No one social tool is responsible for upholding rape culture, including dating apps. As the name implies, it is a cultural phenomenon that is sup-ported by the upholding of toxic heteropatriarchal values. Yet even as we develop ways to deal with the symptoms of such violence, we have a long way to go toward addressing the root causes of patriarchal violence in dating culture. People of color—especially women, femmes, and transgender folx—potentially deal with these harms plus the additional harms that are specific to intersectional experiences. Safety on dating platforms must also account for those potentially negative experiences.

Making the Rules About Safety in Online Dating

One public health definition of safety defines it as "a state in which hazards and conditions leading to physical, psychological or material harm are con-trolled in order to preserve the health and well-being of individuals and the community."[7] To attain safety, individuals and society must cultivate equity in "protecting human rights and freedoms," prevent consequences caused by harm, and respect the physical and psychological integrity of all.[8] Marginal-ized daters—whether queer, transgender, or persons of color, and especially those at any intersection of these experiences—cannot be assured safety on dating platforms if companies are not willing to make provisions for that safety. Spaces where sexual racism flourish are fundamentally unsafe for people of color because they are routinely exposed to conditions that may lead to psycho-logical and physical harm. The problem is, dating companies believe that their products facilitate a mostly safe experience (for the normative White user):

> At *Match Group*, the safety, security, and well-being of our users is some-thing we take very seriously—we consider it a top priority. *While rela-tively few of the hundreds of millions of people that have used our products have been harmed by bad actors,* we believe that any incident of miscon-duct or criminal behavior is one too many.[9]

Because dating platforms do not name sexual racism as a communal threat to safety, they shape the belief that it is normal. Users continue to see sexual racism as an expected, trivial part of the online dating experience. Hence the first way that dating platforms help to automate sexual racism is through meaning making via *inaction*. Experiences of racial fetishization can produce and overlap with sexual harassment in ways that fall outside of community guidelines, and I question the degree to which these policies are intended to protect users and the extent to which they allow unsafe behavior to flourish.

The second form of automating sexual racism speaks to the technological sense of the word "automation." Many dating platforms use algorithmic systems to reinforce their safety efforts, which still largely fail to offer adequate protection for marginalized users. By using automated approaches to safety with known potential for racial and gendered bias, dating platforms literally automate sexual racism. By focusing on some aspects of safety while failing to consider how their own platforms facilitate sexual racism, online dating companies reinforce for users what is acceptable behavior inside and outside of dating platforms. Tech companies have a history of failing to consider race as they make design choices and policy decisions that impact all users.

Ruha Benjamin discusses the broader social and political implications of tech companies' unwillingness to deal with race in *Race After Technology*:

The animating force of the New Jim Code is that tech designers encode judgments into technical systems but claim that the racist results of their designs are entirely exterior to the encoding process. Racism thus becomes doubled—magnified and buried under layers of digital denial.... There are many tech insiders hiding behind the language of free speech, allowing racist and sexist harassment to run rampant in the digital public square and looking the other way as avowedly bad actors deliberately crash into others with reckless abandon. For this reason, we should consider how private industry choices are in fact public policy decisions. They are animated by political values influenced strongly by libertarianism, which extols individual autonomy and corporate freedom from government regulation.[10]

Benjamin's point is that tech companies make decisions about their community guidelines and terms of use that support the expression of racism and sexual harassment while publicly claiming to be working toward the greater good. But tech companies take a hands-off approach when harm comes to their users as a result of the social ecosystem they've developed: acting with the ethos of neoliberalism, it's every person for themselves.

Tech companies allow individuals to act with autonomy while taking no responsibility for building spaces where these kinds of harm thrive. I have been in the room when decisions that privilege autonomy over equity are made. A social media company with a dating platform asked me to informally consult on social equity in their safety policies from my vantage point as a social scientist with expertise at the intersection of technology, race, gender, and popular culture. This large tech company, though well-funded, did not offer to pay for my services (and they did not ask me to sign an NDA either). Yet, they wanted me to do an in-depth review of their community guidelines pertaining to race and racism for their dating platform.

Over several conversations, I gathered that there were no plans for limiting language of racial fetishization. Though they had adopted standard non-discrimination guidelines and anti-hate speech policies, they were hesitant to limit expressions of preference for certain skin tones, race, and other phenotypical features as they saw those preferences as expressions of freedom of speech. They were afraid of being accused of violating individuals' First Amendment rights. Let me save you a Google search on the contents of the First Amendment:

> Congress shall make no law respecting an establishment of religion, or prohibiting the free exercise thereof; or abridging the freedom of speech, or of the press; or the right of the people peaceably to assemble, and to petition the Government for a redress of grievances.

The operative word here is "Congress." This is not a book about freedom of speech, and many have written about the current cultural dialogue on the tension between free speech and hate speech protections.[11] I argue that this tension is unnecessarily weighty and is felt throughout the online dating industry as dating platforms consider protections for users of color. Companies are not governmental bodies and therefore can (and do) freely establish rules about their businesses, including defining what kind of speech is permissible while using their platform.

Choosing to honor freedom of speech or expression above safety of marginalized users is the wrong choice, the White choice, and the choice that is made most often. Sociologist Joe Feagin writes about the impact of White choices. As he argues, the "White racial frame," developed over the past four centuries through systemic racism, deeply pervades American culture and dictates our values.[12] The apparent tension between freedom of expression and hate speech protections is a red herring of sorts, created by the White racial frame. Concerns about free speech for users seem to matter only when hate speech is in play. The real choice is between privileging the comfort of some White users over reducing the harm experienced by a minority of users: people of color and other marginalized user groups. When the frame shifts to safety and freedom from harm for all users, the choice is less laden with political ideologies and more directly grounded in human ethics. Under this logic, tech organizations (online dating companies included) are free to instead choose safety for all as a guiding ethos for community guidelines and harm reduction approaches.

When I was consulting with a social media company with a dating platform, the leadership viewed individuals' preference for "voluptuous Latinas" or Native women with "Pocahontas hair" as expressions of positive desirability and as valid choices that daters should be allowed to state. I explained how racial fetishization has the power to harm and upend safety for some, and I could see dots being connected behind eyes, as though they were considering this possibility for the very first time. This is concerning, given their rank in the corporation and the level of expertise that should accompany that rank. A quick perusal through research on online dating will highlight that racial fetishization, typically defined by scholars as "race-based fixation on a bodily part or characteristic," is a nearly universal experience for daters of color with negative health and social outcomes.[13] Racial fetishization might be confounding for those who don't encounter it (like those at this tech company) because it "involves both idolization and demonization of racial difference."[14]

If you're wondering, or perhaps by this point you know, all of the individuals I spoke with on this leadership team were White presenting. They had quite possibly never considered how the expression of racial fetishization, which they viewed as positive, might be harmful to individuals of color.

Perhaps White leadership at dating companies are unaware of the ramifications of racial fetishization because they themselves do not experience it nor do they have family or friends who encounter fetishizing language. Of the twenty-seven White individuals interviewed while conducting this research, almost all (roughly 94 percent of respondents) said they had never experienced any racial fetishization while using online dating platforms. Two that had—Yasaman, a woman who identified as Iranian and White, and Ilana, a woman who identified as White and Jewish—said they had been pursued by men for stereotypes associated with their nationality or ethnicity. White people believe they are generally free from race-based interactions, unless they initiate them. Emma, another White respondent, was asked if she had ever experienced racial fetishization while using a dating platform. Her response was enlightening:

> I always hear stories [about others], but I've never gotten anything. And I'm like, "Man, my life's boring." [*laughter*] Yeah, no, none at all. It's kinda weird. I mean, no, it's not that I'm like welcoming it [*pause*] but [*trailed off*].

It must be nice to live a safe, boring life free from the agitation of routine racial trauma. Some of us live thrilling lives with ample encounters of jarring unsafety. The truth is though, White people *do* have racialized interactions all the time; they are simply unaware of them because performing Whiteness is the norm. And that performance protects them from unsafety. Inherent to Whiteness is the ability to be safe from consequences of racism.

Policing Black Safety

In 2020, the deaths of George Floyd, Breonna Taylor, and Ahmaud Arbery reminded Black people of our collective inability to be safe from racism. After the resurgence of the movement for Black Lives, suddenly every company seemed to care about race, racism, and, more importantly, the branding that positioned them as being in support of the BLM movement. Black influencers and intellectuals pointed out the glaringly obvious fact that this sudden shift appeared to be driven by the desire to capture the Black dollar rather than a focus on overall wellness and safety of Black people.

Still, there was momentum, ushered in by a new historic moment that held the promise of generating anti-racist action across social structures. A lot of people were asking: Can I be anti-racist?[15] Anti-racist thought involves the knowledge of systematic and widespread racial discrimination and disenfranchisement, an admission that American meritocracy cannot exist in a world where racial disparity is the norm.[16] It involves White people admitting that they are part of a system that upholds racial inequity and that they benefit (in various degrees) from White privilege even if they themselves are not actively espousing racialized beliefs or White supremacist thought. Anti-racist action entails using that knowledge to dismantle existing systems of racial oppression and proactively taking steps to prohibit and inhibit the growth and/or rebuilding of new or adaptable racial systems of oppression.[17] Based on the wisdom of community organizers around the best practices in movement building and adding depth to anti-racist action, individuals and/or corporations should name and claim their personal or organizational responsibility, plan to address or repair past wrongdoing, and communicate ways that they can be held accountable by communities that have been harmed by racial injustice and inequity (on an ongoing and regular basis).[18]

Some dating platforms, attempting to adopt this new-to-them anti-racist ethos, adjusted their platforms to encourage and afford anti-racist thought and action. Several platforms added buttons and filters that would allow users to indicate that they supported Black Lives Matter. Bumble, perhaps taking the most direct anti-racist route, issued an opt-in pledge that same year:

> Bumble stands in solidarity with Black Americans and the Black Lives Matter movement in the fight to end the systematic racism that plagues this country. We urge our community to report racism you see on the app. Racist behavior is not welcome here, and users will be blocked for engaging in hate speech of any kind.

Users had to select "I Agree" before they could continue using the platform.[19] The wording of the opt-in pledge offers a wide interpretation of hate speech, noting that any kind of racism expressed could be considered hate speech by the platform. This move expanded safety and protection for people of color who use the dating service. Bumble also issued a strong public statement redoubling their commitments to racial justice:

> Bumble stands in solidarity with Black Americans and the Black Lives Matter movement in the fight to dismantle white supremacy and end the systemic racism that plagues this country.
>
> We've committed USD $1 million across the following organizations:
>
> - $250,000 to the <u>NAACP Legal Defense and Education Fund</u> to support the end of police brutality on a national scale;
> - $250,000 to the <u>Southern Poverty Law Center</u>, and a new partnership as we work to remove all hate from our platform;
> - $250,000 to the <u>Black Women's Health Imperative</u> to help rectify the health disparities Black women face, especially in this time of heightened stress;
> - $200,000 to community bail funds across the country;
> - $50,000 to the <u>Austin Justice Coalition</u> in support of racial justice in Bumble's hometown.
>
> We'll be matching employee donations to organizations supporting racial justice across our workforce of 700 worldwide. Bumble is also providing flexible, paid time off for those grieving, experiencing trauma, or simply needing to rest amid a climate of fear.
>
> As a mission-driven company with a community of more than 90 million on our app, it's Bumble's duty to ensure our platform is not merely safe and inclusive but actively anti-racist. We've long had a zero-tolerance policy towards hate speech, racism, bigotry, misogyny, and abusive behavior of any kind on our app. Since 2017, we've worked alongside the Anti-Defamation League (ADL), using artificial intelligence to identify hate symbols and using the ADL's research and terminology as our standard.
>
> It's time to double down on our efforts.
>
> We're moving forward with a comprehensive audit across every part of our business, seeking to root out racism, bias, and inequity. We're committed to sharing updates on our progress. We should have embarked on this long ago.
>
> Black Lives Matter.

Bumble's statement takes accountability for benefiting from White privilege, acknowledges the existence of systemic racism, and sets aside funds
to continue the work at national and local governmental levels. Lastly,
they have a plan for protecting users from encountering further racialized
harm, though they fall short in this area. Relying on the Anti-Defamation
League's insight to identify racism is not ideal as the ADL has consistently
come under critique for lacking expertise in this area.[20] They additionally
fall short in another area that matters: providing a documented plan to be in
continual dialogue with marginalized groups about how they can improve.
Still, Bumble provided a decent (though not perfect) approach, attempting
to enact an anti-racist policy for increasing safety of Black users.

Other dating platforms took an approach that was decidedly *not* anti-
racist. On May 31, 2020, just days after the death of George Floyd, Tinder
tweeted: "Take action. Donate here: https://blacklivesmatter.com" with a
public statement attached to the tweet.

Tinder's statement adopts stale, vague language of "injustice" (Figure 5.1).
They do not directly assert that the injustice being experienced is racial; it's

FIGURE 5.1   Public statement on the movement for Black Lives,
posted via Tinder's Twitter account on May 31, 2020.

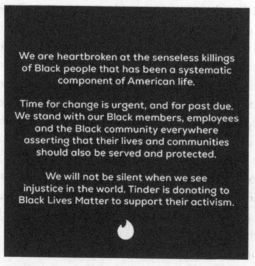

We are heartbroken at the senseless killings
of Black people that has been a systematic
component of American life.

Time for change is urgent, and far past due.
We stand with our Black members, employees
and the Black community everywhere
asserting that their lives and communities
should also be served and protected.

We will not be silent when we see
injustice in the world. Tinder is donating to
Black Lives Matter to support their activism.

Source: https://twitter.com/Tinder/status/1267154771435282432?s=20

simply unjust, not rooted in anything in particular. Murders of Black people have been systematic, but they are not a direct result of systemic racism. This framing matters because Tinder's use of "systematic" here implies routine— killing of Black individuals is regular and expected. It does not make the connection that Black death is a result of systematic oppression and White supremacy. Black individuals should expect that *unsafety* is the standard— and Tinder stands with them in that recognition. It is not enough to simply agree that Black Lives Matter without acknowledging how Tinder contributes to the oppression of and unsafety of Black individuals. Where Bumble had an explicit and detailed plan for anti-racist action, Tinder is standing with "Black members, employees, and the Black community everywhere asserting that their lives should also be served and protected." Except, they're not. After the company issued the statement, users tweeted about being banned for putting BLM in their bio.

A spokesperson from Tinder shared with *BuzzFeed News*:

> "From time to time, our members use Tinder to engage with topics they care about. . . . And while our community guidelines state that we may remove accounts used for promotional purposes, we are dedicated to enforcing our guidelines in line with our values."[21]

What values might those be? Perhaps White supremacist values? Several Tinder users spoke to news outlets about having their accounts reported by individuals who were offended by the use of #BLM or related content in their profiles. One user told *Mashable* that she included ACAB (All Cops Are Bastards) in her bio. ACAB has come to be associated with anti-racist, police abolition movements.[22] The user matched with a police officer, and he said, "I hope the ACAB isn't meant for me." She saw that he had pictures in uniform and explained that "all police/cops are corrupt and even if they do not singlehandedly take part in wrongful murder, the 'good' cops are still watching it happen." The police officer said he'd "unmatch" her, and she was banned from Tinder a day later.[23]

Several stories like these have emerged across news outlets.[24] Some users were able to have their accounts reinstated, and others were not. This is why the last piece of the anti-racist puzzle is so important; plans for accountability and ongoing dialogue are a must for limiting inadvertent racial harm.

Further, Tinder could have been proactive about ignoring reports from users with BLM or other protest phrases in their bio if they had trained profile content moderators according to an anti-racist ethos.[25]

Even though the right to assemble and engage in political protest is protected by law, Tinder is within its rights to set boundaries about how language is used on its platform. Tinder chose to moderate phrases (BLM and ACAB) that alienate some individuals. After being publicly called out, Tinder reversed the decision and informed users that they could freely use BLM in their profiles and in private conversations with other users without fear of being banned. Yet, in the aftermath, many *still* report being kicked off the platform for merely mentioning BLM in their profiles. Tinder's struggle to balance appeasing users with more conservative beliefs, honoring the neo-liberal individualism prized by the tech world, and supporting the movement for Black safety, freedom, and life raises a valuable question: If individuals can be reported and removed for language that poses an affront to White-ness, could similar low- to no-tolerance policies be adopted for language that incites racial harm and racially fetishizes or harasses users of color, resulting in more relative safety for those users?

Certainly the answer is yes—if the weight of White privilege does not oc-clude the company's desire to provide a safe experience for all users. Accord-ing to an industry leader at Match Group, safety for all is a top priority.[26] Yet, this opportunity to privilege safety for all users over White comfort seems particularly difficult for insiders at dating platforms to understand. Let me simplify inclusive approaches to safety by offering an expanded definition of safety. *Safety for all, with an anti-racist lens, means making specific plans for users likely to experience sexual racism including racial fetishization and race-based harassment.* Dating companies claim to be working on better safety reporting mechanisms for users, but these plans should include methods for monitoring and reporting experiences of sexual racism.

Platforms do have some basic safety measures in place, such as teams who manually review user reports and automatic scans of new profiles to check for banned language and prohibited image content (e.g., nude photos, pic-tures of children, etc.), removal of bot or spam accounts, and manual review of suspicious profiles. Beyond these basic measures, all platforms take vary-ing approaches to safety, and some put more onus on the user than others.

In the next section, I'll cover some of the emerging approaches to user safety and highlight how they could better facilitate safety of marginalized users, especially by protecting them from sexual racism.

Navigating the Ick: Trials of Automated Content Moderation

Platform safety in online dating is comprised of steps users take to keep themselves safe while dating and the safety mechanisms dating companies utilize to afford a safe user experience. I like to think of these two areas—individual user caution and platform afforded safety—as existing on a spectrum. Every dating platform has a terms-of-use clause indicating that users assume all risk while dating, but these clauses are buried in the long form agreements that everyone opts into and few ever read completely. Alternatively, public-facing communication about safety and steps that platforms take to reduce harm for users vary widely. Dating platforms like eHarmony and Facebook Dating take a relatively hands-off approach: users are expected to look out for their own safety. OkCupid and Bumble take a more involved approach, carrying relatively more responsibility for user safety. Here are some examples of headliners taken from different platforms' "safety" hubs:

eHarmony Our Trust & Safety team works hard to ensure that you have the best possible experience. We routinely review accounts for inconsistent or suspect behavior. When communicating with or meeting a match, don't ignore your instincts. In any circumstance, your judgment and intuition are necessary to protect yourself.

Bumble At Bumble, the safety of our community is our highest priority. In the five years since our founding, we've introduced a roster of initiatives to help keep you safe while using Bumble Date, Bizz, and BFF.

Facebook Dating We recommend that you read the information below to help keep yourself and the Facebook community safe. You are always the best judge of your own safety, and these guidelines are not intended to be a substitute for your own judgment.

OkCupid Meeting new people is exciting, but you should always be cautious when interacting with someone you don't know. Use your best judgment and put your safety first, whether you are exchanging initial messages or meeting in person. While you can't control the actions of others, there are things you can do to help you stay safe during your OkCupid experience.

For the most part, the safety pages all point to tactics that I hope most daters do regularly, either consciously or unconsciously, such as not sharing money, passwords, or Social Security numbers; exercising caution around initial meetups; having intentional conversations about STI risks; seeking consent before sharing images, and so on. However, Match Group and Bumble, both industry leaders, are setting the tone for advanced platform-afforded safety using a suite of AI-assisted technologies. Importantly, Match Group states,

> We have various brands in our portfolio that employ different tools, processes, and policies to foster respectful communities and environments. . . . Depending on the needs of each platform and the audiences they serve, different tools may be adopted by different brands, but the objective is universal: we are committed to creating a safe and positive experience for all our users on all our platforms.[27]

Because the brands in the Match Group portfolio do not disclose which tactics they employ, I cannot say with certainty which specific platforms are using advanced methods unless it is stated on their website (Figure 5.2). Still, I examine some of the emerging technologies used to reduce harm and question whether these technologies are optimized to reduce harm for marginalized users.[28]

Bumble and Tinder both employ systems that operate on what I call the "ick factor algorithm." Bumble's Private Detector "works by using A.I. to automatically blur a nude image shared within a chat. It'll then alert you that you've been sent something potentially inappropriate."[29] Tinder's "Does This Bother You?" feature was trained on previously submitted user reports and detects potentially insensitive, harmful, hateful, and harassing messages. It works by asking users on both the sending and receiving end about the messages. Before an individual sends a message, users might be prompted with "Are you sure you want to send?" followed by "Think twice—your match may

FIGURE 5.2   Screen capture of Match Group's stated approach to using AI to help ensure safety across brands.

Video and AI Technology

Match Group brands are integrating varying features such as video chat, automated photo review, and photo verification, all of which aid our efforts to help our users ensure that every match is who they say they are. We are also incorporating anti-harassment prompts on our platforms, which use machine learning to automatically screen for potentially offensive messages and prompt the recipient to report the behavior.

Source: https://mtch.com/safety

find this language disrespectful."[30] On the receiving end, users are prompted with "We've detected potentially inappropriate language. Do any of the messages above bother you?"[31]

By interacting with these AI features on dating platforms, users inadvertently train the automated system about their personal ick threshold. Perhaps you don't personally mind an opener of "Hey, wanna fuck?" while someone else might find that terribly offensive. By confirming that a message has or has not offended a user, dating platforms learn about what presents an ick for each individual user. The benefit to these systems is that it means dating companies are becoming more aware of different experiences of sexuality and communication, and they are encouraging users to seek consent before engaging in certain sexual acts. But the ironic downside to these automated systems is that their use confirms that dating platforms are reading all of our messages without our consent.

Ick factor algorithms rely on iterations of natural language processing (NLP) and sentiment analysis. NLP uses rule-based modeling of human language with computational linguistics to process or translate language into computer readable data.[32] Sentiment analysis categorizes data as either being emotionally positive, negative, or neutral. NLP powers Google, Siri, Alexa, Google voice products, automated translator services, and chatbots that offer customer assistance on websites, to name a few examples. Though at times helpful, NLP and sentiment analysis–based systems, like all algorithmically driven technologies, are laden with human biases. Increasingly, algorithmic systems are being trained to detect toxicity, or ick, across social media platforms, discussion boards, and in online dating platforms. Toxic language can include abusive text, insults, offensive wording, profanity, and hate speech. Toxicity is largely dependent on cultural context, hence coders who train AI systems using NLP directly influence who and what might be considered toxic speech and behavior.[33] Toxic speech detection algorithms have been shown to primarily flag minoritized groups and can increase violence toward them.[34] Two well-known tech companies have recently come under fire due to using biased toxicity scoring systems: Google and Twitter.

Google's Counter Abuse Technology Team created Perspective Application Programming Interface (API) in collaboration with Jigsaw to detect toxic language in online discussions. Google and Jigsaw developed ratings of toxicity by collecting millions of online comments and asking multiple panels of ten people to rate comments on a scale from very toxic to very healthy. After training the system on data generated by the panels, the algorithm generates a toxicity score for text present on a given web page.[35] Perspective was intended to help facilitate healthier exchanges of ideas in online discussions. But in 2017, a team of researchers at the University of Washington's Network Security Lab found that the system could be easily manipulated to yield variable toxicity scores based on subtle changes in otherwise toxic language.[36] Further, computer scientists have identified that femme-gendered language is more often categorized as toxic using Perspective.[37]

Perspective's API seems primarily biased against women and feminized language while Twitter's use of toxicity scoring over-detects "offensive" speech from communities of color. Maarten Sap and colleagues found "racial and dialectical bias" in Twitter's language detection system, noting that African American English (AAE) was more likely to be rated as offensive. In their experiment, they demonstrated that Black coders who train language detection systems were less likely to categorize AAE as offensive because they recognized phrasing that is culturally specific (e.g., a Black person tweeting "what's up nigga" versus a White individual using a racial slur to refer to Black individuals).[38] Hence, Sap and colleagues found that phrases that could actually be used in a directly offensive manner by White people were often labeled neutral, redoubling bias in language detection systems.[39]

These findings do not provide much hope that dating platform's ick factor algorithms are equitably reducing harm for users of color. Do the anti-harassment prompts include the ability to detect racial fetishization and sexual racism? In my personal experience, several times I did not receive a "Does This Offend You?" prompt after getting a racially fetishizing remark on Tinder, whereas Bumble generally did ask about these instances of sexual racism. In general, Bumble appears to take a stronger stance on racial fetishization, broad sexual racism, and harm reduction approaches for marginalized groups than other hetero-focused platforms. For example, Bumble provides a resource page for "Microaggressions & Fetishization" and has partnered with Trans Lifeline to provide resources for encountering transphobia and trans fetishization on dating platforms.

Perhaps more platforms have expanded their priorities on safety to include those in the margins in the time since this book was published.[40] If daters of color cannot depend on platforms to accurately detect hate speech and other forms of sexual racism, we must rely on platform-provided reporting mechanisms to regulate these kinds of behaviors, and we can only hope that they take sexual racism seriously. Ideally, dating platforms that claim to be dedicated to protecting Black lives are also dedicated to helping Black people live free from racial harassment and sexual racism. Yet, these ick moderating mechanisms only (unreliably) reduce harm for users within the confines of platform interfaces.[41] What happens when encounters start on dating platforms and result in offline hate crimes?

Online + Offline: Sexual Racism Converges

Brandi, a woman who related a terrifying dating experience, demonstrates the necessity of advanced harm reduction around sexual racism. She responded to a post I made on Tumblr asking women of color to share their best and worst experiences while using online dating platforms. Her story demonstrates that sexual racism is a very real form of racism.

Brandi is a light-skinned Black woman and was a long-time user of Tinder. It is important to note that Brandi can "pass" for White, though when I look at her pictures, I read her as a person of color. It is unclear if the man she went on a date with knew she was a biracial Black woman. I have left her narrative largely unedited (except for clarity) to preserve the reality of her horrific experience (content warning for physical violence and use of racial slurs):

So two years ago I was on Tinder, I matched with a FINE white man, he was in his mid-thirties, had blue eyes, and was completely bald. Honestly, to me he was an absolute dream boat . . . So, we talk for a few days then decide we are ready to meet. I live about an hour from [the city] so we decided he would drive to me. So, the day comes, I'm about to go on a date with this guy that I thought was so amazing and so perfect. I'm at work and he's BLOWING up my phone. So I'm scared something's going on, I call him and he's like "WHY ARE YOU FRIENDS WITH SO MANY BLACK GUYS ON FACEBOOK?" So I'm a bit taken aback like, "EXCUSE ME?" He quickly corrected what he initially said and took it back to say there's so many Black guys commenting on my pictures or whatever and he was jealous. So I explain to him the people I associate myself and have grown up with are predominantly Black. He assures me that he didn't mean it in a racist way, so I'm like okay, whatever let me finish this shift so you can take me out to eat.

Our first date was amazing, he was sweet to me, and didn't try to cross any of my boundaries. So we plan a second date for the very next day. This is when things dramatically changed. So he's talking about Snapchat or whatever and I was like, "Oh, yeah, let's send a picture to my sister she wants to see how cute we are," and he sees my friend Malik sent me a snap. I WILL NEVER FORGET TO THIS DAY IT WAS AN INNOCENT PICTURE OF HIM THAT SAID "GOOD EVENING." So this crazy mother fucker FLIPS OUT, he's like, "I knew you were a 'nigger' lover!'" He then snatched my phone out of my hands and started going through it. Every guy's name he seen in my phone he proceeded to ask me "IS HE A 'NIGGER'?" and "DID YOU FUCK HIM?"

At this point I'm pretty scared, I just want my phone back so I can get out this man's car and walk home. I try to snatch my phone back, but he swipes my hand away. So me, being scared, I grab his keys out of the ignition and try to jump out of the car. BUT HE WON'T LET ME and he snatches his keys back. So now I'm really super uncomfortable and scared. This man throws my brand new IPHONE, I literally got it a week prior, out the window, picks it back up, sees it's not broken, then throws it again. I see the opportunity to jump out of the car and HE TRIES TO HIT ME!! As he was driving away he screamed at me that I was a "nigger" and that I would never amount to anything.

I ran to my phone to see it's shattered beyond repair. I couldn't call out to 911 and Siri wouldn't work. So I walk home, still literally SHAK-ING, and crying because of what just happened. I log onto Facebook and see upwards of twenty+ comments on my pictures, my wall, my sta-tuses calling me a "nigger lover" and a "slut." My iPad had several mes-sages and voicemails from him that just said "NIGGER" and "NIGGER LOVER."

I immediately blocked him on every social media site I had, and un-matched him on Tinder. Later on that night I get a call from an un-known number, it's him. He called me to say how I betrayed him by being a nigger lover and that he would wire me money to pay to fix my phone to right his wrongs. ABSOLUTELY NOT, I DON'T PLAY THAT. I didn't want a dime from him, I didn't want him to know my address. None of that. So a few months pass and I decide to try a differ-ent dating site because after that I was done with Tinder. HE SEES ME AND MESSAGES ME . . . CAN YOU GUESS WHAT HE SAID?!? He called me a "nigger loving slut" and made it so I couldn't message him back. To this day I'm still shaken up by how absolutely DISGUSTING this man was.

When I share this story with White audiences, they are often horrified and cannot believe that explicit racism of this nature still occurs. They be-lieve these moments of racialized terror to be part of a U.S. history from which they are divorced. Brandi's experience is upsetting yet unsurprising for people of color. This kind of racialized violence, whether experienced in person or online, is not an anachronism. The perpetuated belief that explicit racialized violence simply does not happen anymore comes from the same White disbelief about the impact of sexual racism.

Feminist scholar and activist Moya Bailey originated the term "misogy-noir," which describes Black women's unique experience at the intersection of misogyny and anti-Blackness. Bailey argues that digitally meditated mi-sogynoir can result in material experiences of violence.[42] Brandi's experience

in 2016 is one of lived racial terror that is rooted in sexual racism and misogynoir. The term "nigger lover" was originally used to describe White slavery
abolitionists and other White sympathizers.[43] It was also used as an insult
before, during, and after integration for those who associated with and/or
had romantic relationships with Black individuals. A belief in White racial
purity is also bound up with the insidiousness of the slur. White individuals
who have sexual relationships with Black people were thought to be traitors
to the race and were now impure/unclean.[44] This reprehensible White man
asked multiple times if Brandi "fucked" Black men to assess whether she
was morally corrupt and unclean—tainted by Blackness. In his assessment,
her sexual relationships with Black men made her one of "them": "As he was
driving away he screamed at me that I was a 'nigger' and that I would never
amount to anything." To punish her for being a race traitor, he tried to hit
her with his vehicle—an action that could have resulted in her death. This
is the story about how Brandi survived an attempted modern-day lynching,
fueled by the rage of sexual racism and misogynoir.

At the end of Brandi's narrative, she shared that the "absolutely disgusting" man continued to find and harass her across platforms. Match Group
claims to check for known harassers and remove them from their family of
brands. These practices were not in place in 2016. Online dating companies
know that they have to provide a safe experience if they want to maintain
user activity and industry growth. In response to reports of increasing violence related to online dating, companies have adopted several new strategies: optional ID verification, banning of known sex offenders, verifiable
background checks, and partnerships with personal safety companies such
as Noonlight and local law enforcement. In 2020, Tinder was the first of
Match Group's brands to integrate Noonlight, which uses

> proprietary technology and APIs to power new safety features, enabling
> users to access emergency services and transmit highly accurate location
> data within the Noonlight app, without requiring a 911 phone call or the
> ability to talk or text. This service makes personal emergency services
> easily available for a mobile-first audience.[45]

Noonlight allows users to add details about where they plan to meet a
potential match and offers the ability to discreetly signal for help via the

platform if needed (Figure 5.3). If an alert is issued, responders are provided with information submitted about the user, including context and location details about the date. But there are some notable limitations in accessibility. Noonlight works with Tinder, but it is not an embedded feature within Tinder's platform. Users have to download an additional app that only works with iPhones. iPhones are well known to be cost prohibitive, meaning that only those with financial means have access to this additional layer of safety. Second, currently Noonlight is only available in the United States, though the company plans to expand usability to other countries. Third, and most important, safety that is dependent on the use of cell phones can provide a false sense of security.[46] As Brandi's moment of terror highlights, cell phones are not always a reliable safety mechanism, especially if they are broken in an act of violence.

FIGURE 5.3   A diagram produced by Tinder to demonstrate how users might use Noonlight to enhance their safety when meeting up with a match in person.

Source: https://www.help.tinder.com/hc/en-us/articles/360039260031-Noonlight-FAQs-

Where and How Do We Report Sexual Racism?

When all of the advanced safety measures discussed above fail, manual reporting mechanisms provide a final means of harm reduction and harm redress. But to be truly impactful, reporting mechanisms need to be widely available and easily understandable for all users. Further, as Bumble has done, users need to be encouraged, not discouraged, to file reports. Some apps, whether intentionally or unintentionally, do not afford user accessibility to reporting mechanisms. Lastly, users need to know that platforms will act on the issues they report. This means if platforms only act on commonly reported issues such as sexual harassment but not transphobia, or user fraud but not sexual racism, people will not feel empowered to use reporting mechanisms, which results in more of those negative behaviors in dating app communities.

When I asked interviewees of all genders and racial backgrounds if they had ever experienced harassment or sexual violence while using dating platforms or from someone they had met on a dating platform, a themed pattern of response emerged: because dating platforms do not explicitly recognize sexual racism as an area of concern in their safety hubs, people of color have to navigate this additional layer of risk negotiation on their own. Further, the perceptions of accessibility of reporting mechanisms are largely dependent on the positionality of the user. Michelle and Dae recounted their experiences reporting platform-based harassment and/or sexual racism:

> Michelle: Yes, I have actually made reports on the app. . . . So usually on Hinge once you unmatch somebody, you can't—they can't talk to you again. But I guess sometimes it doesn't work that well and they find a way to. Or maybe I just stopped talking to them and deleted the messages and forgot to completely block them or something like that. I don't know. But, um, there have been times where I was on a date and I said no to sex, and he didn't listen. And after I blocked him on the app, he kept talking and kept trying to get me to talk to him again, and so I had to report that.
>
> Apryl: And how did you feel about the process of reporting?
>
> Michelle: It was easy to report. It was just a few quick buttons. It's not the first time that I've reported harassment in my life. Usually my re-

ports are in person. The Navy is unfortunately—Uh, unfortunately, they have a whole lot of men in there with skewed ideas of how to treat women. And I've had to make in-person reports a few times. But on the apps, it was easy. It was quick. It was just, click a button and it's done. Never talk to that person again.

Michelle, who identifies as a Black woman, recounted that it was relatively easy (compared to the complicated militarized bureaucracy of the Navy) to report someone for behavior that made her uncomfortable, and then she'd never have to talk to them again (as opposed to seeing an abuser at one's workplace). Michelle also highlights a common occurrence for users: harassing individuals pop up on the same platform with a new profile or they move to a different platform and find the same individuals to harass again.

Dae, who identifies as a Korean American man, similarly felt that it was relatively easy to report sexual racism. But he also reported seeing the same person with racially fetishizing content on a different dating app:

Apryl: Okay, and have you ever tried to report someone on an online dating platform for race-based bias or harassment?

Dae: Yes.

Apryl: And what was that experience like for you?

Dae: Actually, this was a while ago—there was a White woman's profile and the content was very—she was pretty clear and explicit about her Asian fetish, and kind of like a Koreaboo, K-pop thing—it was weird, and it made me kind of uncomfortable. I think now, that I think back on it, I did match with this person out of sheer curiosity 'cause I hadn't seen something like that before. It was a very uncomfortable and short conversation; there just wasn't really anything to say after yeah, I am an Asian person—I might be a little different than whatever K-pop star you have in your head. But like, I remember it being an uncomfortable interaction, and I think I reported that profile, if I remember correctly.

Apryl: Did you feel that the profile was—that action was taken pretty immediately?

Dae: I never really saw what happened to it, but I did see that account a few months after on a different dating app.

Even White women, who theoretically are the users best served by dating platforms, relay that reporting mechanisms are unsatisfactory. Penelope, who self-identified as a straight White woman, shared about a harasser who followed her on multiple platforms and her attempts to report this and other instances of harassment:

Rachel: Have you ever had any experiences at all with people you met on the apps that you felt like you had to report?

Penelope: Yeah, definitely. I've definitely reported some people. Even, you know, we didn't meet up but we were talking, so I reported people based on just like text exchange things that I felt like were intimidating or harassment. And then, yeah, I did have one encounter with someone that I actually went on a date with. And then I felt very uncomfortable. And so I reported them after going on that date, and blocked them and everything. But that was the only sort of in-person experience. Yeah.

Rachel: And how did you feel about that reporting process?

Penelope: Um, I—So I feel like when it's just, sort of, you're reporting based off of text, it's very unsatisfying because you click a button and then, you know, they're blocked from you. You don't have to see them anymore. Then Tinder is like, "Yeah we won't tell so-and-so that it was you who reported them." You're kind of like, "Okay great. Is this— Are there any consequences? Does this make a difference in any way?" Other than my peace of mind. I don't have to interact with them, that's great.

But when it came to reporting on the person that I actually went out with, they also knew where I lived. They had dropped me off at my house, so you know, there were other sorts of threats tied into it. Um, yeah, maybe it was about a year ago, so I'm trying to remember exactly how the process went. But I did have to send an email, and then I got a response from like—It was like a very vague sort of customer service response. And then I just, I remember that it was never followed up on, and then I never really heard anything. So it was kind of like filing a formal complaint that never—There was no step beyond that. So yeah, that was really unsatisfying.

And I did kind of fear for my situation, just thinking, you know, like, I blocked him on every platform, but he's been to my house, so what do I do there? Nothing ended up coming of it, and he did end up finding me on another app. This was like maybe a couple months, so a very long time, maybe eight or nine months after our initial interaction. So, but in that case, I just blocked him right away on a different app.

If dating platforms cannot protect White women, their prime demographic, then how can we expect them to protect the rest of us? We know that White women are more likely to report sexual harassment or crimes to authorities than women or femmes of color. Research also demonstrates that people of color are less likely to report these kinds of crimes because they don't believe there will be any follow-up.[47] Because there are often no stated guidelines around racial fetishization, users feel as though dating companies do not care about sexual racism. Kevin's experiences demonstrate user fatigue with dating platforms' absence of safety mechanisms for dealing with sexual racism:

> Apryl: Okay, do you feel that you have ever been racially fetishized?
> Kevin: A little bit.
> Apryl: Do you want to describe to me what that feels like or what was said to you that made you feel that way?
> Kevin: [broken audio] A lot of people conflate being Asian with like, K-pop artists and I'm not even Korean. I'm actually Chinese myself, so it's kind of weird because it's like usually the attention is. [broken audio] But every time, it's like—they're not trying to get to know me as a person, it's just like, "Oh, you're Asian, you must like this Asian thing."
> Apryl: I see. So have you ever encountered race-based harassment or violence, either physical or verbal, from someone you met on an online dating platform?
> Kevin: Yeah.
> Apryl: Can you describe what that was like?
> Kevin: [broken audio]
> Apryl: You're breaking up a little bit, so I'm going to repeat what I think I heard you say. Did you say something about penis size?
> Kevin: Yeah, you know, stereotypes. Racist stereotypes.

Apryl: Okay, were you able to report those people on the platforms?

Kevin: No, you can't really report something like that. Tinder or whatever app doesn't do that.

Apryl: Actually some apps do encourage reporting of that type of behavior, but it's interesting that you feel that you can't.

Kevin: I just feel like they don't give a shit. I'm sure you can report it, but it's just like, "Oh, let's ban this user for life."

Apryl: Okay, so you feel like there's a difference in if they would actually care or actually take action?

Kevin: Exactly.

This sentiment, that safety is only prioritized for some, is not relegated to those experiencing sexual racism. Other marginalized groups feel that their safety is not a priority for dating companies and platforms. Jay, who identifies as a White trans man, conveyed that he does not feel supported by platforms and that dating companies are not concerned about people facing transphobia. Jay's perspective draws further attention to the need for safety for all on dating platforms (content warning for transphobia and trans slurs):

Rachel: Have you ever experienced any sort of harassment or violence from somebody you met through a dating app?

Jay: Yes.

Rachel: Yeah? Have you ever tried to report somebody for that sort of behavior on a dating app?

Jay: Reporting really doesn't do anything.

Rachel: No? Can you tell me—?

Jay: I have, but it never did anything.

Rachel: Mm. Can you tell me a little bit about that reporting process? Like, what did you do? What did you hear back? How did you feel about it?

Jay: They would just say—sometimes they would just—like, Facebook Dating—I sometimes go on that, because why not? It'd be like, they do not—It does not—Like, the guidelines, blah blah blah, doesn't work. "They haven't violated any of our guidelines, blah blah blah. Just block them."

Rachel: And how did you feel about that process?

Jay: Not a good process. Because if they're gonna do it to me, why wouldn't they do it to someone else?

Rachel: Sure, I get that fear.

Jay: I've been called the "T" word all the time.

Rachel: If you're comfortable, can you say more about any particular context where that happens?

Jay: Like, they would match with me just because I'm trans and then call me a "tranny." And then block me because they made their point, whatever that means.

Rachel: I'm sorry that you experienced that. Did you report those profiles? Was that on Tinder or Grindr?

Jay: It was Tinder. It didn't—Tinder didn't really do anything.

Rachel: Mm. I'm sorry about that.

Jay: That's okay. I mean, it's not, but, like, you know.

All marginalized users need better protection and deserve to have their safety prioritized. If dating platforms are working towards safety, that must include safety for transgender folx from transphobia on dating platforms. Because I believe survivors, I believe that Facebook Dating communicated to Jay a nonchalance about transphobia, indicating that it fell outside of their community guidelines. I also know that Jay is not alone in being told that a reported act does not violate terms of service.[48] Again, the choice to privilege the comfort of some (in this case, cisgender users) over safety for others (trans and nonbinary users) is a heteropatriarchal choice that upholds gender violence and makes room for other kinds of sexual violence to proliferate on dating platforms and out in the real world.

Equity in Safety

Safety should not be a privileged commodity. Yet in the current structure of most dating platforms' safety priorities, those experiencing harm that falls outside typically reported incidents are at the bottom of the priority list. My dear friend and colleague, Afsaneh Rigot, calls for design from, and for, the margins to increase equity for groups most at risk of experiencing harm in digital environments.[49] Designing from the margins means that the needs of users with experiences like Brandi and Jay, which are often considered "edge cases" or "outliers," drive the priorities of tech companies. Rather than relying on the belief that sexual racism is not really racist, or ignoring it altogether because those who experience it are smaller in number than the majority of users, design from the margins entails focusing on these specific needs to broaden harm reduction approaches for marginalized users from the outset of design.[50]

Equitable, anti-racist approaches to safety might entail, first, incorporating information about sexual racism (inclusive of racial fetishization, microaggressions, and racial harassment) in dating platforms' public-facing safety guides. By publicly acknowledging that these acts are unwelcome in online dating communities, dating companies can help shape the belief that sexual racism is indeed harmful rather than a neutral choice or personal preference. Second, as dating companies are increasingly relying on the use of background check technology to surveil predatory users, they might also consider a shared database of racial harassers. These need not be entangled with law enforcement systems (as law enforcement's approaches to racial harm reduction are lacking). But reports of sexual racism could be stored in a centralized repository to which all platforms have access. It is not enough for Bumble and Match Group to keep a record of known abusers if they do not communicate with each other and other dating companies. Platforms need to be able to note who routinely engages in sexual racism so that they can be removed from the entire online dating population, regardless of which platform they use. Of course, any such system would need to be created with caution and should probably shy away from using automated NLP systems as they are not yet reliably unbiased.[51] Finally, because rehabilitation is possible, there should be a process for review and a tiered system of offenses so that individuals are provided with opportunities to grow but not at the expense of safety for marginalized users. Sexual racism should not be a tolerated part of the online dating experience, and these measures might help reduce harm and increase safety for everyone.

CONCLUSION

All You Need Is Love
(and Transparency, Trust, and Safety)

Sexual racism existed long before dating platforms came to be. But they hide the overtly racist logics of sexual racism, helping to conceal them as personal choice. Further, dating platforms automate sexual racism, making it hyperefficient and routine to swipe in racially curated sexual market-places.[1] Because dating platforms hide the underlying racist sorting and ranking algorithms, people more readily believe that their private racism is a neutral, harmless personal choice with few social implications. Hence automated sexual racism is perceived as more progressive than the outright anti-miscegenation laws, one-drop rules, and racial terrorism that prevented and discouraged interracial coupling in the past.

Right now, automated sexual racism helps to normalize the way we do race, in our intimate lives as well as in our public lives. Discrimination on the basis of race cannot exist in our intimate lives if we are to exist in a truly just society. Justice is a long way away, however. Because technology use deeply pervades our society, the decisions made by those in leadership at tech companies affects us all. Dating companies are mostly led by White tech bros—and although they may claim to be socially liberal, they are algorithmically conservative and anti-regulation of their own businesses. These companies operationalize race in their patented algorithmic sorting systems, which means that this kind of sexual racism is in part protected under the cover of being proprietary.

Dating companies are currently free to manipulate how we think about race, gender, masculinity, and femininity with relative impunity because their processes are opaque, and their industry is unregulated. The legal protection afforded by patented systems means that users can't even truly comprehend the eugenic models that shape their choices. As Ruha Benjamin poignantly adds, when she calls out algorithmic harms as the New Jim Code,

> If private companies are creating public policies by other means, then I think we should stop calling ourselves "users." Users *get used*. We are more like unwitting constituents who, by clicking submit, have authorized tech giants to represent our interests.[2]

So how can we fight back?

Tech companies will say that we don't need to. But we can't trust the companies that built this tech to save us. Dating companies' data use and sorting systems are a combination of math and social beliefs about how the world should work, often framed as magic. But even those within the tech world suffer from their own attempts to subjugate society under the New Jim Code. Recall the legal battle between Match Group and Bumble for patent and trademark infringement of swipe logics (discussed in Chapter 2). Beneath the top layer of heated business negotiations lies a related love story that conveys how personal the stakes are.[3] Tinder's former chief marketing officer, Justin Mateen, claims that his ex-girlfriend, the cofounder of Bumble, Whitney Wolfe Herd, stole the swipe logic and user interface of Tinder while she was dating him—that's right, the leadership of these two companies were literally in bed together! On the other hand, Wolfe Herd asserts that Tinder was a boy's club where women were not allowed to shape the direction of the company and that the organizational culture fostered sexual misconduct and toxic masculinity that went unchecked until she filed sexual assault charges.[4]

Is it any wonder Tinder and Bumble's algorithms reinforce a harmful status quo? If Wolfe Herd's claims are to be believed, Tinder's creations come out of an environment where roughly half of humanity isn't worth listening to. The underlying ethos and programming choices comprise the online dating industry. Those in the industry are committed to maintaining the opaqueness of their platforms. That agreement is at the expense of us users, or unwitting constituents. We are not allowed to know how dating platforms use our data.

What we do know is concerning. One of these companies, Tinder, is part of the Match Group conglomerate. We know that companies within Match Group share data, though, at least theoretically, not for commercial purposes. But Match Group does acknowledge that they "share data for limited and critical purposes, including for corporate audit, analysis and consolidated reporting, to comply with applicable law and to keep our users safe" (Figure C.1). What this means is that when you upload profile information and photos or link your Instagram, Facebook, or Spotify account, forty-plus brands within the Match Group conglomerate may be able to access that data. I do not believe users intended for their data to be used in this way. This data sharing is a breach of user trust. The power of conglomerates is that they have the ability to set the agenda for the sector of the market they have cornered, which means that trust breaches may be central to dating app culture and ethos.[5]

Safiya Noble demonstrates that Google has similar power to shape the tech industry.[6] Despite the public belief that search engine results are or-

FIGURE C.1 Match Group's statement on data sharing, found in the "Data We Collect" subsection.

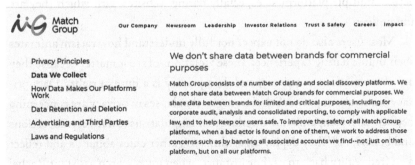

Source: https://mtch.com/privacy#data_we_collect

dered based on popularity or credibility, search engine algorithms produce results in order to drive profit for search engines—even when those results contradict scientific knowledge and threaten to harm public good:

> Information monopolies such as Google have the ability to prioritize web search results on the basis of a variety of topics, such as promoting their own business interests over those of competitors or smaller companies that are less profitable advertising clients than larger multinational corporations are. In this case, the clicks of users, coupled with the commercial processes that allow paid advertising to be prioritized in search results, mean that representations of women are ranked on a search engine page in ways that underscore women's historical and contemporary lack of status in society—a direct mapping of old media traditions into new media architecture.[7]

The search results Noble was referring to carry with them the burden of implicit racial bias and ideologies about gender roles, doubling down on prevailing racialized stereotypes in society. Because of Google's tech giant status, they are able to set the rules for search engine functions, without intervention. When companies operate as if they are untouchable, they disregard the value of user trust.

But trust is a valuable commodity. When consumers trust companies, they are willing to maintain a lifetime of loyalty, generating sustained revenue over time. People trust that Google will return the most relevant web pages, not simply prioritize their own products or neglect to display a competitor's ads. Similarly, users do not expect that their data might be shared across multiple platforms—especially dating websites with which they are unfamiliar.

Most users also do not expect nor fully understand how racism animates their online dating experience. These violations of trust matter because they are also violations of privacy, and data privacy is a human right.[8] Data privacy is also about power. Scholars argue that lapses in privacy are concerning because tech companies use our data to manipulate us toward certain actions and behaviors.[9] They deploy algorithms to gather clues about us and reflect a crafted reality back to us. For instance, when my research assistant Rachel asked Logan if he thought demographics of potential matches were racially diverse, he said, "So the big city I live in, in the southeast, is very much more diverse than other places in the country. But even then, the algorithms, like, figure out pretty quick. I'm like a nerdy White guy, so, it shows me people accordingly." Even in a large urban area, Logan is shown people who look like him because the system makes an assessment, based on his appearance, that he wants mirrored matches. By doing this, they suggest that Logan *should* desire matches who are White like him.

Consumers are growing increasingly weary of the tech giants who seemingly do not value our trust and act as if they can use consumers for profit without consequences and accountability. As we have become skeptical of Meta and others, we must also use that same critical lens on dating companies.[10] We cannot rely on dating apps to act in our best interest. There are several tools that can help us determine if a company is deserving of our trust. The Mozilla Foundation's "Privacy Not Included" project is a consumer guide that covers hundreds of consumer products and services, detailing how data are collected from users (Figure C.2). Mozilla developed a crowdsourced measure that suggests which products, platforms, and services are or are not "creepy." By this measure, most dating apps egregiously disregard user privacy.

FIGURE C.2   The Mozilla Foundation's "Privacy Not Included" consumer guide demonstrating which platforms "creep" on users, violating privacy.

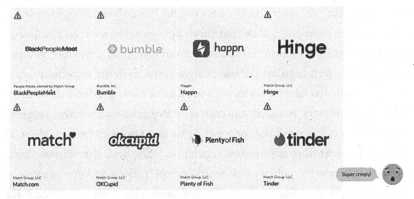

Source: Privacy Not Included, CC BY 4.0, Mozilla Foundation: https://foundation.mozilla.org/en/privacynotincluded/categories/dating-apps/

Which companies earn a privacy ranking of "super creepy"? Well, let's take a look at one of the creepiest: Tinder. For starters, at one point, 70,000 photos of women that were uploaded to Tinder were leaked onto a website known for criminal activity due to Tinder's lack of basic encryption security. Next, Tinder has collected location data and personal information to sell to third parties in a manner that may violate European privacy laws. Finally, if you choose to connect your Facebook account, Tinder and Facebook both have access to that data. As if being "super creepy" weren't enough, Tinder has also been found to engage in discriminatory pricing. Consumers International, with the Mozilla Foundation, found that Tinder was offering up to thirty-one different prices for Tinder Plus (an upgraded plan) within a single country.[11] In the United States, for the exact same service, prices ranged from $4.45 to $25.95. Additionally, the pricing algorithm charged older adults roughly 65 percent more than those aged eighteen to twenty-nine. This is not the first time Tinder was called to account for discriminatory pricing. In 2021, Tinder faced an age discrimination suit in which it agreed to stop charging people higher prices based on age—but only in California and only with the caveat that the company could continue to offer discounts to those in younger age groups.[12]

In an industry-facing paper entitled "Creating Trustworthy AI," several of my colleagues at the Mozilla Foundation describe trustworthy AI as "AI that is demonstrably worthy of trust, tech that considers accountability, agency, and individual and collective well-being."[13] Accountability and collective well-being are central to trustworthy AI. Yet online dating companies are unlikely to suddenly realize that they ought to act more ethically. In addition to pressure for more transparency from consumers, we need governments to effectively regulate the use of algorithmic systems, especially when they operationalize identity categories such as race and gender. Informed by a decade of industry research, my colleague Bogdana Rakova also suggests that tech bro culture and the tone-setting de facto policies for digital social life would benefit from government regulation.[14] She finds that without both internal and external policies that regulate expectations and organizational culture, people working inside tech companies who wish to advocate for marginalized groups face immense pressure not to do so.[15]

My review of industry papers from various tech companies about AI ethics and machine-learning approaches suggests that government regulation is warranted and wanted—by at least a small number of tech company insiders. For example, teams at Meta working on fairness hint at "expectations" of fair and transparent AI throughout their publicly available work.[16] On envisioning transparent algorithmic systems, advocates at the Mozilla Foundation write that there's progress when:

Governments develop the vision and capacity to effectively regulate AI.

There is wider enforcement of existing laws like the GDPR [General Data Protection Regulation in Europe].

Regulators have access to the data they need to scrutinize AI.

Governments develop programs to invest in and procure trustworthy AI.[17]

Transparency is key for trust. Consumers should not trust the words of dating companies or any tech companies without them telling us, in accessible lay terms, where they get our data, what happens to that data, and who has access to that data. But this fight for transparency about our own data likely will not come without governments protecting their citizens and without us, the users of these technologies, advocating for ourselves.

Redesigning Dating Apps, from the Margins

With ownership of Hinge, OkCupid, Plenty of Fish, Pairs, Our Time, Meetic, Hawaya (Muslim dating), Hakuna, Chispa (Latinx daters), and BLK (for Black daters), Match Group clearly understands that diverse cultures likely have different needs. But instead of incorporating knowledge learned from these communities to generate changes that might help all users—such as expanded reporting mechanisms and setting up steps for intentional follow-through—they likely use the same technologies created for mainstream White platforms. I do not intend to say that ethnic and culturally specific dating platforms don't have their place. These dating platforms often serve as safe spaces for users of color who have had too many negative experiences with harassment and racial fetishization on platforms created for mainstream users.[18] But if dating companies recognize that users of color are treated differently, why can't they introduce harm reduction strategies to their platforms designed for mainstream (White) use? The response to this question is grounded in a neo-liberal free speech ethos that suggests that limiting the expression of sexual racism is unfair to those who wish to express their personal taste.

In my research on algorithmic systems, conducted with Jenny Davis and Michael Yang, we argue that fairness framing in the tech world should be thrown out altogether, as it does not serve us particularly well.[19] Instead, we propose adjustments that would make right past wrongs—and guard against future harms—perpetrated by algorithmic systems. This might include taking extra measures to protect groups most at risk of being harmed by irresponsible tech. Under the frame of algorithmic reparation, we urge tech companies to ask what groups might be harmed by using certain technologies and whether it is appropriate to create or implement the use of a specific algorithmic system. Bogdana Rakova suggests that veto power should be adopted by tech culture, where individuals with trained insight have the ability to shut down a newly developed product or technology before it is deployed if it seems suspect.[20]

While consulting for different tech organizations, I've met many people who genuinely want to do good for society and try to reduce harm from within tech spaces. More than that, some people grapple every day with trying to reduce harm from the inside, at large tech companies, or whether it is better to quit altogether and leave their jobs. Industry research shows that pressure to "move fast and break things" is tremendous and that people in tech spaces find it extraordinarily difficult to go against the grain of these fast-moving machines.[21] Rakova's research suggests that those who are working toward the goal of building more responsible and equitable AI struggle to balance internal and external pressure inside tech companies.[22] Opaque channels of communication and status-laden hierarchies in tech companies contribute to blockages, leaving unclear processes for activating change that limits the effectiveness of so-called fairness campaigns in companies. As we've seen with the firing of minoritized folks from large tech companies, people of color—like Timnit Gebru, a former employee at Google—are often doing the hard work on racial equity. Those with relatively less social power are asked to risk their economic safety to usher in safety for the rest of us. And I am thankful for those who choose to take that risk. But the burden to fix companies from the inside should not fall on the same people time and again. Racism, even (or especially) in tech companies, is a White people problem. The people who created the biases in these systems should be tasked with correcting them.

In an effort to guide companies on how to advocate for overlooked users, as a Technology and Public Purpose Fellow at the Harvard Kennedy School, Afsaneh Rigot created *Design from the Margins*.[23] Her research—rooted in social science, legal scholarship, and civil society experience—also advocates for a mix of government regulation and tech-sector self-regulation. Design from the margins is:

> A design process that centers the most impacted and marginalized users from ideation to production, pushes the notion that not only is this something that can and must be done, but also that it is highly beneficial for all users and companies. For this to happen, consumer interest conversations need to be framed outside the "biggest use case" scenarios and United States and European Union-centrisms and refocused on the cases often left in the margins: the decentered cases.[24]

"Decentered cases" include everyone the company fails to consider and protect in product design, implementation, and development. Rigot identifies decentered cases as those "most at risk and under supported" in contexts likely to produce harm. In the case of dating apps, people of color and queer groups are least supported and most likely to find inadequate support for reporting harms.[25] Rigot's framing of decentered users implies that these groups should not exist solely in the margins in the minds of developers; rather, their needs should be centered because design for those most at risk of harm actually enhances safety for all users.

In short, listen to marginalized users.[26] It should not be the case that users do not know how to report sexual harassment. Users should not feel that dating platforms do not care that they experience sexual racism or transphobia. Platforms need to clearly communicate to users what happens when reports are filed and what steps dating apps are taking to ensure their safety moving forward.

Design from the Margins is a forward-looking blueprint for what tech companies could become if they valued marginalized users as much as mainstream users. Often dating platforms refer to non-normative users as edge cases because their experience deviates from the typical user experience. By recentering "edge cases," tech companies would increase privacy, transparency, and safety for all users. For example, Rigot advocated for "edge cases" or atypical users on Grindr in the MENA (Middle East/North Africa) region.[27] She consulted with international experts, technologists, and centered the expertise of queer individuals in Egypt, Lebanon, and Iran. Her needs-based analysis revealed heightened security risks for queer individuals in the region due to penal codes targeting LGBTQIA+ communities. By working iteratively with Grindr throughout the process, Rigot advocated for, and successfully implemented, discreet app icons and a self-destruct function that returns user agency, helping them to protect themselves from police surveillance while still being able to use the app (Figure C.3).[28] Though these

FIGURE C.3   Diagrams demonstrating how Grindr's Discreet App Icon feature can be used to disguise or change the icon on a device to enhance user security.

Source: https://www.muchtech.org/2021/01/how-to-change-grindr-app-icon.html; reprinted with permission from Grindr.

users in this region are only a small portion of Grindr's worldwide user base, these features were adopted because of thoughtful, intentional design. This design is now available to all users and has demonstrated improved safety for even mainstream users.

Rigot's advocacy resulted in expanded protection for marginalized users globally. Though she did the hard work of consulting with these communities about their needs, the expanded protections were only implemented because Grindr was willing to listen to activists, lawyers, and scholars with valuable expertise. Typically, the development of relatively small but hugely impactful changes are blocked before they can even begin because scholars and activists do not know what is happening inside tech companies. Dating companies, especially, are reluctant to share their data with the research community, and this walling off and inability to work with the scholarly community precludes valuable knowledge production and dissemination about potential harm reduction strategies.

(Un)Desired Regulation

Tech companies know that working with researchers has the potential to expand safety for users. In 2021, an industry-backed coalition launched the Digital Trust and Safety Partnership.[29] The group asked companies including Meta, Microsoft, Google, Pinterest, Reddit, and others to report on adherence to "best practices" in safety measures. The report revealed that tech companies are lagging behind other industries when it comes to researcher accessibility. Because the tech industry evades research access, the report also found that the companies do not have the ability to incorporate outside feedback from "credible third party groups, human rights organizations, academics, [or] investors."[30]

Ideally, these findings should support legislation that requires tech companies to share internal data with researchers. Senators Amy Klobuchar, Chris Coons, and Rob Portman proposed a bipartisan bill that would create pathways for researchers to petition a federal agency for access to data from tech platforms for approved studies. At the time of writing, this bill has not been formally introduced, suggesting we are a long way from seeing the adoption of such measures. But this bipartisan effort offers a glimmer of hope and, at the very least, suggests that lawmakers are aware that the tech industry cannot continue to go untamed. Further, the establishment of the European Union's Digital Services Act (DSA) and the General Data Protection Regulation (GDPR) demonstrate how well tech companies play with governments.

The primary aim of the GDPR is to provide consumers with more control over their data in the European Union. The GDPR demands that users know what data are being collected about them, make corrections in data reports, request that data be deleted, request that data be transferred to a different vendor, and file a complaint with EU compliance offices if requests are not met with an appropriate response.[31] But some tech companies, such as Microsoft, have committed to expanding the protections required by the EU to consumers in other locations. Likewise, Facebook decided to allow residents of Canada and Europe to opt into facial recognition features that identify individuals in photos.[32] Outside of these locations, this feature is still set to automatically opt in, meaning that users have little control, whether or not they want their Facebook experience animated by facial recognition technology.

Industry-wide changes initiated by the GDPR reveal two key points relevant to the online dating industry. First, tech companies have the ability to be more transparent about user data—including facial detection systems used to evaluate attractiveness. Every tech company could universally decide that they are going to apply the protections afforded by the GDPR to all users, as Microsoft plans to do. Yet, and this is the second point, tech companies choose to exclude prime markets from these protections because doing so would impact their revenue.[33] How the tech industry has responded to the GDPR means that, if faced with government regulation, the industry would indeed move towards more comprehensive safety, accessibility, and transparency about data and data processes for users; but without that regulation, there is little incentive to do so here in the United States. Tech companies exploit users and our data, knowing that doing so poses a risk to our safety and, in some cases, our democracy, in pursuit of the all-American dollar.

Hence safety for all users—concerning data transparency, content moderation, and automated sexual racism—are not issues of ability but desire. Developers have to *want* to reduce harm by creating platforms that protect marginalized users. As indicated by the language in their patent, Match Group is primarily concerned with creating a user experience that encourages continued play. They are reluctant to introduce features or remove features that may turn away their mainstream users because doing so is a threat to their revenue.

While my ultimate goal in conducting this research is to amplify the voices of marginalized users and help readers to become more informed about their own biases, a secondary goal is to hold online dating companies accountable for their part in automating sexual racism by creating environments where racial bias thrives. To do that, I hope to draw them into a future where decentered users are recentered. Design from the margins might look like expanded ick factor algorithms that are trained to capture, recognize, and flag subtly encoded sexual racism and to seek user feedback about this implementation. To do this well, dating companies would need to hire teams with expertise in diverse linguistic patterns. Platforms should also make clear in user guidelines that sexual racism and racial fetishization are not tolerated. Accordingly, users who encounter sexual racism should be supported in reporting incidents, and platforms should follow up with them. Further, dating companies (and all tech companies) should tell users, in lay terms, how, when, and where their data are used and collected. Lastly, dating companies need to explain to users how their algorithms work to create the automated dating experience. Design from the margins means that all users regain agency. These goals also coincide with the movement for thriving Black Lives. Users of color can thrive when they are not subjected to automated sexual racism without recourse.

Ruha Benjamin, as well as many other activists and scholars, provides us with tools for abolishing the covert harms that hallmark the New Jim Code.[34] First, we have to understand that countering racist technologies does not simply mean being concerned with how these technologies are developed but also with how we talk about and use these tools in our everyday lives.[35] Context matters. Right now, the context is that dating platforms are untrustworthy and use racist matching and sorting algorithms. Within broader social context, dating platforms' automated sexual racism stands at odds with the broader movement for Black Lives. Though many people think about Black Lives Matter as a movement to end police brutality and extralegal murder of Black people, it is also a movement for thriving, not just surviving. Black people and other folks of color cannot thrive in systems where they lack protection from the most intimate kinds of racism.

If we are to abolish the New Jim Code and, with it, sexual racism couched in personal choice narratives, our abolitionist toolkit must include both computational interventions and narrative strategies.[36] Data points are comprised of actions made by individuals, yet stories told by big data are often incomplete. We must shape how we talk about dating platforms, the data they collect, the racism inherent to their sorting systems, and the matches they create. To realize this goal, we need a "justice-oriented, emancipatory approach to data production, analysis, and public engagement."[37]

I propose one approach that might establish accessible communication with users, center marginalized users as experts on their own harm reduction measures, and demonstrate transparency, if implemented alongside governmental regulation of tech companies. I envision a cooperative, user-generated rating system of accountability for online dating platforms and dating companies. In this system, users are provided with factual and accessible reports about how and when data are tracked, details about what kind of data are collected, and with which companies' user data are shared. Users also vote on dating platforms' safety ecosystems in accordance with best practices established by experts from marginalized communities. Users' experience of safety and the safety of their data go hand in hand. This kind of system might encourage cooperation with government regulation and induce self-regulating measures if companies begin to lose users because of receiving a lower overall safety evaluation from them. But, as discussed previously, we cannot expect companies to act in consumer interest without support from our government. Without regulation, the described system would run the risk of concealing and creating new types of racial inequity.

"Fair" Play

I've often wondered if I need to, like, take a class to improve my algorithm. . . . I've definitely been curious about that because I mean there is, there's some, you know, algorithm they use to match people, and I don't know. I feel like I know a lot of people that work at these kind of, like, tech companies and, I don't know, a lot of them are—like, a lot of the product people aren't quite the best people

in the world. So, I'm sure there's probably ways they could improve the apps.
[Laughs] I mean, the thing about that is people with biases make technology.
So algorithms are fundamentally flawed because they are made by flawed
people with biases. So those things determine it. Like you just can't help that.
Those things would dictate how any kind of algorithm performs.

JAMIE, INTERVIEWED IN 2020

Jamie's right about one thing: people with biases make technology, and therefore technologies are fundamentally flawed. Though many companies are establishing or renewing commitments to fair AI, we have to acknowledge that AI and algorithmic systems can never be fair.[38] Because society is fundamentally unjust and built to uphold White supremacy, our technologies are also unjust.

But Jamie's wrong about these systems being unfixable, especially in the case of dating platforms. Dating platforms, unlike other automated digital technologies, have a singular primary function. Of course, we sometimes make friends or work connections through dating platforms (especially with apps like Bumble Bizz and Bumble BFF), but they are not multimodal in the same way as social media platforms like Pinterest, Facebook, and Instagram.

Dating companies exist to help us find romantic and sexual connections. Dating companies think that we don't have other alternatives for finding relationships. Currently, the online dating industry does not have incentives to change, but it might if we started to impact profits. There are things we can do as individuals to disrupt these systems:

1. If you are in a position of power (meaning not a minoritized person seeking to reduce your encounters with sexual racism), stop using race filters and stop paying for them.

2. Glitch the system. Intentionally confuse dating platforms' algorithms by deliberately engaging with those whom you ordinarily would not. Who knows, you may just find a love match (keeping in mind the old adage that opposites attract). By feeding algorithmic systems information that does not fit within expected patterns, you can disrupt the "efficiency" of ranking and sorting systems.

3. Ask dating companies for your data. Most dating companies will provide users with at least some of the stored data. Though the process

for acquiring your data might be unduly burdensome, seeing the vast amount of data stored about whom you've matched with, all of your text-based exchanges, and other descriptive data might make you think twice about continuing to use online dating services.

4. Following up on the third item, once you start to question what happens to all of this data, write to companies to ask them! If dating companies begin to receive these requests en masse (i.e., consumers become a nuisance to them), they may reconsider their policies around what data are collected and how that information is shared with users.

5. Lastly, tech companies are so deeply committed to neo-liberal ethos that they will not seek out regulation—in fact, they will resist it. Push back by demanding that your local and state representatives craft tech sector relevant legislation that centers the experiences of marginalized and/or harmed users as a matter of equity and social justice.

For being in the relationship business, online dating companies do not appear to have what it takes to be in a healthy relationship. Would you stay in a relationship that lacked trust and in which you did not feel safe? The reality is, sometimes the answer is yes. People stay in unsafe relationships when they don't feel like they have other options, or when they don't know that they could do better. We do have other options, and we can do better. The steps above may be a start. But perhaps it's time for us to all take stock of our relationship with dating companies and determine if we really need them, if they make us feel safe, and if we trust them. If the answer is no, maybe we need to swipe left on dating apps altogether until they commit to real accountability.

TABLE A.1 Demographic Characteristics of Participants

RACE	PERCENT	COUNT
Black	26%	26
White	27%	27
Asian	25%	25
Latinx (Hispanic)	22%	22
Total responses		100

AGE*	PERCENT	COUNT
20–29	60%	60
30–39	30%	30
40–49	6%	6
50–63	4%	4
Total responses		100

RESIDENCE	PERCENT	COUNT
Urban	75%	53
Suburban	11%	8
Rural	14%	10
Total responses		71

INTERSECTIONAL GENDER AND RACE	PERCENT	COUNT
Black/Men	7%	7
Black/Women	19%	19
White/Men	11%	11
White/Women	16%	16
White nonbinary	1%	1
Asian/Men	11%	11
Asian/Women	13%	13
Latinx (Hispanic)/Men	10%	10
Latinx (Hispanic)/Women	12%	12
Total responses		100

SEXUAL ORIENTATION	PERCENT	COUNT
Heterosexual	75%	75
Homosexual	8%	8
Bisexual	12%	12
Pansexual	2%	2
Demisexual	3%	3
Total responses		100

* Mean age 29.27

Introduction

1. Kathy O'Neil, *Weapons of Math Destruction: How Big Data Increases Inequality and Threatens Democracy* (New York: Broadway Books, 2016).

2. Patricia Hill Collins, *Black Feminist Thought: Knowledge, Consciousness, and the Politics of Empowerment* (New York: Routledge, 2002).

3. Judith Butler, *Gender Trouble: Feminism and the Subversion of Identity* (New York: Routledge, 2002).

4. Monica Anderson, Emily A. Vogels, and Erica Turner, "The Virtues and Downsides of Online Dating," *Pew Research Center*, February 6, 2020. https://www.pew research.org/internet/2020/02/06/the-virtues-and-downsides-of-online-dating/

5. Afsaneh Rigot, *Design from the Margins: Centering the Most Marginalized and Impacted in Design Processes—from Ideation to Production*, Belfer Center for Science and International Affairs, May 13, 2022. https://www.belfercenter.org/publication/ design-margins

6. Denton Callander, Christy E. Newman, and Martin Holt, "Is Sexual Racism *Really* Racism? Distinguishing Attitudes Toward Sexual Racism and Generic Racism Among Gay and Bisexual Men," *Archives of Sexual Behavior* 44, no. 7 (2015): 1991–2000; Jesús Gregorio Smith et al., "Is Sexual Racism Still Really Racism? Revisiting Callander et al. (2015) in the USA," *Archives of Sexual Behavior* 51, no. 6 (2022): 3049–3062.

7. The original OkCupid website with this data has been taken down. The data

are available at Reddit: https://www.reddit.com/r/Okcupid /comments/n1hdmm/ okcupid _quickmatch_scores_based_on_race/

8. Sonu Bedi, *Private Racism* (Cambridge, UK: Cambridge University Press, 2019).

9. Celeste Vaughan Curington, Jennifer Hickes Lundquist, and Ken-Hou Lin, *The Dating Divide: Race and Desire in the Era of Online Romance* (Oakland: University of California Press, 2021); Collins, *Black Feminist*.

10. Curington, Lundquist, and Lin, *Dating Divide*; Eduardo Bonilla-Silva, *Racism Without Racists: Color-Blind Racism and the Persistence of Racial Inequality in the United States* (Lanham, MD: Rowman & Littlefield, 2008).

11. Austin Carr, "I Found Out My Secret Internal Tinder Rating and Now I Wish I Hadn't," *Fast Company*, January 11, 2016. https://www.fastcompany.com/30 54871/whats-your-tinder-score-inside-the-apps-internal-ranking-system

12. Match Group, "Privacy," 2023. https://mtch.com/privacy/#data_we_collect

13. Christian Rudder, *Dataclysm: Who We Are (When We Think No One's Looking)* (New York: Crown, 2014).

14. Rudder, *Dataclysm*, 705.

15. Alexis Kleinman, "Black People and Asian Men Have a Much Harder Time Dating on OkCupid ," *HuffPost*, September 12, 2014. https://www.huffpost.com/en try/okcupid -race_n_5811840

16. Andrew Leonard, "OkCupid Founder: 'I Wish People Exercised More Humanity' on OkCupid ," *Salon*, September 12, 2014. https://www.salon.com/2014/09 /12/okcupid _founder_i_wish_people_exercised_more_humanity_on_okcupid /

17. Leonard, "OkCupid Founder."

18. Sen_Mendoza,"How Race Affects the Reply Rate Among OkCupid Members," Reddit: r/dataisbeautiful, March 24, 2014. https://www.reddit.com/r/datais beautiful/comments/217vtn/how_race_affects_the_reply_rate_among_okcupid /

19. Melissa Pandika, "Are Your Dating Preferences Racist?," *Mic*, July 1, 2021. https://www.mic.com/life/are-your-dating-preferences-racist-82343271

20. Joseph L. Graves Jr., "Great Is Their Sin: Biological Determinism in the Age of Genomics," *Annals of the American Academy of Political and Social Science* 661, no. 1 (2015): 24–50.

21. Cited in Pandika, "Are Your Dating Preferences Racist?"

22. Melissa R. Herman and Mary E. Campbell, "I Wouldn't, But You Can: Attitudes Toward Interracial Relationships," *Social Science Research* 41, no. 2 (2012): 343–358.

23. Jeremy Hunsinger, "Critical Internet Studies," in *Second International Handbook of Internet Research*, eds. Jeremy Hunsinger, Matthew M. Allen, and Lizbeth Klastrup (New York: Springer International, 2020), 263–279.

24. Collins, *Black Feminist*, 11.

25. Collins, *Black Feminist*, 79.

26. Safiya Umoja Noble, *Algorithms of Oppression: How Search Engines Reinforce Racism* (New York: New York University Press, 2018).

27. Mireille Miller-Young, *A Taste for Brown Sugar: Black Women in Pornography* (Durham: Duke University Press, 2014).

28. Noble, *Algorithms*.

29. Derek Kenji Iwamoto and William Ming Liu, "Asian American Men and Asianized Attribution: Intersections of Masculinity, Race, and Sexuality," in *Asian American Psychology*, eds. Nita Tewari and Alvin N. Alvarez (New York: Psychology Press, 2008), 261–282; Kevin K. Kumashiro, "Supplementing Normalcy and Otherness: Queer Asian American Men Reflect on Stereotypes, Identity, and Oppression," *Qualitative Studies in Education* 12 (1999): 491–508; Yen Ling Shek, "Asian American Masculinity: A Review of the Literature," *Journal of Men's Studies* 14, no. 3 (2007): 379–391.

30. Shek, "Asian American," 380.

31. Shek, "Asian American," 381; Yen Le Espiritu, *Asian American Women and Men: Labor, Laws, and Love* (Thousand Oaks, CA: Sage, 1997).

32. Kumashiro, "Supplementing."

33. Yarden Katz, *Artificial Whiteness: Politics and Ideology in Artificial Intelligence* (New York: Columbia University Press, 2020), 154.

34. Katz, *Artificial Whiteness*, 155.

35. Beth Coleman, "Race as Technology," *Camera Obscura: Feminism, Culture, and Media Studies* 24, no. 1 (2009): 177–207; André Brock Jr., "Distributed Blackness," in *Distributed Blackness: African American Cybercultures* (New York: New York University Press, 2020).

36. Sara Ahmed, "A Phenomenology of Whiteness," in *Fanon, Phenomenology, and Psychology*, eds. Leswin Laubscher, Derek Hook, and Miraj U. Desai (New York: Routledge, 2021), 229–246.

37. Bonilla-Silva, *Racism*; Samuel L. Gaertner and John F. Dovidio, "Understanding and Addressing Contemporary Racism: From Aversive Racism to the Common Ingroup Identity Model," *Journal of Social Issues* 61, no. 3 (2005): 615–639; Joel Kovel, *White Racism: A Psychohistory* (New York: Columbia University Press, 1984).

38. O'Neil, *Weapons*; Ruha Benjamin, *Race After Technology: Abolitionist Tools for the New Jim Code* (Medford, MA: Polity Press, 2019).

39. Noble, *Algorithms*, 1.

40. Benjamin, *Race After Technology*; Wendy Hui Kyong Chun, *Discriminating Data: Correlation, Neighborhoods, and the New Politics of Recognition* (Cambridge, MA: MIT Press, 2021).

41. Benjamin, *Race After Technology*.

42. Benjamin, *Race After Technology*.

43. O'Neil, *Weapons*, 26.

44. Benjamin, *Race After Technology*, 3.

45. Richard Delgado and Jean Stefancic, *Critical Race Theory: An Introduction*, 3rd ed. (New York: New York University Press, 2017).

46. Benjamin, *Race After Technology*; Winifred R. Poster, "Racialized Surveillance in the Digital Service Economy," in *Captivating Technology: Race, Carceral Technoscience, and Liberatory Imagination in Everyday Life*, ed. Ruha Benjamin (Durham: Duke University Press, 2019), 133–169.

47. O'Neil, *Weapons*, 8.

48. Thomas M. Shapiro, *The Hidden Cost of Being African American: How Wealth Perpetuates Inequality* (New York: Oxford University Press, 2004); Delgado and Stefancic, *Critical Race*.

49. Tamara Nopper, "Digital Character in 'The Scored Society': FICO, Social Networks, and Competing Measurements of Creditworthiness," in *Captivating Technology: Race, Carceral Technoscience, and Liberatory Imagination in Everyday Life*, ed. Ruha Benjamin (Durham: Duke University Press, 2019), 170–187; O'Neil, *Weapons*.

50. O'Neil, *Weapons*; Devah Pager and Hana Shepherd, "The Sociology of Discrimination: Racial Discrimination in Employment, Housing, Credit, and Consumer Markets," *Annual Review of Sociology* 34 (2008): 181–209.

51. O'Neil, *Weapons*, 165; italics in original.

52. André Brock, "From the Blackhand Side: Twitter as a Cultural Conversation," *Journal of Broadcasting & Electronic Media* 56, no. 4 (2012): 529–49; Brock, "Distributed Blackness"; Jessie Daniels, "'My Brain Database Doesn't See Skin Color': Color-Blind Racism in the Technology Industry and in Theorizing the Web," *American Behavioral Scientist* 59, no. 11 (2015): 1377–1393; Noble, *Algorithms*; Katz, *Artificial Whiteness*; Tara J. Yosso, "Whose Culture Has Capital? A Critical Race Theory Discussion of Community Cultural Wealth," *Race Ethnicity and Education* 8, no. 1 (2005): 69–91.

53. Mozilla, "New Research: Tinder's Opaque, Unfair Pricing Algorithm Can Charge Users Up to Five-Times More for Same Service," *Mozilla* (blog), February 8, 2022. https://foundation.mozilla.org/en/blog/new-research-tinders-opaque-unfair-pricing-algorithm-can-charge-users-up-to-five-times-more-for-same-service/

54. Vanessa Gonlin, "Come Back Home, Sista!: Reactions to Black Women in Interracial Relationships with White Men," *Ethnic and Racial Studies* (2023): 1–23.

55. The Bibliography includes a listing of helpful websites for more information.

56. Benjamin, *Race After Technology*.

57. Rigot, *Design from the Margins*.

Chapter 1

1. Kyung-Hee Choi et al., "Experiences of Discrimination and Their Impact on the Mental Health Among African American, Asian and Pacific Islander, and Latino Men Who Have Sex with Men," *American Journal of Public Health* 103, no. 5 (2013): 868–874; Chong-suk Han, "A Qualitative Exploration of the Relationship Between Racism and Unsafe Sex Among Asian Pacific Islander Gay Men," *Archives of Sexual Behavior* 37 (2008): 827–837; Chirk Jenn Ng, Hui Meng Tan, and Wah Yun Low, "What Do Asian Men Consider as Important Masculinity Attributes? Findings from the Asian Men's Attitudes to Life Events and Sexuality (MALES) Study," *Journal of Men's Health*, 5, no. 4 (2008): 350–355; Yen Ling Shek, "Asian American Masculinity: A Review of the Literature," *Journal of Men's Studies* 14, no. 3 (2007): 379–391.

2. Shantel Gabrieal Buggs, "Color, Culture, or Cousin? Multiracial Americans and Framing Boundaries in Interracial Relationships," *Journal of Marriage and Family* 81, no. 5 (2019): 1221–1236; Shantel Gabrieal Buggs, "Dating in the Time of #BlackLivesMatter: Exploring Mixed-Race Women's Discourses of Race and Racism," *Sociology of Race and Ethnicity* 3, no. 4 (2017): 538–551; Matthew H. Rafalow, Cynthia Feliciano, and Belinda Robnett, "Racialized Femininity and Masculinity in the Preferences of Online Same-Sex Daters," *Social Currents* 4, no. 4 (2017): 306–321; Brandon Andrew Robinson, "'Personal Preference' as the New Racism: Gay Desire and Racial Cleansing in Cyberspace," *Sociology of Race and Ethnicity* 1, no. 2 (2015): 317–330; Jesús Gregorio Smith and Gabriel Amaro, "'No Fats, No Femmes, and No Blacks or Asians': The Role of Body-Type, Sex Position, and Race on Condom Use Online," *AIDS and Behavior* 25, no. 7 (2021): 2166–2176.

3. Patricia Hill Collins, *Black Feminist Thought: Knowledge, Consciousness, and the Politics of Empowerment* (New York: Routledge, 2002).

4. Mike Donaldson, "What Is Hegemonic Masculinity?," *Theory and Society* 22, no. 5 (1993): 643–657.

5. Maria DelGreco and Amanda Denes, "You Are Not as Cute as You Think You Are: Emotional Responses to Expectancy Violations in Heterosexual Online Dating Interactions," *Sex Roles* 82, no. 9 (2020): 622–632.

6. Laura Thompson, "'I Can Be Your Tinder Nightmare': Harassment and Misogyny in the Online Sexual Marketplace," *Feminism & Psychology* 28, no. 1 (2018): 69–89.

7. Frances Shaw, "'Bitch I Said Hi': The *Bye Felipe* Campaign and Discursive Activism in Mobile Dating Apps," *Social Media+ Society*, 2 no. 4 (2016): 1–10.

8. Ng, Tan, and Low, "What Do Asian Men Consider"; Shek, "Asian American."

9. Thomas A. Foster, "The Sexual Abuse of Black Men Under American Slavery," *Journal of the History of Sexuality* 20, no. 3 (2011): 445–464; Collins, *Black Feminist*; Michael Pass, Ellen Benoit, and Eloise Dunlap, "'I Just Be Myself': Contradicting

Hyper Masculine and Hyper Sexual Stereotypes Among Low-Income Black Men in New York City," in *Hyper Sexual, Hyper Masculine? Gender, Race and Sexuality in the Identities of Contemporary Black Men*, eds. Brittany C. Slatton and Kamesha Spates (London: Routledge, 2014), 165–181; Busi Makoni, "Labelling Black Male Genitalia and the 'New Racism': The Discursive Construction of Sexual Racism by a Group of Southern African College Students," *Gender and Language* 10, no. 1 (2016): 48–72.

10. Collins, *Black Feminist*; Foster, "Sexual Abuse of Black Men."

11. Rachel F. Moran, *Interracial Intimacy: The Regulation of Race and Romance* (Chicago: University of Chicago Press, 2001); Russell K. Robinson and David M. Frost, "LGBT Equality and Sexual Racism," *Fordham Law Review* 86, no. 6 (2018): 2739–2754; Jesús Gregorio Smith, Maria Cristina Morales, and Chong-suk Han, "The Influence of Sexual Racism on Erotic Capital: A Systemic Racism Perspective," in *Handbook of the Sociology of Racial and Ethnic Relations*, eds. P. Batur and J. R. Feagin (New York: Springer, 2018), 389–399; Frank Howard, "Social Matching Systems, Intimate Personal Data, and Romantic Compatibility on Internet Dating Sites and Apps," *Journal of Research in Gender Studies* 10, no. 1 (2020): 80–86; Joe R. Feagin, *The White Racial Frame: Centuries of Racial Framing and Counter-Framing* (New York: Routledge, 2020).

12. Feagin, *White Racial Frame*.

13. Foster, "Sexual Abuse of Black Men"; Howard C. Stevenson Jr., "The Psychology of Sexual Racism and AIDS: An Ongoing Saga of Distrust and the 'Sexual Other,'" *Journal of Black Studies* 25, no. 1 (1994): 62–80.

14. Foster, "Sexual Abuse of Black Men."

15. Stevenson, "Psychology of Sexual Racism and AIDS."

16. John D'Emilio and Estelle B. Freedman, *Intimate Matters: A History of Sexuality in America* (New York: Harper & Row, 1988); Stevenson, "Psychology of Sexual Racism and AIDS."

17. Kenneth James Lay, "Sexual Racism: A Legacy of Slavery," *National Black Law Journal* 13, no. 1–2 (1993): 165.

18. Lay, "Sexual Racism," 167.

19. Lay, "Sexual Racism," 167.

20. Sonu Bedi, *Private Racism* (Cambridge, UK: Cambridge University Press, 2019); Stevenson, "Psychology of Sexual Racism and AIDS."

21. Collins, *Black Feminist*, 79.

22. Feagin, *White Racial Frame*.

23. Collins, *Black Feminist*, 79.

24. Collins, citing Omolade, in *Black Feminist*, 145.

25. Collins, *Black Feminist*.

26. Smith and Amaro, "No Fats."

27. Han, "Relationship Between Racism and Unsafe Sex"; David J. Brennan et

al., "'Never Reflected Anywhere': Body Image Among Ethnoracialized Gay and Bisexual Men," *Body Image* 10, no. 3 (2013): 389–398; Yash Bhambhani et al., "The Role of Psychological Flexibility as a Mediator Between Experienced Sexual Racism and Psychological Distress Among Men of Color Who Have Sex with Men," *Archives of Sexual Behavior* 49, no. 2 (2020): 711–720; Stevenson, "Psychology of Sexual Racism and AIDS"; Mary Dianne Plummer, "Sexual Racism in Gay Communities: Negotiating the Ethnosexual Marketplace," PhD dissertation (University of Washington, 2008); Michael Thai, "Sexual Racism Is Associated with Lower Self-Esteem and Life Satisfaction in Men Who Have Sex with Men," *Archives of Sexual Behavior* 49, no. 1 (2020): 347–353.

28. Collins, *Black Feminist*; Kimberlé Crenshaw, "Mapping the Margins: Intersectionality, Identity Politics, and Violence Against Women of Color," *Stanford Law Review* 43, no. 6 (1993): 1241.

29. Foster, "Sexual Abuse of Black Men"; Lay, "Sexual Racism."

30. David A. Hollinger, "The One Drop Rule and the One Hate Rule," *Daedalus* 134, no. 1 (2005): 18–28.

31. Daniel J. Sharfstein, "Crossing the Color Line: Racial Migration and the One-Drop Rule, 1600–1860." *Minnesota Law Review* 91 (2007): 592; Hollinger, "One Drop."

32. W. E. B. Du Bois, *The Souls of Black Folk* (Chicago: A. C. McClurg & Co., 1903).

33. Moya Bailey, "Misogynoir Transformed," in *Misogynoir Transformed* (New York: New York University Press, 2021).

34. Bedi, *Private Racism*; Buggs, "Dating."

35. Collins, *Black Feminist*.

36. Safiya Umoja Noble, *Algorithms of Oppression: How Search Engines Reinforce Racism* (New York: New York University Press, 2018).

37. Collins, *Black Feminist*; Noble, *Algorithms*.

38. Jenny L. Davis, Apryl Williams, and Michael W. Yang, "Algorithmic Reparation," *Big Data & Society* 8, no. 2 (2021): 1–12; Jeffrey Dastin, "Amazon Scraps Secret AI Recruiting Tool That Showed Bias Against Women," *Reuters*, October 10, 2018. https://www.reuters.com/article/us-amazon-com-jobs-automation-insight/amazon-scraps-secret-ai-recruiting-tool-that-showed-bias-against-women-idUSKCN1MK08G

39. Helen Mayer Hacker, "The New Burdens of Masculinity," *Marriage and Family Living* 19, no. 3 (1957): 227–233; R. W. Connell and James W. Messerschmidt, "Hegemonic Masculinity: Rethinking the Concept," *Gender & Society* 19, no. 6 (2005): 829–859.

40. Judith Butler, *Gender Trouble: Feminism and the Subversion of Identity* (New York: Routledge, 2002), 13.

41. Smith and Amaro, "No Fats."

42. Tressie McMillan Cottom, *Thick: And Other Essays* (New York: New Press, 2018); Sonu Bedi, "Sexual Racism: Intimacy as a Matter of Justice," *Journal of Politics* 77, no. 4 (2015): 998–1011.

43. R. W. Connell, *Masculinities*, 2nd ed. (Cambridge, UK: Polity Press, 2005).

44. Connell and Messerschmidt, "Hegemonic Masculinity"; Diana M. Hechavarria and Amy E. Ingram, "The Entrepreneurial Gender Divide: Hegemonic Masculinity, Emphasized Femininity and Organizational Forms," *International Journal of Gender and Entrepreneurship* 8, no. 3 (2016): 242–281.

45. Connell and Messerschmidt, "Hegemonic Masculinity."

46. Donaldson, "What Is Hegemonic Masculinity?"

47. Alice Marwick, "There's a Beautiful Girl Under All of This: Performing Hegemonic Femininity in Reality Television," *Critical Studies in Media Communication*, 27, no. 3 (2010): 251–266.

48. Shelley Budgeon, "The Dynamics of Gender Hegemony: Femininities, Masculinities and Social Change," *Sociology* 48, no. 2 (2014): 317–334; Carrie Paechter, "Rethinking the Possibilities for Hegemonic Femininity: Exploring a Gramscian Framework," *Women's Studies International Forum* 68 (2018): 121–128.

49. Paechter, "Rethinking Possibilities for Hegemonic Femininity."

50. Michel Foucault, *Discipline and Punish: The Birth of the Prison* (Durham: Duke University Press, 2007), 445–471.

51. Angela King, "The Prisoner of Gender: Foucault and the Disciplining of the Female Body," *Journal of International Women's Studies* 5, no. 2 (2004): 29–39; Monique Deveaux, "Feminism and Empowerment: A Critical Reading of Foucault, *Feminist Studies* 20, no. 2 (1994): 223–247; Anne Balsamo, *Technologies of the Gendered Body: Reading Cyborg Women* (Durham: Duke University Press, 1996).

52. Cottom, *Thick*; Bedi, "Sexual Racism."

53. Deveaux, "Feminism and Empowerment."

54. DelGreco and Denes, "You Are Not as Cute."

55. Ng, Tan, and Low, "What Do Asian Men Consider."

56. Khoa Phan Howard, "The Creepy White Guy and the Helpless Asian: How Sexual Racism Persists in a Gay Interracial Friendship Group," *Social Problems* (2021): 1–17; Denton Callander, Christy E. Newman, and Martin Holt, "Is Sexual Racism *Really* Racism? Distinguishing Attitudes Toward Sexual Racism and Generic Racism Among Gay and Bisexual Men," *Archives of Sexual Behavior* 44, no. 7 (2015): 1991–2000; Makoni, "Labelling Black Male Genitalia"; Thai, "Sexual Racism."

57. Callander, Newman, and Holt, "Is Sexual Racism *Really* Racism?"

58. Callander, Newman, and Holt, "Is Sexual Racism *Really* Racism?"

59. Robin DiAngelo, *White Fragility: Why It's So Hard for White People to Talk About Racism* (Boston: Beacon Press, 2018).

60. Callander, Newman, and Holt, "Is Sexual Racism *Really* Racism?," 1995; emphasis added.

61. Callander, Newman, and Holt, "Is Sexual Racism *Really* Racism?"

62. Pass, Benoit, and Dunlap, "'I Just Be Myself'"; William L. Jeffries IV, "A Comparative Analysis of Homosexual Behaviors, Sex Role Preferences, and Anal Sex Proclivities in Latino and Non-Latino Men," *Archives of Sexual Behavior* 38 (2009): 765–778.

63. Callander, Newman, and Holt, "Is Sexual Racism *Really* Racism?"

64. Smith et al., "Is Sexual Racism Still Really Racism?"

65. Callander, Newman, and Holt, "Is Sexual Racism *Really* Racism?"

66. Afsaneh Rigot, *Design from the Margins: Centering the Most Marginalized and Impacted in Design Processes—from Ideation to Production*, Belfer Center for Science and International Affairs, May 13, 2022. https://www.belfercenter.org/publication/design-margins

67. Phan Howard, "Creepy White Guy."

68. Lawrence Stacey and TehQuin D. Forbes, "Feeling Like a Fetish: Racialized Feelings, Fetishization, and the Contours of Sexual Racism on Gay Dating Apps," *Journal of Sex Research* 59, no. 3 (2022): 372–384.

69. Stacey and Forbes, "Feeling Like a Fetish"; Molly Silvestrini, "'It's Not Something I Can Shake': The Effect of Racial Stereotypes, Beauty Standards, and Sexual Racism on Interracial Attraction," *Sexuality & Culture* 24 (2020): 305–325.

70. Han, "Relationship Between Racism and Unsafe Sex"; Chong-suk Han et al., "Stress and Coping with Racism and Their Role in Sexual Risk for HIV Among African American, Asian/Pacific Islander, and Latino Men Who Have Sex with Men," *Archives of Sexual Behavior* 44 (2015): 411–420; Brennan et al., "'Never Reflected Anywhere'"; Bhambhani, "The Role of Psychological Flexibility"; Stevenson, "Psychology of Sexual Racism and AIDS"; Plummer, "Sexual Racism in Gay Communities"; Thai, "Sexual Racism."

71. Han, "Relationship Between Racism and Unsafe Sex"; David Malebranche et al., "Masculine Socialization and Sexual Risk Behaviors Among Black Men Who Have Sex with Men: A Qualitative Exploration," *Men and Masculinities* 12, no. 1 (2007): 90–112; Smith and Amaro, "No Fats."

72. Han, "Relationship Between Racism and Unsafe Sex"; Bhambhani, "The Role of Psychological Flexibility"; Annie Ro et al., "Dimensions of Racism and Their Impact on Partner Selection Among Men of Colour Who Have Sex with Men: Understanding Pathways to Sexual Risk," *Culture, Health & Sexuality* 15, no. 7 (2013): 836–850; Ilan H. Meyer, "Resilience in the Study of Minority Stress and Health of Sexual and Gender Minorities," *Psychology of Sexual Orientation and Gender Diversity* 2, no. 3 (2015): 209–213.

73. Eduardo Bonilla-Silva, *Racism Without Racists: Color-Blind Racism and the*

Persistence of Racial Inequality in the United States (Lanham, MD: Rowman & Little-field Publishers, 2008).

74. Buggs, "Dating."

75. Bonilla-Silva, *Racism*, 76.

76. Collins, *Black Feminist*.

77. Bonilla-Silva, *Racism*.

78. E. Benjamin Skinner, "The Fight to End Global Slavery," *World Policy Journal* 26, no. 2 (2009): 33–41.

79. Rachel McCurdy, "Did Slavery Ever Really End? An Analysis of Institutional Racism and the Prison Industrial Complex in America," PhD dissertation (University of Hull, 2021); Diane Bailey, *The Emancipation Proclamation and the End of Slavery in America* (Buffalo: Rosen Publishing, 2014).

80. Antoinette Harrell and Justin Fornal, "Black People in the US Were Enslaved Well into the 1960s," *Vice*, February 28, 2018. https://www.vice.com/en/article/437573/blacks-were-enslaved-well-into-the-1960s; McCurdy, "Did Slavery Ever Really End?"

81. Bonilla-Silva, *Racism*.

82. Ruha Benjamin, *Race After Technology: Abolitionist Tools for the New Jim Code* (Medford, MA: Polity Press, 2019).

83. Paul F. Lazarsfeld and Robert K. Merton, "Friendship as a Social Process: A Substantive and Methodological Analysis," *Freedom and Control in Modern Society* 18, no. 1 (1954): 18–66; Donna L. Berry et al., "Understanding Health Decision Making: An Exploration of Homophily," *Social Science & Medicine* 214 (2018): 118–124.

84. Celeste Vaughan Curington, Jennifer Hickes Lundquist, and Ken-Hou Lin, *The Dating Divide: Race and Desire in the Era of Online Romance* (Oakland: University of California Press, 2021), 84–85.

85. Christian Rudder, *Dataclysm: Who We Are (When We Think No One's Looking)* (New York: Crown, 2014).

86. Belinda Robnett and Cynthia Feliciano, "Patterns of Racial-Ethnic Exclusion by Internet Daters," *Social Forces* 89, no. 3 (2011): 807–828; Rafalow, Feliciano, and Robnett, "Racialized Femininity and Masculinity."

87. Celeste Vaughan Curington and Jennifer Hickes, "Romantic Apartheid: Digital Sexual Racism in Online Dating," in *Introducing the New Sexuality Studies,* 4th ed., eds. Nancy L. Fischer, Laurel Westbrook, and Steven Seidman (London: Routledge, 2022), 214–223.

88. Curington, Lundquist, and Lin, *Dating Divide*, 44.

89. Curington, Lundquist, and Lin, *Dating Divide*.

90. Curington, Lundquist, and Lin, *Dating Divide*, 4–5; italics in original.

Chapter 2

1. Austin Carr, "I Found Out My Secret Internal Tinder Rating and Now I Wish I Hadn't," *Fast Company*, January 11, 2016. https://www.fastcompany.com/3054871/whats-your-tinder-score-inside-the-apps-internal-ranking-system

2. Carr, "I Found My Tinder Rating."

3. Match Group, "Privacy," 2023. https://mtch.com/privacy/#data_we_collect

4. Ruha Benjamin, *Race After Technology: Abolitionist Tools for the New Jim Code* (Medford, MA: Polity Press, 2019).

5. Match Group, U.S. Patent 10,203,854, "Matching Process System and Method." Inventors: Sean Rad, Todd M. Carrico, Kenneth B. Hoskins, James C. Stone, and Jonathan Badeen, Current assignee: Match Group LLC. Filed April 3, 2018; issued February 12, 2019. https://patents.google.com/patent/US10203854B2/en?oq=10%2c203%2c854

6. Match Group, U.S. Patent 10,203,854.

7. Match Group, U.S. Patent 10,203,854.

8. Match Group, U.S. Patent 10,203,854.

9. Cynthia L. Robinson-Moore, "Beauty Standards Reflect Eurocentric Paradigms—So What? Skin Color, Identity, and Black Female Beauty," *Journal of Race & Policy* 4, no. 1 (2008): 66–85; Peggy Chin Evans and Allen R. McConnell, "Do Racial Minorities Respond in the Same Way to Mainstream Beauty Standards? Social Comparison Processes in Asian, Black, and White Women," *Self and Identity* 2, no. 2 (2003): 153–167.

10. Match Group, U.S. Patent 10,203,854.

11. Match Group, U.S. Patent 10,203,854.

12. Xaiyi Li, "The Gamification of Dating: Tinder and Game-Playing on Reddit Communities," MA thesis (University of Melbourne, 2017). Christina Brown, "It's a Match! The Procedural Rhetoric of Gaming and Online Dating in Tinder," *Student Research Submissions* (2018): 1–21.

13. Mozilla, "New Research: Tinder's Opaque, Unfair Pricing Algorithm Can Charge Users Up to Five-Times More for Same Service," *Mozilla* (blog), February 8, 2022. https://foundation.mozilla.org/en/blog/new-research-tinders-opaque-unfair-pricing-algorithm-can-charge-users-up-to-five-times-more-for-same-service/

14. Match Group, U.S. Patent 10,203,854.

15. Match Group, U.S. Patent 10,203,854. Emphasis added.

16. Clare Duffy, "State Attorneys General Launch Investigation into Meta-Owned Instagram's Impact on Kids," *CNN*, November 18, 2021. https://www.cnn.com/2021/11/18/tech/meta-instagram-kids-attorneys-general-investigation/index.html., 2020; Kate Duffy, "Facebook Spied on Instagram Users Through Their iPhone Cameras, a New Lawsuit Claims," *Business Insider*, September 18, 2020.

https://www.businessinsider.com/facebook-spied-on-instagram-users-through
-iphone-cameras-lawsuit-says-2020-9

17. Kim Lyons, "An Instagram Bug Showed a 'Camera on' Indicator for IOS 14 Devices Even When Users Weren't Taking Photos," *The Verge*, July 25, 2020. https://www.theverge.com/2020/7/25/21338151/instagram-bug-camera-privacy-ios14-apple

18. Brendan F. Klare et al., "Face Recognition Performance: Role of Demographic Information," *IEEE Transactions on Information Forensics and Security* 7, no. 6 (2012): 1789–1801; Joy Buolamwini and Timnit Gebru, "Gender Shades: Intersectional Accuracy Disparities in Commercial Gender Classification," *Proceedings of Machine Learning Research* 81 (2018): 1–15; James Coe and Mustafa Atay, "Evaluating Impact of Race in Facial Recognition Across Machine Learning and Deep Learning Algorithms," *Computers* 10, no. 9 (2021): 1–24; P. Jonathon Phillips et al., "An Other-Race Effect for Face Recognition Algorithms," *ACM Transactions on Applied Perception (TAP)* 8, no. 2 (2011): 1–11.

19. James Vincent, "Google 'Fixed' Its Racist Algorithm by Removing Gorillas from Its Image-Labeling Tech," *The Verge*, January 12, 2018. https://www.theverge.com/2018/1/12/16882408/google-racist-gorillas-photo-recognition-algorithm-ai

20. Ally Jarmanning, "Boston Bans Use of Facial Recognition Technology. It's the 2nd-Largest City to Do So," *WBUR*, June 24, 2020. https://www.wbur.org/news/2020/06/23/boston-facial-recognition-ban

21. Coe and Atay, "Evaluating Impact of Race."

22. Buolamwini and Gebru, "Gender Shades"; Patrick J. Grother, P. Jonathon Phillips, and George W. Quinn, *Report on the Evaluation of 2D Still-Image Face Recognition Algorithms* (Washington, DC: U.S. Department of Commerce, National Institute of Standards and Technology, 2011); Neeru Narang and Thirimachos Bourlai, "Gender and Ethnicity Classification Using Deep Learning in Heterogeneous Face Recognition," in *2016 International Conference on Biometrics (ICB)* (IEEE, 2016), 1–8.

23. Klare et al., "Face Recognition Performance"; Hoo Keat Wong, Ian D. Stephen, and David R. T. Keeble, "The Own-Race Bias for Face Recognition in a Multiracial Society," *Frontiers in Psychology* 11 (2020): 1–16.

24. V. Siju, "A Survey on Machine Learning Algorithms for Face Recognition," *International Research Journal of Engineering and Technology* 7 (2008): 1072–1075; Shailaja A. Patil and P. J. Deore, "Face Recognition: A Survey," *Informatics Engineering: An International Journal* 1, no. 1 (2013): 31–41; Mei Wang and Weihong Deng, "Deep Face Recognition: A Survey," *Neurocomputing* 429 (2021): 215–244.

25. Cynthia M. Cook et al., "Demographic Effects in Facial Recognition and Their Dependence on Image Acquisition: An Evaluation of Eleven Commercial Systems," *IEEE Transactions on Biometrics, Behavior, and Identity Science* 1, no. 1 (2019): 32–41.

26. Hee Jung Ryu, Hartwig Adam, and Margaret Mitchell, "InclusiveFaceNet: Improving Face Attribute Detection with Race and Gender Diversity," in *Workshop on Fairness, Accountability, and Transparency in Machine Learning (FAT/ML 2018)* (Stockholm, Sweden, 2018), 1–6; Siju, "Survey on Machine Learning Algorithms"; Phillips et al., "An Other-Race Effect;" Coe and Atay, "Evaluating Impact of Race."

27. Coe and Atay, "Evaluating Impact of Race."

28. Wesley L. Passos, Igor M. Quintanilha, and Gabriel M. Araujo, "Real-Time Deep-Learning-Based System for Facial Recognition," *Simpósio Brasileiro de Telecomunicações e Processamento de Sinais (SBrT)* 37 (2018): 895–899.

29. Coe and Atay, "Evaluating Impact of Race."

30. Klare et al., "Face Recognition Performance."

31. Neeraj Kumar et al., "Describable Visual Attributes for Face Verification and Image Search," *IEEE Transactions on Pattern Analysis and Machine Intelligence* 33, no. 10 (2011): 1962–1977.

32. Match Group, U.S. Patent 10,203,854. Emphasis added.

33. Michael Omi and Howard Winant, *Racial Formation in the United States* (New York: Routledge, 2014); Wendy Hui Kyong Chun, *Discriminating Data: Correlation, Neighborhoods, and the New Politics of Recognition* (Cambridge, MA: MIT Press, 2021).

34. Daniel J. Kevles, "Eugenics and Human Rights," *BMJ* 319, no. 7207 (1999): 435–438.

35. Benjamin, *Race After Technology.*

36. Ajitha Reddy, "The Eugenic Origins of IQ Testing: Implications for Post-Atkins Litigation," *DePaul Law Review* 57 (2008): 667–678; Kevles, "Eugenics and Human Rights."

37. Darcell P. Scharff et al., "More Than Tuskegee: Understanding Mistrust About Research Participation," *Journal of Health Care for the Poor and Underserved* 21 no. 3 (2010): 879–897.

38. Scharff et al., "More Than Tuskegee."

39. Sasha Costanza-Chock, *Design Justice: Community-Led Practices to Build the Worlds We Need* (Cambridge, MA: MIT Press, 2020), 99.

40. Match Group, U.S. Patent 10,203,854. Emphasis added.

41. Reddy, "Eugenic Origins of IQ Testing," 674.

42. Reddy, "Eugenic Origins of IQ Testing."

43. Susan Harden, "Comparison of Readability Indices with Grades 1–5 Narrative and Expository Texts," PhD dissertation (Wayne State University, 2018).

44. J. Philippe Rushton and C. Davison Ankney, "Whole Brain Size and General Mental Ability: A Review," *International Journal of Neuroscience* 119, no. 5 (2009): 692–732; Richard Lynn, "The Role of Nutrition in Secular Increases in Intelligence, *Personality and Individual Differences* 11, no. 3 (1990): 273–285.

45. Belinda Robnett and Cynthia Feliciano, "Patterns of Racial-Ethnic Exclusion by Internet Daters," *Social Forces* 89, no. 3 (2011): 807–828; Celeste Vaughan Curington, Jennifer Hickes Lundquist, and Ken-Hou Lin, *The Dating Divide: Race and Desire in the Era of Online Romance* (Oakland: University of California Press, 2021); Matthew H. Rafalow, Cynthia Feliciano, and Belinda Robnett, "Racialized Femininity and Masculinity in the Preferences of Online Same-Sex Daters," *Social Currents* 4, no. 4 (2017): 306–321.

46. Match Group, U.S. Patent 10,203,854.

47. Match Group, U.S. Patent 10,203,854. Emphasis added.

48. Match Group, U.S. Patent 10,203,854.

49. Trond Viggo Grøntvedt et al., "Hook, Line and Sinker: Do Tinder Matches and Meet Ups Lead to One-Night Stands?," *Evolutionary Psychological Science* 6, no. 2 (2020): 109–118.

50. Match Group, U.S. Patent 10,203,854.

51. Match Group, U.S. Patent 10,203,854.

52. Jenny L. Davis, *How Artifacts Afford: The Power and Politics of Everyday Things* (Cambridge, MA: MIT Press, 2020).

53. Jenny L. Davis and James B. Chouinard, "Theorizing Affordances: From Request to Refuse," *Bulletin of Science, Technology & Society* 36, no. 4 (2016): 241–248.

54. Davis, *How Artifacts Afford*.

55. Davis and Chouinard, "Theorizing Affordances," 243.

56. Davis and Chouinard, "Theorizing Affordances," 243.

57. Davis and Chouinard, "Theorizing Affordances," 243.

58. George Ritzer, *The McDonaldization of Society* (Los Angeles: Sage, 2013).

59. Sebastian Deterding et al., "From Game Design Elements to Gamefulness: Defining 'Gamification,'" in *Proceedings of the 15th International Academic MindTrek Conference* (Tampere, Finland, 2011), 9–15.

60. Elisabeth Timmermans and Ellen De Caluwé, "Development and Validation of the Tinder Motives Scale (TMS)," *Computers in Human Behavior* 70 (2017): 341–350.

61. Benjamin, *Race After Technology*, 3.

62. Safiya Umoja Noble, *Algorithms of Oppression: How Search Engines Reinforce Racism* (New York: New York University Press, 2018).

63. Benjamin, *Race After Technology*, 4.

Chapter 3

1. Robin DiAngelo, "White Fragility: Why It's So Hard to Talk to White People About Racism," *The Good Men Project*, April 9, 2015. https://goodmenproject.com/featured-content/white-fragility-why-its-so-hard-to-talk-to-white-people-about-racism-twlm/; Katy Waldman, "A Sociologist Examines the 'White Fragility' That

Prevents White Americans from Confronting Racism," *The New Yorker*, July 23, 2018. https://www.newyorker.com/books/page-turner/a-sociologist-examines-the -white-fragility-that-prevents-white-americans-from-confronting-racism

2. Jesús Gregorio Smith et al., "Is Sexual Racism Still Really Racism? Revisiting Callander et al. (2015) in the USA," *Archives of Sexual Behavior* 51, no. 6 (2022): 3049–3062.

3. George Lipsitz, *The Possessive Investment in Whiteness: How White People Profit from Identity Politics* (Philadelphia: Temple University Press, 1998); Safiya Umoja Noble, *Algorithms of Oppression: How Search Engines Reinforce Racism* (New York: New York University Press, 2018).

4. Noble, *Algorithms*, 59.

5. Ruha Benjamin, *Race After Technology: Abolitionist Tools for the New Jim Code* (Medford, MA: Polity Press, 2019).

6. Yarden Katz, *Artificial Whiteness: Politics and Ideology in Artificial Intelligence* (New York: Columbia University Press, 2020).

7. Benjamin, *Race After Technology*.

8. Match Group, U.S. Patent 10,203,854, "Matching Process System and Method." Inventors: Sean Rad, Todd M. Carrico, Kenneth B. Hoskins, James C. Stone, and Jonathan Badeen, Current assignee: Match Group LLC. Filed April 3, 2018; issued February 12, 2019, 10–11. https://patents.google.com/patent/ US10203854B2/en?oq=10%2c203%2c854

9. Barbara Applebaum, "Comforting Discomfort as Complicity: White Fragility and the Pursuit of Invulnerability," *Hypatia* 32, no. 4 (2017): 862–875; Kristian D. Stewart and Daniela Gachago, "Step into the Discomfort: (Re)orienting the White Gaze and Strategies to Disrupt Whiteness in Educational Spaces," *Whiteness and Education* 7, no. 1 (2022): 18–31.

10. DiAngelo, "White Fragility."

11. Waldman, "A Sociologist Examines 'White Fragility'"; DiAngelo, "White Fragility"; Stewart and Gachago, "Step into the Discomfort."

12. Eduardo Bonilla-Silva, *Racism Without Racists: Color-Blind Racism and the Persistence of Racial Inequality in the United States* (Lanham, MD: Rowman & Littlefield, 2008).

13. Melvin A. Whitehead, "Whiteness, Anti-Blackness, and Trauma: A Grounded Theory of White Racial Meaning Making," *Journal of College Student Development* 62, no. 3 (2021): 310–326; Jessie Daniels, *Nice White Ladies: The Truth About White Supremacy, Our Role in It, and How We Can Help Dismantle It* (New York: Seal Press, 2021); Theresa J. Guess, "The Social Construction of Whiteness: Racism by Intent, Racism by Consequence," *Critical Sociology* 32, no. 4 (2006): 649–73; Lipsitz, *Possessive Investment in Whiteness*.

14. Cheryl E. Matias and Robin DiAngelo, "Beyond the Face of Race: Emo-

Cognitive Explorations of White Neurosis and Racial Cray-Cray," *Educational Foundations* 27, no. 3–4 (2013): 3–20.

15. Jessie Daniels, "The Trouble with White Feminism: Whiteness, Digital Feminism and the Intersectional Internet," *SSRN: Digital Feminism and the Intersectional Internet* (2015): 1–37.

16. Joe R. Feagin, *The White Racial Frame: Centuries of Racial Framing and Counter-Framing* (New York: Routledge, 2020).

17. Feagin, *White Racial Frame.*

18. Zizi Papacharissi, "Democracy Online: Civility, Politeness, and the Democratic Potential of Online Political Discussion Groups," *New Media & Society* 6, no. 2 (2004): 259–283.

19. DiAngelo, "White Fragility."

20. Bonilla-Silva, *Racism.*

21. Mei-Po Kwan, "Beyond Space (As We Knew It): Toward Temporally Integrated Geographies of Segregation, Health, and Accessibility," *Annals of the Association of American Geographers* 103, no. 5 (2013): 1078–1086.

22. Lindsey L. Almond and Jacquelyn K. Mallette, "Intentions, Results, and Disuse of Online Dating for Religious and Non-Religious Emerging Adults," *Journal of Media and Religion* 21, no. 1 (2022): 38–54; Gregory A. Huber and Neil Malhotra, "Political Homophily in Social Relationships: Evidence from Online Dating Behavior," *Journal of Politics* 79, no. 1 (2017): 269–283; Shantel Gabrieal Buggs, "Dating in the Time of #BlackLivesMatter: Exploring Mixed-Race Women's Discourses of Race and Racism," *Sociology of Race and Ethnicity* 3, no. 4 (2017): 538–551; Farah Hasan, "Keep It Halal! A Smartphone Ethnography of Muslim Dating," *Journal of Religion, Media and Digital Culture* 10, no. 1 (2021): 135–154; Sylvia Niehuis et al., "Guilty Pleasure? Communicating Sexually Explicit Content on Dating Apps and Disillusionment with App Usage," *Human Communication Research* 46, no. 1 (2020): 55–85; Günter J. Hitsch, Ali Hortaçsu, and Dan Ariely, "What Makes You Click?—Mate Preferences in Online Dating," *Quantitative Marketing and Economics* 8, no. 4 (2010): 393–427; Stephen Whyte, Ho Fai Chan, and Benno Torgler, "Do Men and Women Know What They Want? Sex Differences in Online Daters' Educational Preferences," *Psychological Science* 29, no. 8 (2018): 1370–1375.

23. Arianne E. Miller and Lawrence Josephs, "Whiteness as Pathological Narcissism," *Contemporary Psychoanalysis* 45, no. 1 (2009): 93–119.

24. Miller and Josephs, "Whiteness"; Sigmund Freud, "A Special Type of Choice of Object Made by Men (Contributions to the Psychology of Love I)," in *The Standard Edition of the Complete Psychological Works of Sigmund Freud, Volume XI (1910): Five Lectures on Psycho-Analysis, Leonardo Da Vinci and Other Works* (New York: W. W. Norton, 1957), 163–176.

25. Miller and Josephs, "Whiteness."

26. Frantz Fanon, *Black Skin, White Masks* (New York: Grove Press, 1967); Cheryl E. Matias, "White Skin, Black Friend," in *Feeling White: Whiteness, Emotionality, and Education*, ed. Cheryl E. Matias (Rotterdam: Sense Publishers, 2016), 83–97.

27. Jennifer C. Mueller and DyAnna K. Washington, "Anticipating White Futures: The Ends-Based Orientation of White Thinking," *Symbolic Interaction* 45, no. 1 (2022): 21.

28. Mueller and Washington, "Anticipating."

29. Zeus Leonardo and Michalinos Zembylas, "Whiteness as Technology of Affect: Implications for Educational Praxis," *Equity & Excellence in Education* 46, no. 1 (2013): 150–165.

30. Leonardo and Zembylas, "Whiteness as Technology of Affect."

31. Beth Coleman, "Race as Technology," *Camera Obscura: Feminism, Culture, and Media Studies* 24, no. 1 (2009): 177–207.

32. Gina Castle Bell and Sally O. Hastings, "Exploring Parental Approval and Disapproval for Black and White Interracial Couples," *Journal of Social Issues* 71, no. 4 (2015): 755–771.

33. Bell and Hastings, "Exploring Parental Approval"; Kimberly Jacobs and Alan Sillars, "Sibling Support During Post-Divorce Adjustment: An Idiographic Analysis of Support Forms, Functions, and Relationship Types," *Journal of Family Communication* 12 (2012): 167–187.

34. Bell and Hastings, "Exploring Parental Approval."

35. Daniels, *Nice White Ladies*.

36. "Immigration and Nationality Act of 1952 (The McCarran-Walter Act)," *Immigration History*, 2019. https://immigrationhistory.org/item/immigration-and-nationality-act-the-mccarran-walter-act/

37. Jessie Daniels, *White Lies: Race, Class, Gender, and Sexuality in White Supremacist Discourse* (New York: Routledge, 2016); Ruth Frankenberg, *White Women, Race Matters: The Social Construction of Whiteness* (Santa Cruz: University of California, 1988).

38. Howard Schuman et al., *Racial Attitudes in America: Trends and Interpretations*, 2nd ed. (Cambridge, MA: Harvard University Press, 1997); Melissa R. Herman and Mary E. Campbell, "I Wouldn't, But You Can: Attitudes Toward Interracial Relationships," *Social Science Research* 41, no. 2 (2012): 343–358.

39. Herman and Campbell, "I Wouldn't"; Terri A. Karis, "How Race Matters and Does Not Matter for White Women in Relationships with Black Men," *Journal of Couple & Relationship Therapy* 2, no. 2–3 (2003): 23–40.

40. Herman and Campbell, "I Wouldn't"; Diane N. Lye and Ingrid Waldron, "Attitudes Toward Cohabitation, Family, and Gender Roles: Relationships to Values and Political Ideology," *Sociological Perspectives* 40, no. 2 (1997): 199–225;

George Yancey, "Homogamy over the Net: Using Internet Advertisements to Discover Who Interracially Dates," *Journal of Social and Personal Relationships* 24, no. 6 (2007): 913–930.

41. Herman and Campbell, "I Wouldn't"; Buggs, "Dating."

42. Herman and Campbell, "I Wouldn't"; Yancey, "Homogamy"; Cynthia Feliciano, Belinda Robnett, and Golnaz Komaie, "Gendered Racial Exclusion Among White Internet Daters," *Social Science Research* 38, no. 1 (2009): 39–54.

43. Herman and Campbell, "I Wouldn't."

44. Richard Alba and Victor Nee, *Remaking the American Mainstream: Assimilation and Contemporary Immigration* (Cambridge, MA: Harvard University Press, 2009); Bonilla-Silva, *Racism*.

45. Dario Moreno and Christopher Warren, "The Conservative Enclave Revisited: Cuban Americans in Florida," in *Ethnic Ironies: Latino Politics in the 1992 Elections*, eds. Rodolfo O. de la Garza and Louis DeSipio (New York: Routledge, 2018), 169–184; Alejandro Portes and Rafael Mozo, "The Political Adaptation Process of Cubans and Other Ethnic Minorities in the United States: A Preliminary Analysis," *International Migration Review* 19, no. 1 (1985): 35–63.

46. Alba and Nee, *Remaking the American Mainstream*; Bonilla-Silva, *Racism*.

47. Herman and Campbell, "I Wouldn't."

48. Celeste Vaughan Curington, Jennifer Hickes Lundquist, and Ken-Hou Lin, *The Dating Divide: Race and Desire in the Era of Online Romance* (Oakland: University of California Press, 2021); Feliciano, Robnett, and Komaie, "Gendered Racial Exclusion"; Belinda Robnett and Cynthia Feliciano, "Patterns of Racial-Ethnic Exclusion by Internet Daters," *Social Forces* 89, no. 3 (2011): 807–828.

49. Zhiqiu Benson Zhou, "Compulsory Interracial Intimacy: Why Does Removing the Ethnicity Filter on Dating Apps Not Benefit Racial Minorities?," *Media, Culture & Society* 44, no. 5 (2022): 1034–1043.

50. This language has been redacted in an effort to reduce harm to people with Down syndrome.

51. Jessica Strubel and Trent A. Petrie, "Love Me Tinder: Body Image and Psychosocial Functioning Among Men and Women, *Body Image* 21 (2017): 34–38; Aaron S. Breslow et al., "Adonis on the Apps: Online Objectification, Self-Esteem, and Sexual Minority Men," *Psychology of Men & Masculinities* 21, no. 1 (2020): 25–35.

52. Alice E. Marwick and danah boyd, "I Tweet Honestly, I Tweet Passionately: Twitter Users, Context Collapse, and the Imagined Audience," *New Media & Society* 13, no. 1 (2010): 114–133.

53. Abiola Abrams, "Intimacy Intervention: My Husband Uses Racial Slurs During Sex," *Essence*, October 28, 2020. https://www.essence.com/love/intimacy-intervention-my-husband-uses-racial-slurs-during-sex/.

54. Ibram X. Kendi, *How to Be an Antiracist* (New York: One World, 2021).

55. Applebaum, "Comforting Discomfort"; Michalinos Zembylas, "Affect, Race, and White Discomfort in Schooling: Decolonial Strategies for 'Pedagogies of Discomfort,'" *Ethics and Education* 13, no. 1 (2018): 86–104.

56. Benjamin Blaisdell, "Beyond Discomfort? Equity Coaching to Disrupt Whiteness," *Whiteness and Education* 3, no. 2 (2018): 162–181; Stewart and Gachago, "Step into the Discomfort."

57. Kendi, *How to Be Antiracist.*

58. Karen L. Suyemoto et al., "Becoming and Fostering Allies and Accomplices Through Authentic Relationships: Choosing Justice over Comfort," *Research in Human Development* 18, no. 1–2 (2021): 1–28.

59. Applebaum, "Comforting Discomfort"; DiAngelo, "White Fragility."

Chapter 4

1. Jasmine Banks and Miranda Reynaga are advanced graduate students in the Department of Psychology at the University of Michigan. Mel Monier is an advanced graduate student in the Department of Communication and Media Studies at the University of Michigan.

2. Lawrence Stacey and TehQuin D. Forbes, "Feeling Like a Fetish: Racialized Feelings, Fetishization, and the Contours of Sexual Racism on Gay Dating Apps," *Journal of Sex Research* 59, no. 3 (2022): 372–384. Chong-suk Han et al., "Stress and Coping with Racism and Their Role in Sexual Risk for HIV Among African American, Asian/Pacific Islander, and Latino Men Who Have Sex with Men," *Archives of Sexual Behavior* 44 (2015): 411–420; David J. Brennan et al., "'Never Reflected Anywhere': Body Image Among Ethnoracialized Gay and Bisexual Men," *Body Image* 10, no. 3 (2013): 389–398; Yash Bhambhani et al., "The Role of Psychological Flexibility as a Mediator Between Experienced Sexual Racism and Psychological Distress Among Men of Color Who Have Sex with Men," *Archives of Sexual Behavior* 49, no. 2 (2020): 711–720; Howard C. Stevenson Jr., "The Psychology of Sexual Racism and AIDS: An Ongoing Saga of Distrust and the 'Sexual Other,'" *Journal of Black Studies* 25, no. 1 (1994): 62–80; Mary Dianne Plummer, "Sexual Racism in Gay Communities: Negotiating the Ethnosexual Marketplace," PhD dissertation (University of Washington, 2008); Michael Thai, "Sexual Racism Is Associated with Lower Self-Esteem and Life Satisfaction in Men Who Have Sex with Men," *Archives of Sexual Behavior* 49, no. 1 (2020): 347–353.

3. Rosemary Briseño, "Unmasked Horror in Idyllic Places: America as a 'Sunken Place,'" in *The Spaces and Places of Horror*, eds. Francesco Pascuzzi and Sandra Waters (Wilmington, DE: Vernon Press, 2020), 237–250; Chayla Haynes and Floyd Cobb, "I Write You from the Sunken Place," *International Journal of Qualitative Studies in Education* 35, no. 4 (2022): 425–437.

4. Dionne R. Powell, "From the Sunken Place to the Shitty Place: The Film *Get*

Out, Psychic Emancipation and Modern Race Relations from a Psychodynamic Clinical Perspective," *Psychoanalytic Quarterly* 89, no. 3 (2020): 414–445.

5. Abiola Abrams, "Intimacy Intervention: My Husband Uses Racial Slurs During Sex," *Essence,* October 28, 2020. https://www.essence.com/love/intimacy-intervention-my-husband-uses-racial-slurs-during-sex/

6. Shantel Gabrieal Buggs, "Does (Mixed-)Race Matter? The Role of Race in Interracial Sex, Dating, and Marriage," *Sociology Compass* 11, no. 11 (2017): 1–13.

7. Brandon Andrew Robinson, "'Personal Preference' as the New Racism: Gay Desire and Racial Cleansing in Cyberspace," *Sociology of Race and Ethnicity* 1, no. 2 (2015): 317–330.

8. David M. Kopp, "Workforce Diversity," in *Human Resource Management in the Pornography Industry: Business Practices in a Stigmatized Trade* (Cham: Palgrave Macmillan, 2020), 49–58.

9. Taia N. Pollock, "With Love: Designing with Love to Create Space for Healing," MA thesis (Pratt Institute, 2021); Aliya Chaudhry, "How Dating Apps Feed into Racism, Sexism, and 'Rape Culture.'" *Slate,* June 4, 2021. https://slate.com/culture/2021/06/nancy-jo-sales-interview-i-think-dating-apps-are-rape-culture.html

10. Caren M. Holmes, "The Colonial Roots of the Racial Fetishization of Black Women," *Black & Gold* 2 (2016): 1–11; Linda Meyer Williams, "Race and Rape: The Black Woman as Legitimate Victim," 1986. https://files.eric.ed.gov/fulltext/ED294970.pdf; Patricia Hill Collins, *From Black Power to Hip Hop: Racism, Nationalism, and Feminism* (Philadelphia: Temple University Press, 2006).

11. Reema Sood, "Biases Behind Sexual Assault: A Thirteenth Amendment Solution to Under-Enforcement of the Rape of Black Women," *University of Maryland Law Journal of Race, Religion, Gender* 18, no. 2 (2018): 405–428; Jennifer Katz et al., "White Female Bystanders' Responses to a Black Woman at Risk for Incapacitated Sexual Assault," *Psychology of Women Quarterly* 41, no. 2 (2017): 273–285; Holmes, "Colonial Roots"; Kali Nicole Gross, "African American Women, Mass Incarceration, and the Politics of Protection," *Journal of American History* 102, no. 1 (2015): 25–33.

12. Robin Zheng, "Why Yellow Fever Isn't Flattering: A Case Against Racial Fetishes," *Journal of the American Philosophical Association* 2, no. 3 (2016): 400–419.

13. Hanyu Chwe, Apryl Williams, and Ronald E. Robertson, "'Hey Beautiful': Race and Gender on Tinder," in *Proceedings of the 56th Hawaii International Conference on System Sciences,* 2041–2050, 2023. https://hdl.handle.net/10125/102886

14. Chwe, Williams, and Robertson, "Race and Gender on Tinder."

15. Marco Benoît Carbone, "Beauty and the Octopus: Close Encounters with the Other-Than-Human," in *Beasts of the Deep: Sea Creatures and Popular Culture,* eds. Jon Hackett and Seán Harrington (Herts, UK: John Libbey, 2018), 59–77; Joel Powell Dahlquist and Lee Garth Vigilant, "Way Better Than Real: Manga Sex to

Tentacle Hentai," in *Net.SeXXX: Readings on Sex, Pornography, and the Internet*, ed. Dennis D. Waskul (New York: Peter Lang, 2004), 91–103; Daniel E. Josephy-Hernández, "Fansubbing Hentai Anime: Users, Distribution, Censorship and Ethics," in *Non-Professional Subtitling*, eds. David Orrego-Carmona and Yvonne Lee (Newcastle upon Tyne, UK: Cambridge Scholars, 2017), 171–198.

16. Grace Kao, Kelly Stamper Balistreri, and Kara Joyner, "Asian American Men in Romantic Dating Markets," *Contexts* 17, no. 4 (2018): 48–53.

17. Cynthia Feliciano and Jessica M. Kizer, "Reinforcing the Racial Structure: Observed Race and Multiracial Internet Daters' Racial Preferences," *Social Forces* 99, no. 4 (2021): 1457–1486.

18. Beatriz Aldana Marquez et al., "The Discourse of Deservingness: Racialized Framing During Rumored ICE Raids," *Ethnicities* 22, no. 2 (2022): 318–342; Cecilia Menjivar, "Global Processes and Local Lives: Guatemalan Women's Work and Gender Relations at Home and Abroad," *International Labor and Working-Class History* 70, no. 1 (2006): 86–105.

19. Margaret L. Hunter, "'If You're Light You're Alright': Light Skin Color as Social Capital for Women of Color," *Gender and Society* 16, no. 2 (2002): 175–193.

20. Shantel Gabriel Buggs, "Color, Culture, or Cousin? Multiracial Americans and Framing Boundaries in Interracial Relationships," *Journal of Marriage and Family* 81, no. 5 (2019): 1221–1236.

21. Richard Alba and Victor Nee, *Remaking the American Mainstream: Assimilation and Contemporary Immigration* (Cambridge, MA: Harvard University Press, 2009); Eva H. Telzer and Heidie A. Vazquez Garcia, "Skin Color and Self-Perceptions of Immigrant and U.S.-Born Latinas: The Moderating Role of Racial Socialization and Ethnic Identity," *Hispanic Journal of Behavioral Sciences* 31, no. 3 (2009): 357–374; Tanya Golash-Boza and William Darity Jr., "Latino Racial Choices: The Effects of Skin Colour and Discrimination on Latinos' and Latinas' Racial Self-Identifications," *Ethnic and Racial Studies* 31, no. 5 (2008): 899–934.

22. Betina Cutaia Wilkinson and Emily Earle, "Taking a New Perspective to Latino Racial Attitudes: Examining the Impact of Skin Tone on Latino Perceptions of Commonality with Whites and Blacks," *American Politics Research* 41, no. 5 (2013): 783–818; Margaret L. Hunter, "The Persistent Problem of Colorism: Skin Tone, Status, and Inequality," *Sociology Compass* 1, no. 1 (2007): 237–254.

23. Feliciano and Kizer, "Reinforcing the Racial Structure."

24. Theresa A. Mok, "Asian American Dating: Important Factors in Partner Choice," *Cultural Diversity and Ethnic Minority Psychology* 5, no. 2 (1999): 103–117.

25. Glenn Tsunokai, Allison R. McGrath, and Jillian Kavanagh, "Online Dating Preferences of Asian Americans," *Journal of Social and Personal Relationships* 31, no. 6 (2014): 796–814.

26. Dasol Kim, "The Growing up Asian American Tag: An Asian American

Networked Counterpublic on YouTube," *International Journal of Communication*, no. 15 (2021): 123–142.

27. Trinity Alexander, "Internalized Racism and Gender Colorism Among African Americans: A Study of Intra-Group Bias, Perceived Discrimination, and Psychological Well-Being," PhD dissertation (American University, 2021).

28. Frank F. Montalvo and George Edward Codina, "Skin Color and Latinos in the United States," *Ethnicities* 1, no. 13 (2001): 321–341.

29. Alba and Nee, *Remaking the American Mainstream*.

30. Brenda Gambol, "Changing Racial Boundaries and Mixed Unions: The Case of Second-Generation Filipino Americans," *Ethnic and Racial Studies* 39, no. 14 (2016): 2621–2640.

31. Divya Anand and Laura Hsu, "COVID-19 and Black Lives Matter: Examining Anti-Asian Racism and Anti-Blackness in US Education," *International Journal of Multidisciplinary Perspectives in Higher Education* 5, no. 1 (2020): 190–199.

32. Vilna Bashi, "Globalized Anti-Blackness: Transnationalizing Western Immigration Law, Policy, and Practice," *Ethnic and Racial Studies* 27, no. 4 (2004): 584–606.

33. Bashi, "Globalized Anti-Blackness."

34. Adam Bledsoe and Willie Jamaal Wright, "The Anti-Blackness of Global Capital," *Environment and Planning D: Society and Space* 37, no. 1 (2018): 8–26.

35. Beth L. Bailey, *From Front Porch to Back Seat: Courtship in Twentieth-Century America* (Baltimore: Johns Hopkins University Press, 1989).

36. Brenna M. Henn et al., "Hunter-Gatherer Genomic Diversity Suggests a Southern African Origin for Modern Humans," in *Proceedings of the National Academy of Sciences* 108, no. 13 (2011): 5154–5162; John A. L. Armour et al., "Minisatellite Diversity Supports a Recent African Origin for Modern Humans," *Nature Genetics* 13, no. 2 (1996): 154–160; Yuehai Ke et al., "African Origin of Modern Humans in East Asia: A Tale of 12,000 Y Chromosomes," *Science* 292, no. 5519 (2001): 1151–1153; Satoshi Horai et al., "Recent African Origin of Modern Humans Revealed by Complete Sequences of Hominoid Mitochondrial DNAs," *Proceedings of the National Academy of Sciences* 92, no. 2 (1995): 532–536.

37. Hunter, "'Light Skin Color as Social Capital."

38. Holmes, "Colonial Roots."

Chapter 5

1. Hillary Flynn, Keith Cousins, and Elizabeth Naismith Picciani, "Tinder Lets Known Sex Offenders Use the App. It's Not the Only One," *ProPublica*, December 2, 2019. https://www.propublica.org/article/tinder-lets-known-sex-offenders-use-the-app-its-not-the-only-one

2. Elena Cama, "Understanding Experiences of Sexual Harms Facilitated

Through Dating and Hook Up Apps Among Women and Girls," in *The Emerald International Handbook of Technology-Facilitated Violence and Abuse*, eds. Jane Bailey, Asher Flynn, and Nicola Henry (Bingley, UK: Emerald Publishing, 2021), 333–350.

3. Ritesh Chugh and Marika Guggisberg, "Stalking and Other Forms of Dating Violence: Lessons Learned from You in Relation to Cyber Safety," *Journal of Interpersonal Violence* 37, no. 9–10 (2022): NP6760–NP6784.

4. Erika Borrajo, Manuel Gámez-Guadix, and Esther Calvete, "Cyber Dating Abuse: Prevalence, Context, and Relationship with Offline Dating Aggression," *Psychological Reports* 116, no. 2 (2015): 565–585; Molly Branson and Evita March, "Dangerous Dating in the Digital Age: Jealousy, Hostility, Narcissism, and Psychopathy as Predictors of Cyber Dating Abuse," *Computers in Human Behavior* 119 (2021): 1–8; Evita March et al., "Trolling on Tinder® (and Other Dating Apps): Examining the Role of the Dark Tetrad and Impulsivity," *Personality and Individual Differences* 110 (2017): 139–143.

5. Ari Ezra Waldman, "Law, Privacy, and Online Dating: 'Revenge Porn' in Gay Online Communities," *Law & Social Inquiry* 44, no. 4 (2019): 987–1018.

6. Aliya Chaudhry, "How Dating Apps Feed into Racism, Sexism, and 'Rape Culture,'" *Slate*, June 4, 2021. https://slate.com/culture/2021/06/nancy-jo-sales-interview-i-think-dating-apps-are-rape-culture.html

7. Government of Québec, "Definition of the Concept of Safety," INSPQ Public Health Expertise and Reference Centre, August 17, 2018. https://www.inspq.qc.ca/en/quebec-collaborating-centre-safety-promotion-and-injury-prevention/definition-concept-safety

8. Government of Québec, "Definition of the Concept of Safety."

9. "Safety," *Match Group*. https://mtch.com/safety; emphasis added.

10. Ruha Benjamin, *Race After Technology: Abolitionist Tools for the New Jim Code* (Medford, MA: Polity Press, 2019), 6.

11. See Michael Bérubé and Jennifer Ruth, *It's Not Free Speech: Race, Democracy, and the Future of Academic Freedom* (Baltimore: Johns Hopkins University Press, 2022); Mari J. Matsuda et al., *Words That Wound: Critical Race Theory, Assaultive Speech, and the First Amendment* (New York: Routledge, 1993).

12. Joe R. Feagin, *The White Racial Frame: Centuries of Racial Framing and Counter-Framing* (New York: Routledge, 2020).

13. Robin Zheng, "Why Yellow Fever Isn't Flattering: A Case Against Racial Fetishes," *Journal of the American Philosophical Association* 2, no. 3 (2016): 400–419; Christopher C. Lim and Ryan C. Anderson, "Effect of Sexual Racism on Partner Desirability in Gay Asian Men," *Journal of Homosexuality* 70, no. 2 (2021): 329–346; Ryan M. Wade and Gary W. Harper, "Racialized Sexual Discrimination (RSD) in the Age of Online Sexual Networking: Are Young Black Gay/Bisexual Men

(YBGBM) at Elevated Risk for Adverse Psychological Health?," *American Journal of Community Psychology* 65, no. 3–4 (2019): 504–523.

14. Lawrence Stacey and TehQuin D. Forbes, "Feeling Like a Fetish: Racialized Feelings, Fetishization, and the Contours of Sexual Racism on Gay Dating Apps," *Journal of Sex Research* 59, no. 3 (2022): 372–384.

15. Anna North, "What It Means to Be Anti-Racist," *Vox*, June 3, 2020. https://www.vox.com/2020/6/3/21278245/antiracist-racism-race-books-resources-antiracism

16. Jenny L. Davis, Apryl Williams, and Michael W. Yang, "Algorithmic Reparation," *Big Data & Society* 8, no. 2 (2021): 1–12.

17. Ibram X. Kendi, *How to Be an Antiracist* (New York: One World, 2019); North, "What It Means to Be Anti-Racist."

18. Davis, Williams, and Yang, "Algorithmic Reparation."

19. Dominic Whitlock, "Bumble Makes Users Take Pledge to Support Black Lives Matter," *Global Dating Insights*, June 25, 2020. https://www.globaldatinginsights.com/news/bumble-makes-users-take-pledge-to-support-black-lives-matter/

20. Emmaia Gelman, "The Anti-Defamation League Is Not What It Seems," *Boston Review*, May 23, 2019. https://bostonreview.net/articles/emmaia-gelman-anti-defamation-league/

21. Julia Reinstein, "Tinder Will Stop Banning Users for Fundraising for Black Lives Matter and Bail Funds," *BuzzFeed News*, June 7, 2020. https://www.buzzfeednews.com/article/juliareinstein/tinder-ends-ban-blm-fundraisers

22. Colin Groundwater, "A Brief History of ACAB," *GQ*, June 10, 2020. https://www.gq.com/story/history-of-acab

23. Anna Iovine, "Tinder Users Still Getting Banned After Showing Support for Black Lives Matter," *Mashable*, July 11, 2020. https://mashable.com/article/tinder-ban-black-lives-matter

24. Paige Leskin, "Some Tinder Users Say They've Been Banned from the App for Encouraging Others to Donate to Black Lives Matter," *Business Insider*, June 9, 2020. https://www.businessinsider.com/tinder-ban-users-fundraising-promoting-black-lives-matter-bail-funds-2020-6; Reinstein, "Tinder Will Stop Banning Users."

25. Matthew W. Hughey and Jessie Daniels, "Racist Comments at Online News Sites: A Methodological Dilemma for Discourse Analysis," *Media, Culture & Society* 35, no. 3 (2013): 332–347.

26. Arit John, "Harassment Is the Status Quo on Dating Sites. This Woman Is Trying to Change That," *Los Angeles Times*, August 19, 2021. https://www.latimes.com/lifestyle/story/2021-08-19/how-one-woman-boosting-safety-match-tinder-hinge

27. "Safety," *Match Group.* https://mtch.com/safety

28. Afsaneh Rigot, *Design from the Margins: Centering the Most Marginalized and Impacted in Design Processes—from Ideation to Production,* Belfer Center for Science and International Affairs, May 13, 2022. https://www.belfercenter.org/publication/design-margins

29. Bumble, "With Bumble's Private Detector, You Have Control over Unsolicited Nudes." https://bumble.com/en-us/the-buzz/privatedetector

30. Gian De Poloni, "Tinder's New Anti-Harassment Tool Is Here, but Will It Stop Abuse?," *ABC Triple J Hack,* May 21, 2021. https://www.abc.net.au/triplej/programs/hack/tinder-introduces-new-anti-harassment-feature-are-you-sure/13354190

31. Arielle Pardes, "Tinder Asks 'Does This Bother You'?," *Wired,* January 27, 2020. https://www.wired.com/story/tinder-does-this-bother-you-harassment-tools/

32. IBM Topics, "What Is Natural Language Processing (NLP)? https://www.ibm.com/topics/natural-language-processing

33. Xiao Ma, Trishala Neeraj, and Mor Naaman, "A Computational Approach to Perceived Trustworthiness of Airbnb Host Profiles," *Proceedings of the International AAAI Conference on Web and Social Media* 11, no. 1 (2017): 604–607; Tommi Gröndahl et al., "All You Need Is 'Love': Evading Hate Speech Detection," in *Proceedings of the 11th ACM Workshop on Artificial Intelligence and Security,* 2–12, 2018. https://doi.org/10.1145/3270101.3270103

34. Maarten Sap et al., "The Risk of Racial Bias in Hate Speech Detection," in *Proceedings of the 57th Annual Meeting of the Association for Computational Linguistics* (Florence, Italy, 2018), 1668–1678; Gwenn Schurgin O'Keeffe, Kathleen Clarke-Pearson, and Council on Communications and Media, "The Impact of Social Media on Children, Adolescents, and Families," *Pediatrics* 127, no. 4 (2011): 800–804; James Cleland, "Racism, Football Fans, and Online Message Boards: How Social Media Has Added a New Dimension to Racist Discourse in English Football," *Journal of Sport and Social Issues* 38, no. 5 (2014): 415–431; Paul Mozur, "A Genocide Incited on Facebook, with Posts from Myanmar's Military," *New York Times,* October 15, 2018. https://www.nytimes.com/2018/10/15/technology/myanmar-facebook-genocide.html; Dasol Kim, "The Growing up Asian American Tag: An Asian American Networked Counterpublic on YouTube," *International Journal of Communication,* no. 15 (2021): 123–142; Abishrant Panday and Joyce Tian, "Algorithmic Fairness in Post-Processed Toxicity Text Classification," 1–7, 2020. https://abishrantpanday.com/documents/226.pdf

35. Hossein Hosseini et al., "Deceiving Google's Perspective API Built for Detecting Toxic Comments," *arXiv* (2017): 1–4.

36. Hosseini et al., "Deceiving Google's Perspective API."

37. Tolga Bolukbasi et al., "Man Is to Computer Programmer as Woman Is to

Homemaker? Debiasing Word Embeddings," *Advances in Neural Information Processing Systems* 29 (2016): 4349–4357; Ji Ho Park, Jamin Shin, and Pascale Fung, "Reducing Gender Bias in Abusive Language Detection," *arXiv* (2018): 1–6.

38. Sap et al., "Racial Bias in Hate Speech Detection."

39. Sap et al., "Racial Bias in Hate Speech Detection."

40. Rigot, *Design from the Margins.*

41. Pardes, "Tinder Asks 'Does This Bother You'?."

42. Moya Bailey, "Misogynoir Transformed," in *Misogynoir Transformed* (New York: New York University Press, 2021).

43. M. A. Quayum, "July's People: Gordimer's Radical Critique of White 'Liberal' Attitude," *English Studies in Africa* 39, no. 1 (1996): 13–24.

44. Phoebe Godfrey, "'Sweet Little (White) Girls'? Sex and Fantasy Across the Color Line and the Contestation of Patriarchal White Supremacy," *Equity & Excellence in Education* 37, no. 3 (2004): 204–218.

45. Cision PR Newswire, "Match Group Invests in Noonlight to Integrate First-of-Its-Kind Safety Technology Across Portfolio, Beginning with Tinder." https://www.prnewswire.com/news-releases/match-group-invests-in-noonlight-to-integrate-first-of-its-kind-safety-technology-across-portfolio-beginning-with-tinder-300992052.html

46. Benjamin Tkach and Apryl A. Williams, "Mobile (in)Security? Exploring the Realities of Mobile Phone Use in Conflict Areas," *Information, Communication & Society* 21, no. 11 (2018): 1639–1654.

47. Martie Thompson et al., "Reasons for Not Reporting Victimizations to the Police: Do They Vary for Physical and Sexual Incidents?," *Journal of American College Health* 55, no. 5 (2007): 277–282.

48. Chris Riotta, "Tinder Still Banning Transgender People Despite Pledge of Inclusivity," *The Independent*, December 12, 2019. https://www.independent.co.uk/news/world/americas/tinder-ban-trans-account-block-report-lawsuit-pride-gender-identity-a9007721.html

49. Rigot, *Design from the Margins.*

50. Rigot, *Design from the Margins*; Sasha Costanza-Chock, *Design Justice: Community-Led Practices to Build the Worlds We Need* (Cambridge, MA: MIT Press, 2020).

51. Pardes, "Tinder Asks 'Does This Bother You'?."

Conclusion

1. George Ritzer, *The McDonaldization of Society* (Los Angeles: Sage, 2013).

2. Ruha Benjamin, *Race After Technology: Abolitionist Tools for the New Jim Code* (Medford, MA: Polity Press, 2019), 7; italics in original.

3. Chloe Malle, "Inside Dating-App Bumble's Bid for Global Domination,"

Vogue, April 18, 2019. https://www.vogue.com/article/bumble-india-whitney-wolfe
-herd-interview-may-2019-issue

4. Charlotte Alter, "How Whitney Wolfe Herd Turned a Vision of a Better Internet into a Billion-Dollar Brand," *Time*, March 19, 2021. https://time.com/5947727
/whitney-wolfe-herd-bumble/

5. Molly Niesen, "Love, Inc.: Toward Structural Intersectional Analysis of Online Dating Sites and Applications," in *The Intersectional Internet: Race, Sex, Class and Culture Online*, eds. Safiya Umoja Nobel and Brendesha M. Tynes (New York: Peter Lang, 2016), 161–178.

6. Safiya Umoja Noble, *Algorithms of Oppression: How Search Engines Reinforce Racism* (New York: New York University Press, 2018).

7. Noble, *Algorithms of Oppression*, 24.

8. Yvonne McDermott, "Conceptualising the Right to Data Protection in an Era of Big Data," *Big Data & Society* 4, no. 1 (2016): 1–7.

9. Neil Richards, *Intellectual Privacy: Rethinking Civil Liberties in the Digital Age* (New York: Oxford University Press, 2015).

10. Laura F. Bright, Gary B. Wilcox, and Hayley Rodriguez, "#DeleteFacebook and the Consumer Backlash of 2018: How Social Media Fatigue, Consumer (Mis) Trust and Privacy Concerns Shape the New Social Media Reality for Consumers," *Journal of Digital & Social Media Marketing* 7, no. 2 (2019): 177–188.

11. Mozilla, "New Research: Tinder's Opaque, Unfair Pricing Algorithm Can Charge Users Up to Five-Times More for Same Service," *Mozilla* (blog), February 8, 2022. https://foundation.mozilla.org/en/blog/new-research-tinders-opaque-unfair
-pricing-algorithm-can-charge-users-up-to-five-times-more-for-same-service/

12. Holly Barker, "Tinder's 24 Million Deal to End Age Discrimination Suit Undone," *Bloomberg Law*, August 17, 2021. https://news.bloomberglaw.com/us-law
-week/tinders-24-million-deal-to-end-age-discrimination-suit-undone

13. Becca Ricks, Mark Surman, and Contributors, "Creating Trustworthy AI," *Mozilla Foundation*, December 15, 2020. https://foundation.mozilla.org/en/insights
/trustworthy-ai-whitepaper/

14. Bogdana Rakova, "Challenges for Responsible AI Practitioners and the Importance of Solidarity," *Partnership on AI*, March 8, 2021. https://partnershiponai.
org/challenges-for-responsible-ai-practitioners/

15. Rakova, "Challenges for Responsible AI Practitioners."

16. See Virginie Do et al., "Two-Sided Fairness in Rankings via Lorenz Dominance," *Advances in Neural Information Processing Systems* 34 (2021): 8596–8608; Chavez Procope et al., "System-Level Transparency of Machine Learning," *Meta Research*, February 23, 2022. https://research.facebook.com/file/3015640278652885/
System-Level-Transparency-of-Machine-Learning.pdf

17. Ricks, Surman, and Contributors, "Creating Trustworthy AI."

18. Zhiqiu Benson Zhou, "Compulsory Interracial Intimacy: Why Does Removing the Ethnicity Filter on Dating Apps Not Benefit Racial Minorities?," *Media, Culture & Society* 44, no. 5 (2022): 1034–1043.

19. Jenny L. Davis, Apryl Williams, and Michael W. Yang, "Algorithmic Reparation," *Big Data & Society* 8, no. 2 (2021): 1–12.

20. Rakova, "Challenges for Responsible AI Practitioners."

21. Rakova, "Challenges for Responsible AI Practitioners"; Afsaneh Rigot, *Design from the Margins: Centering the Most Marginalized and Impacted in Design Processes—from Ideation to Production*, Belfer Center for Science and International Affairs, May 13, 2022. https://www.belfercenter.org/publication/design-margins

22. Rakova, "Challenges for Responsible AI Practitioners."

23. Rigot, *Design from the Margins.*

24. Rigot, *Design from the Margins*, 1.

25. Rigot, *Design from the Margins.*

26. Sasha Costanza-Chock, *Design Justice: Community-Led Practices to Build the Worlds We Need* (Cambridge, MA: MIT Press, 2020).

27. Rigot, *Design from the Margins.*

28. Rigot, *Design from the Margins*, 34.

29. Christiano Lima and Aaron Schaffer, "Tech's Blind Spots: Sharing with Researchers and Listening to Users," *Washington Post*, July 25, 2022. https://www.washingtonpost.com/politics/2022/07/25/techs-blind-spots-sharing-with-researchers-listening-users/

30. Lima and Schaffer, "Tech's Blind Spots."

31. Government Technology News Staff, "Tech Companies Embrace Some GDPR Privacy Practices Outside of Europe," *Government Technology*, n.d. https://www.govtech.com/policy/tech-companies-embrace-some-gdpr-privacy-practices-outside-of-europe.html

32. Government Technology News Staff, "Tech Companies Embrace."

33. Giorgio Presidente and Carl Benedikt Frey, "The GDPR Effect: How Data Privacy Regulation Shaped Firm Performance Globally," *Vox EU*, March 10, 2022. https://cepr.org/voxeu/columns/gdpr-effect-how-data-privacy-regulation-shaped-firm-performance-globally

34. Benjamin, *Race After Technology.*

35. Benjamin, *Race After Technology.*

36. Benjamin, *Race After Technology.*

37. Benjamin, *Race After Technology.*

38. Davis, Williams, and Yang, "Algorithmic Reparation."

Helpful Websites
Bumble–Black Lives Matter: https://bumble.com/en-us/the-buzz/
  blacklivesmatter
Bumble–microaggressions/fetishization: https://bumble.com/en/help/
  microaggressions---fetishization
Bumble–photo verification feature: https://bumble.com/the-buzz/request
  -verification
Bumble–Private Detector: https://bumble.com/en-us/the-buzz/privatedetector
Bumble–safety: https://bumble.com/en/help/safety-irl
Bumble–sexual harassment policy: https://bumble.com/en-us/the-buzz/bumble
  -sexual-harassment-policy
Bumble–support for trans women: https://bumble.com/en/help/what-to-do-after
  -being-fetishized-as-a-trans-woman
eHarmony–dating safety tips: https://www.eharmony.com/safe-online-dating/
eHarmony–terms and conditions: https://www.eharmony.com/
  termsandconditions/
Facebook Dating–safety tips: https://www.facebook.com/dating/safety-tips/
Match Group–commitment to safety: https://mtch.com/safety#our_commitment
  _to_safety
Match Group–press release on safety: https://ir.mtch.com/news-and-events/press
  -releases/press-release-details/2020/Match-Group-Invests-In-Noonlight-To

-Integrate-First-of-its-Kind-Safety-Technology-Across-Portfolio-Beginning
-With-Tinder/default.aspx

Match Group–privacy: https://mtch.com/privacy/#data_we_collect

Match Group–safety: https://mtch.com/safety

Natural language processing: https://www.ibm.com/cloud/learn/natural-language
-processing

Noonlight: https://www.noonlight.com/noonlight-app#Pricing

Noonlight–FAQs: https://www.help.tinder.com/hc/en-us/articles/360039260031
-What-is-Noonlight-#:~:text=Tinder%20has%20partnered%20with%
20Noonlight,IRL%20via%20Noonlight's%20Timeline%20feature

OkCupid–safety tips: https://www.okcupid.com/legal/safety-tips

Perspective API: https://www.perspectiveapi.com/how-it-works/

Tinder–Are You Sure?: https://www.tinderpressroom.com/2021-05-20-Tinder
-Introduces-Are-You-Sure-,-an-Industry-First-Feature-That-is-Stopping
-Harassment-Before-It-Starts

Tinder—personal data hacked: https://www.theguardian.com/technology/2017/
sep/26/tinder-personal-data-dating-app-messages-hacked-sold

Sources

Abrams, Abiola. "Intimacy Intervention: My Husband Uses Racial Slurs During
Sex." *Essence*. October 28, 2020. https://www.essence.com/love/intimacy-inter
vention-my-husband-uses-racial-slurs-during-sex/

Ahmed, Sara. "A Phenomenology of Whiteness." In *Fanon, Phenomenology, and Psychology*, edited by Leswin Laubscher, Derek Hook, and Miraj U. Desai, 229–246.
New York: Routledge, 2021.

Alba, Richard, and Victor Nee. *Remaking the American Mainstream: Assimilation
and Contemporary Immigration*. Cambridge, MA: Harvard University Press,
2009.

Alexander, Trinity. "Internalized Racism and Gender Colorism Among African
Americans: A Study of Intra-Group Bias, Perceived Discrimination, and Psychological Well-Being." PhD dissertation. American University, 2021. http://hdl
.handle.net/1961/auislandora:95202

Almond, Lindsey L., and Jacquelyn K. Mallette. "Intentions, Results, and Disuse of
Online Dating for Religious and Non-Religious Emerging Adults." *Journal of
Media and Religion* 21, no. 1 (2022): 38–54.

Alter, Charlotte. "How Whitney Wolfe Herd Turned a Vision of a Better Internet
into a Billion-Dollar Brand." *Time*. March 19, 2021. https://time.com/5947727/
whitney-wolfe-herd-bumble/

Anand, Divya, and Laura Hsu. "COVID-19 and Black Lives Matter: Examining
Anti-Asian Racism and Anti-Blackness in US Education." *International Journal*

of Multidisciplinary Perspectives in Higher Education 5, no. 1 (2020): 190–199. https://doi.org/10.32674/jimphe.v5i1.2656

Anderson, Monica, Emily A. Vogels, and Erica Turner. "The Virtues and Downsides of Online Dating." *Pew Research Center*. February 6, 2020. https://www.pewresearch.org/internet/2020/02/06/the-virtues-and-downsides-of-online-dating/

Applebaum, Barbara. "Comforting Discomfort as Complicity: White Fragility and the Pursuit of Invulnerability." *Hypatia* 32, no. 4 (2017): 862–875.

Armour, John A. L., Tiiu Anttinen, Celia A. May, Emilce E. Vega, Antti Sajantila, Judith R. Kidd, Kenneth K. Kidd, Jaume Bertranpetit, Svante Pääbo, and Alec J. Jeffreys. "Minisatellite Diversity Supports a Recent African Origin for Modern Humans." *Nature Genetics* 13, no. 2 (1996): 154–160.

Bailey, Beth L. *From Front Porch to Back Seat: Courtship in Twentieth-Century America*. Baltimore: Johns Hopkins University Press, 1989.

Bailey, Diane. *The Emancipation Proclamation and the End of Slavery in America*. Buffalo: Rosen Publishing, 2014.

Bailey, Moya. "Misogynoir Transformed." In *Misogynoir Transformed*. New York: New York University Press, 2021.

Balsamo, Anne. *Technologies of the Gendered Body: Reading Cyborg Women*. Durham: Duke University Press, 1996.

Barker, Holly. "Tinder's 24 Million Deal to End Age Discrimination Suit Undone." *Bloomberg Law*. August 17, 2021. https://news.bloomberglaw.com/us-law-week/tinders-24-million-deal-to-end-age-discrimination-suit-undone

Bashi, Vilna. "Globalized Anti-Blackness: Transnationalizing Western Immigration Law, Policy, and Practice." *Ethnic and Racial Studies* 27, no. 4 (2004): 584–606. https://doi.org/10.1080/0141987042000216726

Bedi, Sonu. *Private Racism*. Cambridge, UK: Cambridge University Press, 2019.

———. "Sexual Racism: Intimacy as a Matter of Justice." *Journal of Politics* 77, no. 4 (2015): 998–1011.

Bell, Gina Castle, and Sally O. Hastings. "Exploring Parental Approval and Disapproval for Black and White Interracial Couples." *Journal of Social Issues* 71, no. 4 (2015): 755–771.

Benjamin, Ruha. *Race After Technology: Abolitionist Tools for the New Jim Code*. Medford, MA: Polity Press, 2019.

Berry, Donna L., Traci M. Blonquist, Rachel Pozzar, and Manan M. Nayak. "Understanding Health Decision Making: An Exploration of Homophily." *Social Science & Medicine* 214 (2018): 118–124. https://doi.org/10.1016/j.socscimed.2018.08.026

Bérubé, Michael, and Jennifer Ruth. *It's Not Free Speech: Race, Democracy, and the Future of Academic Freedom*. Baltimore: Johns Hopkins University Press, 2022.

Bhambhani, Yash, Maureen K. Flynn, Kate Kellum Karen, and Kelly G. Wilson.

"The Role of Psychological Flexibility as a Mediator Between Experienced Sexual Racism and Psychological Distress Among Men of Color Who Have Sex with Men." *Archives of Sexual Behavior* 49, no. 2 (2020): 711–720. https://doi.org/10.1007/s10508-018-1269-5

Blaisdell, Benjamin. "Beyond Discomfort? Equity Coaching to Disrupt Whiteness." *Whiteness and Education* 3, no. 2 (2018): 162–181.

Bledsoe, Adam, and Willie Jamaal Wright. "The Anti-Blackness of Global Capital." *Environment and Planning D: Society and Space* 37, no. 1 (2018): 8–26. https://doi.org/10.1177/0263775818805102

Bolukbasi, Tolga, Kai-Wei Chang, James Y. Zou, Venkatesh Saligrama, and Adam T. Kalai. "Man Is to Computer Programmer as Woman Is to Homemaker? Debiasing Word Embeddings." *Advances in Neural Information Processing Systems* 29 (2016): 4349–4357. https://arxiv.org/abs/1607.06520

Bonilla-Silva, Eduardo. *Racism Without Racists: Color-Blind Racism and the Persistence of Racial Inequality in the United States.* Lanham, MD: Rowman & Littlefield, 2008.

Borrajo, Erika, Manuel Gámez-Guadix, and Esther Calvete. "Cyber Dating Abuse: Prevalence, Context, and Relationship with Offline Dating Aggression." *Psychological Reports* 116, no. 2 (2015): 565–585. https://doi.org/10.2466/21.16.PR0.116k22w4

Branson, Molly, and Evita March. "Dangerous Dating in the Digital Age: Jealousy, Hostility, Narcissism, and Psychopathy as Predictors of Cyber Dating Abuse." *Computers in Human Behavior* 119 (2021): 1–8. https://doi.org/10.1016/j.chb.2021.106711

Brennan, David J., Kenta Asakura, Clemon George, Peter A. Newman, Sulaimon Giwa, Trevor A. Hart, Rusty Souleymanov, and Gerardo Betancourt. "'Never Reflected Anywhere': Body Image Among Ethnoracialized Gay and Bisexual Men." *Body Image* 10, no. 3 (2013): 389–398. https://doi.org/10.1016/j.bodyim.2013.03.006

Breslow, Aaron S., Riddhi Sandil, Melanie E. Brewster, Mike C. Parent, Anthea Chan, Aysegul Yucel, Nicholas Bensmiller, and Elizabeth Glaeser. "Adonis on the Apps: Online Objectification, Self-Esteem, and Sexual Minority Men." *Psychology of Men & Masculinities* 21, no. 1 (2020): 25–35. https://doi.org/10.1037/men0000202

Bright, Laura F., Gary B. Wilcox, and Hayley Rodriguez. "#DeleteFacebook and the Consumer Backlash of 2018: How Social Media Fatigue, Consumer (Mis)Trust and Privacy Concerns Shape the New Social Media Reality for Consumers." *Journal of Digital & Social Media Marketing* 7, no. 2 (2019): 177–188. https://hstalks.com/article/5137/deletefacebook-and-the-consumer-backlash-of-2018-h/

Briseño, Rosemary. "Unmasked Horror in Idyllic Places: America as a 'Sunken Place.'" In *The Spaces and Places of Horror*, edited by Francesco Pascuzzi and Sandra Waters, 237–250. Wilmington, DE: Vernon Press, 2020.

Brock Jr., André. "Distributed Blackness." In *Distributed Blackness: African American Cybercultures*. New York: New York University Press, 2020.

———. "From the Blackhand Side: Twitter as a Cultural Conversation." *Journal of Broadcasting & Electronic Media* 56, no. 4 (2012): 529–549.

Brown, Christina. "It's a Match! The Procedural Rhetoric of Gaming and Online Dating in Tinder." *Student Research Submissions* (2018): 1–21. https://scholar.umw.edu/student_research/246

Budgeon, Shelley. "The Dynamics of Gender Hegemony: Femininities, Masculinities and Social Change." *Sociology* 48, no. 2 (2014): 317–334. https://doi.org/10.1177/0038038513490358

Buggs, Shantel Gabrieal. "Color, Culture, or Cousin? Multiracial Americans and Framing Boundaries in Interracial Relationships." *Journal of Marriage and Family* 81, no. 5 (2019): 1221–1236. https://doi.org/10.1111/jomf.12583

———. "Dating in the Time of #BlackLivesMatter: Exploring Mixed-Race Women's Discourses of Race and Racism." *Sociology of Race and Ethnicity* 3, no. 4 (2017): 538–551. https://doi.org/10.1177/2332649217702658

———. "Does (Mixed-)Race Matter? The Role of Race in Interracial Sex, Dating, and Marriage." *Sociology Compass* 11, no. 11 (2017): 1–13. https://doi.org/10.1111/soc4.12531

Bumble. "With Bumble's Private Detector, You Have Control over Unsolicited Nudes." https://bumble.com/en-us/the-buzz/privatedetector

Buolamwini, Joy, and Timnit Gebru. "Gender Shades: Intersectional Accuracy Disparities in Commercial Gender Classification." In *Conference on Fairness, Accountability and Transparency*, 77–91. *Proceedings of Machine Learning Research* 81 (2018): 1–15. https://proceedings.mlr.press/v81/buolamwini18a/buolamwini18a.pdf

Butler, Judith. *Gender Trouble: Feminism and the Subversion of Identity*. New York: Routledge, 2002.

Callander, Denton, Christy E. Newman, and Martin Holt. "Is Sexual Racism Really Racism? Distinguishing Attitudes Toward Sexual Racism and Generic Racism Among Gay and Bisexual Men." *Archives of Sexual Behavior* 44, no. 7 (2015): 1991–2000.

Cama, Elena. "Understanding Experiences of Sexual Harms Facilitated Through Dating and Hook Up Apps Among Women and Girls." In *The Emerald International Handbook of Technology-Facilitated Violence and Abuse*, edited by Jane Bailey, Asher Flynn, and Nicola Henry, 333–350. Bingley, UK: Emerald Publishing, 2021.

Carbone, Marco Benoît. "Beauty and the Octopus: Close Encounters with the Other-Than-Human." In *Beasts of the Deep: Sea Creatures and Popular Culture*, edited by Jon Hackett and Seán Harrington, 59–77. Herts, UK: John Libbey, 2018.

Carr, Austin. "I Found Out My Secret Internal Tinder Rating and Now I Wish I Hadn't." *Fast Company*. January 11, 2016. https://www.fastcompany.com/3054871/whats-your-tinder-score-inside-the-apps-internal-ranking-system

Chaudhry, Aliya. "How Dating Apps Feed into Racism, Sexism, and 'Rape Culture.'" *Slate*. June 4, 2021. https://slate.com/culture/2021/06/nancy-jo-sales-interview-i-think-dating-apps-are-rape-culture.html

Choi, Kyung-Hee, Jay Paul, George Ayala, Ross Boylan, and Steven E. Gregorich. "Experiences of Discrimination and Their Impact on the Mental Health Among African American, Asian and Pacific Islander, and Latino Men Who Have Sex with Men." *American Journal of Public Health* 103, no. 5 (2013): 868–874. https://doi.org/10.2105/AJPH.2012.301052

Chugh, Ritesh, and Marika Guggisberg. "Stalking and Other Forms of Dating Violence: Lessons Learned from You in Relation to Cyber Safety." *Journal of Interpersonal Violence* 37, no. 9–10 (2022): NP6760–NP6784. https://doi.org/10.1177/0886260520966674

Chun, Wendy Hui Kyong. *Discriminating Data: Correlation, Neighborhoods, and the New Politics of Recognition*. Cambridge, MA: MIT Press, 2021.

Chwe, Hanyu, Apryl Williams, and Ronald E. Robertson. "'Hey Beautiful': Race and Gender on Tinder." In *Proceedings of the 56th Hawaii International Conference on System Sciences*, 2041–2050. 2023. https://hdl.handle.net/10125/102886

Cision PR Newswire. "Match Group Invests in Noonlight to Integrate First-of-Its-Kind Safety Technology Across Portfolio, Beginning with Tinder." https://www.prnewswire.com/news-releases/match-group-invests-in-noonlight-to-integrate-first-of-its-kind-safety-technology-across-portfolio-beginning-with-tinder-300992052.html

Cleland, James. "Racism, Football Fans, and Online Message Boards: How Social Media Has Added a New Dimension to Racist Discourse in English Football." *Journal of Sport and Social Issues* 38, no. 5 (2014): 415–431. https://doi.org/10.1177/0193723513499922

Coe, James, and Mustafa Atay. "Evaluating Impact of Race in Facial Recognition Across Machine Learning and Deep Learning Algorithms." *Computers* 10, no. 9 (2021): 1–24 https://doi.org/10.3390/computers10090113

Coleman, Beth. "Race as Technology." *Camera Obscura: Feminism, Culture, and Media Studies* 24, no. 1 (2009): 177–207.

Collins, Patricia Hill. *Black Feminist Thought: Knowledge, Consciousness, and the Politics of Empowerment*. New York: Routledge, 2002.

————. *From Black Power to Hip Hop: Racism, Nationalism, and Feminism.* Philadelphia: Temple University Press, 2006.

Connell, R. W. *Masculinities,* 2nd ed. Cambridge, UK: Polity Press, 2005.

Connell, R. W., and James W. Messerschmidt. "Hegemonic Masculinity: Rethinking the Concept." *Gender & Society* 19, no. 6 (2005): 829–859. https://doi.org/10.1177/0891243205278639

Cook, Cynthia M., John J. Howard, Yevgeniy B. Sirotin, Jerry L. Tipton, and Arun R. Vemury. "Demographic Effects in Facial Recognition and Their Dependence on Image Acquisition: An Evaluation of Eleven Commercial Systems." *IEEE Transactions on Biometrics, Behavior, and Identity Science* 1, no. 1 (2019): 32–41. https://doi.org/10.1109/TBIOM.2019.2897801

Costanza-Chock, Sasha. *Design Justice: Community-Led Practices to Build the Worlds We Need.* Cambridge, MA: MIT Press, 2020.

Cottom, Tressie McMillan. *Thick: And Other Essays.* New York: New Press, 2018.

Crenshaw, Kimberlé. "Mapping the Margins: Intersectionality, Identity Politics, and Violence Against Women of Color." *Stanford Law Review* 43, no. 6 (1993): 1241–1299. https://doi.org/10.2307/1229039

Curington, Celeste Vaughan, and Jennifer Hickes. "Romantic Apartheid: Digital Sexual Racism in Online Dating." In *Introducing the New Sexuality Studies,* 4th ed., edited by Nancy L. Fischer, Laurel Westbrook, and Steven Seidman, 214–223. London: Routledge, 2022.

Curington, Celeste Vaughan, Jennifer Hickes Lundquist, and Ken-Hou Lin. *The Dating Divide: Race and Desire in the Era of Online Romance.* Oakland: University of California Press, 2021.

Dahlquist, Joel Powell, and Lee Garth Vigilant. "Way Better Than Real: Manga Sex to Tentacle Hentai." In *Net.SeXXX: Readings on Sex, Pornography, and the Internet,* edited by Dennis D. Waskul, 91–103. New York: Peter Lang, 2004.

Daniels, Jessie. "'My Brain Database Doesn't See Skin Color': Color-Blind Racism in the Technology Industry and in Theorizing the Web." *American Behavioral Scientist* 59, no. 11 (2015): 1377–1393.

————. *Nice White Ladies: The Truth About White Supremacy, Our Role in It, and How We Can Help Dismantle It.* New York: Seal Press, 2021.

————. "The Trouble with White Feminism: Whiteness, Digital Feminism and the Intersectional Internet." *SSRN: Digital Feminism and the Intersectional Internet* (2015): 1–37. https://academicworks.cuny.edu/gc_pubs/194/

————. *White Lies: Race, Class, Gender, and Sexuality in White Supremacist Discourse.* New York: Routledge, 2016.

Dastin, Jeffrey. "Amazon Scraps Secret AI Recruiting Tool That Showed Bias Against Women." *Reuters.* October 10, 2018. https://www.reuters.com/article/us

-amazon-com-jobs-automation-insight/amazon-scraps-secret-ai-recruiting-tool
-that-showed-bias-against-women-idUSKCN1MK08G

Davis, Jenny L. *How Artifacts Afford: The Power and Politics of Everyday Things.* Cambridge, MA: MIT Press, 2020.

Davis, Jenny L., and James B. Chouinard. "Theorizing Affordances: From Request to Refuse." *Bulletin of Science, Technology & Society* 36, no. 4 (2016): 241–248.

Davis, Jenny L., Apryl Williams, and Michael W. Yang. "Algorithmic Reparation." *Big Data & Society* 8, no. 2 (2021): 1–12. https://doi.org/10.1177/20539517211044808

Delgado, Richard, and Jean Stefancic. *Critical Race Theory: An Introduction*, 3rd ed. New York: New York University Press, 2017.

DelGreco, Maria, and Amanda Denes. "You Are Not as Cute as You Think You Are: Emotional Responses to Expectancy Violations in Heterosexual Online Dating Interactions. *Sex Roles* 82, no. 9 (2020): 622–632.

D'Emilio, John, and Estelle B. Freedman. *Intimate Matters: A History of Sexuality in America.* New York: Harper & Row, 1988.

De Poloni, Gian. "Tinder's New Anti-Harassment Tool Is Here, but Will It Stop Abuse?" *ABC Triple J Hack.* May 21, 2021. https://www.abc.net.au/triplej/programs /hack/tinder-introduces-new-anti-harassment-feature-are-you-sure/13354190

Deterding, Sebastian, Dan Dixon, Rilla Khaled, and Lennart Nacke. "From Game Design Elements to Gamefulness: Defining 'Gamification.'" In *Proceedings of the 15th International Academic MindTrek Conference*, 9–15. Tampere, Finland, 2011. https://doi.org/10.1145/2181037.2181040

Deveaux, Monique. "Feminism and Empowerment: A Critical Reading of Foucault." *Feminist Studies* 20, no. 2 (1994): 223–247. https://doi.org/10.2307/3178151

DiAngelo, Robin. *White Fragility: Why It's So Hard for White People to Talk About Racism.* Boston: Beacon Press, 2018.

———. "White Fragility: Why It's So Hard to Talk to White People About Racism." *The Good Men Project.* April 9, 2015. https://goodmenproject.com/ featured-content/white-fragility-why-its-so-hard-to-talk-to-white-people-about -racism-twlm/

Do, Virginie, Sam Corbett-Davies, Jamal Atif, and Nicolas Usunier. "Two-Sided Fairness in Rankings via Lorenz Dominance." *Advances in Neural Information Processing Systems* 34 (2021): 8596–8608.

Donaldson, Mike. "What Is Hegemonic Masculinity?" *Theory and Society* 22, no. 5 (1993): 643–657. https://www.jstor.org/stable/657988

Du Bois, W. E. B. *The Souls of Black Folk.* Chicago: A. C. McClurg & Co., 1903.

Duffy, Clare. "State Attorneys General Launch Investigation into Meta-Owned Instagram's Impact on Kids." *CNN.* November 18, 2021. https://www.cnn.com/2021/ 11/18/tech/meta-instagram-kids-attorneys-general-investigation/index.html

Duffy, Kate. "Facebook Spied on Instagram Users Through Their iPhone Cameras,

a New Lawsuit Claims." *Business Insider.* September 18, 2020. https://www.busi
nessinsider.com/facebook-spied-on-instagram-users-through-iphone-cameras
-lawsuit-says-2020-9

Espiritu, Yen Le. *Asian American Women and Men: Labor, Laws, and Love.* Thousand Oaks, CA: Sage, 1997.

Evans, Peggy Chin, and Allen R. McConnell. "Do Racial Minorities Respond in the
Same Way to Mainstream Beauty Standards? Social Comparison Processes in
Asian, Black, and White Women." *Self and Identity* 2, no. 2 (2003): 153–167. https:
//doi.org/10.1080/15298860309030

Fanon, Frantz. *Black Skin, White Masks.* New York: Grove Press, 1967.

Feagin, Joe R. *The White Racial Frame: Centuries of Racial Framing and Counter-
Framing.* New York: Routledge, 2020.

Feliciano, Cynthia, and Jessica M. Kizer. "Reinforcing the Racial Structure: Observed Race and Multiracial Internet Daters' Racial Preferences." *Social Forces*
99, no. 4 (2021): 1457–1486. https://doi.org/10.1093/sf/soaa065

Feliciano, Cynthia, Belinda Robnett, and Golnaz Komaie. "Gendered Racial Exclusion Among White Internet Daters." *Social Science Research* 38, no. 1 (2009): 39–
54. https://doi.org/10.1016/j.ssresearch.2008.09.004

Flynn, Hillary, Keith Cousins, and Elizabeth Naismith Picciani. "Tinder Lets
Known Sex Offenders Use the App. It's Not the Only One." *ProPublica.* December 2, 2019. https://www.propublica.org/article/tinder-lets-known-sex-offenders
-use-the-app-its-not-the-only-one

Foster, Thomas A. "The Sexual Abuse of Black Men Under American Slavery."
Journal of the History of Sexuality 20, no. 3 (2011): 445–464. https://doi.org/10
.5555/jhs.2011.20.3.445

Foucault, Michel. *Discipline and Punish: The Birth of the Prison.* Durham: Duke University Press, 2007.

Frankenberg, Ruth. *White Women, Race Matters: The Social Construction of Whiteness.* Santa Cruz: University of California, 1988.

Freud, Sigmund. "A Special Type of Choice of Object Made by Men (Contributions
to the Psychology of Love I)." In *The Standard Edition of the Complete Psychological Works of Sigmund Freud, Volume XI (1910): Five Lectures on Psycho-Analysis,
Leonardo Da Vinci and Other Works,* 163–176. New York: W. W. Norton, 1957.

Gaertner, Samuel L., and John F. Dovidio. "Understanding and Addressing Contemporary Racism: From Aversive Racism to the Common Ingroup Identity
Model." *Journal of Social Issues* 61, no. 3 (2005): 615–639.

Gambol, Brenda. "Changing Racial Boundaries and Mixed Unions: The Case of
Second-Generation Filipino Americans." *Ethnic and Racial Studies* 39, no. 14
(2016): 2621–2640.

Gelman, Emmaia. "The Anti-Defamation League Is Not What It Seems." *Boston*

Review. May 23, 2019. https://bostonreview.net/articles/emmaia-gelman-anti-de famation-league/

Godfrey, Phoebe. "'Sweet Little (White) Girls'? Sex and Fantasy Across the Color Line and the Contestation of Patriarchal White Supremacy." *Equity & Excellence in Education* 37, no. 3 (2004): 204–218. https://doi.org/10.1080/10665680490491506

Golash-Boza, Tanya, and William Darity Jr. "Latino Racial Choices: The Effects of Skin Colour and Discrimination on Latinos' and Latinas' Racial Self-Identifications." *Ethnic and Racial Studies* 31, no. 5 (2008): 899–934. https://doi.org/10.1080/01419870701568858

Gonlin, Vanessa. "Come Back Home, Sista!: Reactions to Black Women in Interracial Relationships with White Men." *Ethnic and Racial Studies* (2023): 1–23.

Government of Québec. "Definition of the Concept of Safety." INSPQ Public Health Expertise and Reference Centre. August 17, 2018. https://www.inspq.qc .ca/en/quebec-collaborating-centre-safety-promotion-and-injury-prevention/ definition-concept-safety

Government Technology News Staff. "Tech Companies Embrace Some GDPR Privacy Practices Outside of Europe." *Government Technology*. n.d. https://www. govtech.com/policy/tech-companies-embrace-some-gdpr-privacy-practices -outside-of-europe.html

Graves Jr., Joseph L. "Great Is Their Sin: Biological Determinism in the Age of Genomics." *Annals of the American Academy of Political and Social Science* 661, no. 1 (2015): 24–50.

Gröndahl, Tommi, Luca Pajola, Mika Juuti, Mauro Conti, and N. Asokan. "All You Need Is 'Love': Evading Hate Speech Detection." In *Proceedings of the 11th ACM Workshop on Artificial Intelligence and Security*, 2–12, 2018. https://doi.org/10.1145 /3270101.3270103

Grøntvedt, Trond Viggo, Mons Bendixen, Ernst O. Botnen, and Leif Edward Ottesen Kennair. "Hook, Line and Sinker: Do Tinder Matches and Meet Ups Lead to One-Night Stands?" *Evolutionary Psychological Science* 6, no. 2 (2020): 109–118.

Gross, Kali Nicole. "African American Women, Mass Incarceration, and the Politics of Protection." *Journal of American History* 102, no. 1 (2015): 25–33. https://doi .org/10.1093/jahist/jav226

Grother, Patrick J., P. Jonathon Phillips, and George W. Quinn. *Report on the Evaluation of 2D Still-Image Face Recognition Algorithms*. Washington, DC: U.S. Department of Commerce, National Institute of Standards and Technology, 2011.

Groundwater, Colin. "A Brief History of ACAB." *GQ*. June 10, 2020. https://www .gq.com/story/history-of-acab

Guess, Theresa J. "The Social Construction of Whiteness: Racism by Intent, Racism by Consequence." *Critical Sociology* 32, no. 4 (2006): 649–673.

Hacker, Helen Mayer. "The New Burdens of Masculinity." *Marriage and Family Living* 19, no. 3 (1957): 227–233. https://doi.org/10.2307/348873

Han, Chong-suk. "A Qualitative Exploration of the Relationship Between Racism and Unsafe Sex Among Asian Pacific Islander Gay Men." *Archives of Sexual Behavior* 37 (2008): 827–837. https://doi.org/10.1007/s10508-007-9308-7

Han, Chong-suk, et al. "Stress and Coping with Racism and Their Role in Sexual Risk for HIV Among African American, Asian/Pacific Islander, and Latino Men Who Have Sex with Men." *Archives of Sexual Behavior* 44 (2015): 411–420. https://doi.org/10.1007/s10508-014-0331-1

Harden, Susan. "Comparison of Readability Indices with Grades 1–5 Narrative and Expository Texts." PhD dissertation. Wayne State University, 2018.

Harrell, Antoinette, and Justin Fornal. "Black People in the US Were Enslaved Well into the 1960s." *Vice*. February 28, 2018. https://www.vice.com/en/article/437573/blacks-were-enslaved-well-into-the-1960s

Hasan, Farah. "Keep It Halal! A Smartphone Ethnography of Muslim Dating." *Journal of Religion, Media and Digital Culture* 10, no. 1 (2021): 135–154.

Haynes, Chayla, and Floyd Cobb. "I Write You from the Sunken Place." *International Journal of Qualitative Studies in Education* 35, no. 4 (2022): 425–437. https://doi.org/10.1080/09518398.2021.2003900

Hechavarria, Diana M., and Amy E. Ingram. "The Entrepreneurial Gender Divide: Hegemonic Masculinity, Emphasized Femininity and Organizational Forms." *International Journal of Gender and Entrepreneurship* 8, no. 3 (2016): 242–281. https://doi.org/10.1108/IJGE-09-2014-0029

Henn, Brenna M., et al. "Hunter-Gatherer Genomic Diversity Suggests a Southern African Origin for Modern Humans." In *Proceedings of the National Academy of Sciences* 108, no. 13 (2011): 5154–5162. https://doi.org/10.1073/pnas.1017511108

Herman, Melissa R., and Mary E. Campbell. "I Wouldn't, But You Can: Attitudes Toward Interracial Relationships." *Social Science Research* 41, no. 2 (2012): 343–358.

Hess, Aaron, and Carlos Flores. "Simply More Than Swiping Left: A Critical Analysis of Toxic Masculine Performances on Tinder Nightmares." *New Media & Society* 20, no. 3 (2018): 1085–1102.

Hitsch, Günter J., Ali Hortaçsu, and Dan Ariely. "What Makes You Click?—Mate Preferences in Online Dating." *Quantitative Marketing and Economics* 8, no. 4 (2010): 393–427.

Hollinger, David A. "The One Drop Rule and the One Hate Rule." *Daedalus* 134, no. 1 (2005): 18–28. https://www.jstor.org/stable/20027957

Holmes, Caren M. "The Colonial Roots of the Racial Fetishization of Black Women." *Black & Gold* 2 (2016): 1–11. https://openworks.wooster.edu/blackandgold/vol2/iss1/2

Horai, Satoshi, Kenji Hayasaka, Rumi Kondo, Kazuo Tsugane, and Naoyuki Taka-hata. "Recent African Origin of Modern Humans Revealed by Complete Se-quences of Hominoid Mitochondrial DNAs." *Proceedings of the National Academy of Sciences* 92, no. 2 (1995): 532–536. https://doi.org/10.1073/pnas.92.2.532

Hosseini, Hossein, Sreeram Kannan, Baosen Zhang, and Radha Poovendran. "De-ceiving Google's Perspective API Built for Detecting Toxic Comments." *arXiv* (2017): 1–4. https://doi.org/10.48550/arXiv.1702.08138

Howard, Frank. "Social Matching Systems, Intimate Personal Data, and Romantic Compatibility on Internet Dating Sites and Apps." *Journal of Research in Gender Studies* 10, no. 1 (2020): 80–86. https://doi.org/10.22381/JRGS10120208

Huber, Gregory A., and Neil Malhotra. "Political Homophily in Social Relation-ships: Evidence from Online Dating Behavior." *Journal of Politics* 79, no. 1 (2017): 269–283.

Hughey, Matthew W., and Jessie Daniels. "Racist Comments at Online News Sites: A Methodological Dilemma for Discourse Analysis." *Media, Culture & Society* 35, no. 3 (2013): 332–347. https://doi.org/10.1177/0163443712472089

Hunsinger, Jeremy. "Critical Internet Studies." In *Second International Handbook of Internet Research*, edited by Jeremy Hunsinger, Matthew M. Allen, and Lizbeth Klastrup, 263–279. New York: Springer International, 2020.

Hunter, Margaret L. "'If You're Light You're Alright': Light Skin Color as Social Capital for Women of Color." *Gender and Society* 16, no. 2 (2002): 175–193. http://www.jstor.org/stable/3081860

———. "The Persistent Problem of Colorism: Skin Tone, Status, and Inequality." *Sociology Compass* 1, no. 1 (2007): 237–254. https://doi.org/10.1111/j.1751-9020.2007.00006.x

IBM Topics. "What Is Natural Language Processing (NLP)?" https://www.ibm.com/topics/natural-language-processing

"Immigration and Nationality Act of 1952 (The McCarran-Walter Act)." *Immigra-tion History*. 2019. https://immigrationhistory.org/item/immigration-and-na tionality-act-the-mccarran-walter-act/

Iovine, Anna. "Tinder Users Still Getting Banned After Showing Support for Black Lives Matter." *Mashable*. July 11, 2020. https://mashable.com/article/tinder-ban-black-lives-matter

Iwamoto, Derek Kenji, and William Ming Liu. "Asian American Men and Asian-ized Attribution: Intersections of Masculinity, Race, and Sexuality." In *Asian American Psychology*, edited by Nita Tewari and Alvin N. Alvarez, 261–282. New York: Psychology Press, 2008.

Jacobs, Kimberly, and Alan Sillars. "Sibling Support During Post-Divorce Adjust-ment: An Idiographic Analysis of Support Forms, Functions, and Relationship Types." *Journal of Family Communication* 12 (2012): 167–187.

Jarmanning, Ally. "Boston Bans Use of Facial Recognition Technology. It's the 2nd-Largest City to Do So." *WBUR*. June 24, 2020. https://www.wbur.org/news/2020/06/23/boston-facial-recognition-ban

Jeffries IV, William L. "A Comparative Analysis of Homosexual Behaviors, Sex Role Preferences, and Anal Sex Proclivities in Latino and Non-Latino Men." *Archives of Sexual Behavior* 38 (2009): 765–778. https://doi.org/10.1007/s10508-007-9254-4

John, Arit. "Harassment Is the Status Quo on Dating Sites. This Woman Is Trying to Change That." *Los Angeles Times*. August 19, 2021. https://www.latimes.com/lifestyle/story/2021-08-19/how-one-woman-boosting-safety-match-tinder-hinge

Josephy-Hernández, Daniel E. "Fansubbing Hentai Anime: Users, Distribution, Censorship and Ethics." In *Non-Professional Subtitling*, edited by David Orrego-Carmona and Yvonne Lee, 171–198. Newcastle upon Tyne, UK: Cambridge Scholars, 2017.

Kao, Grace, Kelly Stamper Balistreri, and Kara Joyner. "Asian American Men in Romantic Dating Markets." *Contexts* 17, no. 4 (2018): 48–53. https://doi.org/10.1177/1536504218812869

Karis, Terri A. "How Race Matters and Does Not Matter for White Women in Relationships with Black Men." *Journal of Couple & Relationship Therapy* 2, no. 2–3 (2003): 23–40.

Katz, Jennifer, Christine Merrilees, Jill C. Hoxmeier, and Marisa Motisi. "White Female Bystanders' Responses to a Black Woman at Risk for Incapacitated Sexual Assault." *Psychology of Women Quarterly* 41, no. 2 (2017): 273–285. https://doi.org/10.1177/0361684316689367

Katz, Yarden. *Artificial Whiteness: Politics and Ideology in Artificial Intelligence*. New York: Columbia University Press, 2020.

Ke, Yuehai, et al. "African Origin of Modern Humans in East Asia: A Tale of 12,000 Y Chromosomes." *Science* 292, no. 5519 (2001): 1151–1153. https://doi.org/10.1126/science.1060011

Kendi, Ibram X. *How to Be an Antiracist*. New York: One World, 2021.

Kevles, Daniel J. "Eugenics and Human Rights." *BMJ* 319, no. 7207 (1999): 435–438.

Kim, Dasol. "The Growing up Asian American Tag: An Asian American Networked Counterpublic on YouTube." *International Journal of Communication*, no. 15 (2021): 123–142.

King, Angela. "The Prisoner of Gender: Foucault and the Disciplining of the Female Body." *Journal of International Women's Studies* 5, no. 2 (2004): 29–39. https://vc.bridgew.edu/jiws/vol5/iss2/4

Klare, Brendan F., Mark J. Burge, Joshua C. Klontz, Richard W. V. Bruegge, and Anil K. Jain. "Face Recognition Performance: Role of Demographic Information." *IEEE Transactions on Information Forensics and Security* 7, no. 6 (2012): 1789–1801.

Kleinman, Alexis. "Black People and Asian Men Have a Much Harder Time Dating on OkCupid." *HuffPost*. September 12, 2014. https://www.huffpost.com/entry/okcupid-race_n_5811840

Kopp, David M. "Workforce Diversity." In *Human Resource Management in the Pornography Industry: Business Practices in a Stigmatized Trade*, 49–58. Cham: Palgrave Macmillan, 2020. https://doi.org/10.1007/978-3-030-37659-8_5

Kovel, Joel. *White Racism: A Psychohistory*. New York: Columbia University Press, 1984.

Kumar, Neeraj, Alexander Berg, Peter N. Belhumeur, and Shree Nayar. "Describable Visual Attributes for Face Verification and Image Search." *IEEE Transactions on Pattern Analysis and Machine Intelligence* 33, no. 10 (2011): 1962–1977.

Kumashiro, Kevin K. "Supplementing Normalcy and Otherness: Queer Asian American Men Reflect on Stereotypes, Identity, and Oppression." *Qualitative Studies in Education* 12 (1999): 491–508.

Kwan, Mei-Po. "Beyond Space (As We Knew It): Toward Temporally Integrated Geographies of Segregation, Health, and Accessibility." *Annals of the Association of American Geographers* 103, no. 5 (2013): 1078–1086. https://doi.org/10.1080/00045608.2013.792177

Lay, Kenneth James. "Sexual Racism: A Legacy of Slavery." *National Black Law Journal* 13, no. 1–2 (1993): 165–183.

Lazarsfeld, Paul F., and Robert K. Merton. "Friendship as a Social Process: A Substantive and Methodological Analysis." *Freedom and Control in Modern Society* 18, no. 1 (1954): 18–66.

Leonard, Andrew. "OkCupid Founder: 'I Wish People Exercised More Humanity' on OkCupid." *Salon*. September 12, 2014. https://www.salon.com/2014/09/12/okcupid_founder_i_wish_people_exercised_more_humanity_on_okcupid/

Leonardo, Zeus, and Michalinos Zembylas. "Whiteness as Technology of Affect: Implications for Educational Praxis." *Equity & Excellence in Education* 46, no. 1 (2013): 150–165.

Leskin, Paige. "Some Tinder Users Say They've Been Banned from the App for Encouraging Others to Donate to Black Lives Matter." *Business Insider*. June 9, 2020. https://www.businessinsider.com/tinder-ban-users-fundraising-promoting-black-lives-matter-bail-funds-2020-6

Li, Xaiyi. "The Gamification of Dating: Tinder and Game-Playing on Reddit Communities." MA thesis. University of Melbourne, 2017.

Lim, Christopher C., and Ryan C. Anderson. "Effect of Sexual Racism on Partner Desirability in Gay Asian Men." *Journal of Homosexuality* 70, no. 2 (2021): 329–346. https://doi.org/10.1080/00918369.2021.1948772

Lima, Christiano, and Aaron Schaffer. "Tech's Blind Spots: Sharing with Researchers and Listening to Users." *Washington Post*. July 25, 2022. https://www.washing

tonpost.com/politics/2022/07/25/techs-blind-spots-sharing-with-researchers
-listening-users/

Lipsitz, George. *The Possessive Investment in Whiteness: How White People Profit from Identity Politics*. Philadelphia: Temple University Press, 1998.

Lye, Diane N., and Ingrid Waldron. "Attitudes Toward Cohabitation, Family, and Gender Roles: Relationships to Values and Political Ideology." *Sociological Perspectives* 40, no. 2 (1997): 199–225.

Lynn, Richard. "The Role of Nutrition in Secular Increases in Intelligence." *Personality and Individual Differences* 11, no. 3 (1990): 273–285.

Lyons, Kim. "An Instagram Bug Showed a 'Camera on' Indicator for IOS 14 Devices Even When Users Weren't Taking Photos." *The Verge*. July 25, 2020. https://www.theverge.com/2020/7/25/21338151/instagram-bug-camera-privacy-ios14-apple

Ma, Xiao, Trishala Neeraj, and Mor Naaman. "A Computational Approach to Perceived Trustworthiness of Airbnb Host Profiles." *Proceedings of the International AAAI Conference on Web and Social Media* 11, no. 1 (2017): 604–607. https://doi.org/10.1609/icwsm.v11i1.14937

Makoni, Busi. "Labelling Black Male Genitalia and the 'New Racism': The Discursive Construction of Sexual Racism by a Group of Southern African College Students." *Gender and Language* 10, no. 1 (2016): 48–72. https://doi.org/10.1558/genl.v10i1.21434

Malebranche, David J., Errol L. Fields, Lawrence O. Bryant, and Shaun R. Harper. "Masculine Socialization and Sexual Risk Behaviors Among Black Men Who Have Sex with Men: A Qualitative Exploration." *Men and Masculinities* 12, no. 1 (2007): 90–112. https://doi.org/10.1177/1097184X07309504

Malle, Chloe. "Inside Dating-App Bumble's Bid for Global Domination." *Vogue*. April 18, 2019. https://www.vogue.com/article/bumble-india-whitney-wolfe-herd-interview-may-2019-issue

March, Evita, Rachel Grieve, Jessica Marrington, and Peter K. Jonason. "Trolling on Tinder® (and Other Dating Apps): Examining the Role of the Dark Tetrad and Impulsivity." *Personality and Individual Differences* 110 (2017): 139–143.

Marquez, Beatriz Aldana, Apryl A. Williams, Nancy Plankey-Videla, and Selene I. Diaz. "The Discourse of Deservingness: Racialized Framing During Rumored ICE Raids." *Ethnicities* 22, no. 2 (2022): 318–342.

Marwick, Alice. "There's a Beautiful Girl Under All of This: Performing Hegemonic Femininity in Reality Television." *Critical Studies in Media Communication* 27, no. 3 (2010): 251–266. https://doi.org/10.1080/15295030903583515

Marwick, Alice E., and danah boyd. "I Tweet Honestly, I Tweet Passionately: Twitter Users, Context Collapse, and the Imagined Audience." *New Media & Society* 13, no. 1 (2010): 114–133.

Match Group. "Privacy." 2023. https://mtch.com/privacy/#data_we_collect

Match Group. U.S. Patent 10,203,854. "Matching Process System and Method." Inventors: Sean Rad, Todd M. Carrico, Kenneth B. Hoskins, James C. Stone, and Jonathan Badeen, Current assignee: Match Group LLC. Filed April 3, 2018; issued February 12, 2019. https://patents.google.com/patent/US10203854B2/en?oq=10%2c203%2c854

Matias, Cheryl E. "White Skin, Black Friend." In *Feeling White: Whiteness, Emotionality, and Education*, edited by Cheryl E. Matias, 83–97. Rotterdam: Sense Publishers, 2016.

Matias, Cheryl E., and Robin DiAngelo. "Beyond the Face of Race: Emo-Cognitive Explorations of White Neurosis and Racial Cray-Cray." *Educational Foundations* 27, no. 3–4 (2013): 3–20. https://files.eric.ed.gov/fulltext/EJ1065640.pdf

Matsuda, Mari J., Charles R. Lawrence III, Richard Delgado, and Kimberlé Williams Crenshaw. *Words That Wound: Critical Race Theory, Assaultive Speech, and the First Amendment*. New York: Routledge, 1993.

McCurdy, Rachel. "Did Slavery Ever Really End? An Analysis of Institutional Racism and the Prison Industrial Complex in America." PhD dissertation. University of Hull, 2021.

McDermott, Yvonne. "Conceptualising the Right to Data Protection in an Era of Big Data." *Big Data & Society* 4, no. 1 (2016): 1–7. https://doi.org/10.1177/2053951 71668699

Menjivar, Cecilia. "Global Processes and Local Lives: Guatemalan Women's Work and Gender Relations at Home and Abroad." International Labor and Working-Class History 70, no. 1 (2006): 86–105.

Meyer, Ilan H. "Resilience in the Study of Minority Stress and Health of Sexual and Gender Minorities." *Psychology of Sexual Orientation and Gender Diversity* 2, no. 3 (2015): 209–213. https://doi.org/10.1037/sgd0000132

Miller, Arianne E., and Lawrence Josephs. "Whiteness as Pathological Narcissism." *Contemporary Psychoanalysis* 45, no. 1 (2009): 93–119.

Miller-Young, Mireille. *A Taste for Brown Sugar: Black Women in Pornography.* Durham: Duke University Press, 2014.

Mok, Theresa A. "Asian American Dating: Important Factors in Partner Choice." *Cultural Diversity and Ethnic Minority Psychology* 5, no. 2 (1999): 103–117. https://doi.org/10.1037/1099-9809.5.2.103

Montalvo, Frank F., and G. Edward Codina. "Skin Color and Latinos in the United States." *Ethnicities* 1, no. 13 (2001): 321–341.

Moran, Rachel F. *Interracial Intimacy: The Regulation of Race and Romance.* Chicago: University of Chicago Press, 2001.

Moreno, Dario, and Christopher Warren. "The Conservative Enclave Revisited: Cuban Americans in Florida." In *Ethnic Ironies: Latino Politics in the 1992 Elec-*

tions, edited by Rodolfo O. de la Garza and Louis DeSipio, 169–184. New York: Routledge, 2018.

Mozilla. "New Research: Tinder's Opaque, Unfair Pricing Algorithm Can Charge Users Up to Five-Times More for Same Service." *Mozilla* (blog). February 8, 2022. https://foundation.mozilla.org/en/blog/new-research-tinders-opaque-unfair -pricing-algorithm-can-charge-users-up-to-five-times-more-for-same-service/

Mozur, Paul. "A Genocide Incited on Facebook, with Posts from Myanmar's Military." *New York Times.* October 15, 2018. https://www.nytimes.com/2018/10/15/ technology/myanmar-facebook-genocide.html

Mueller, Jennifer C., and DyAnna K. Washington. "Anticipating White Futures: The Ends-Based Orientation of White Thinking." *Symbolic Interaction* 45, no. 1 (2022): 3–26.

Narang, Neeru, and Thirimachos Bourlai. "Gender and Ethnicity Classification Using Deep Learning in Heterogeneous Face Recognition." In *2016 International Conference on Biometrics (ICB)*, 1–8. IEEE, 2016.

Ng, Chirk Jenn, Hui Meng Tan, and Wah Yun Low. "What Do Asian Men Consider as Important Masculinity Attributes? Findings from the Asian Men's Attitudes to Life Events and Sexuality (MALES) Study." *Journal of Men's Health* 5, no. 4 (2008): 350–355. https://doi.org/10.1016/j.jomh.2008.10.005

Niehuis, Sylvia, Alan Reifman, Dana A. Weiser, Narissa M. Punyanunt-Carter, Jeanne Flora, Vladimir S. Arias, and C. Rebecca Oldham. "Guilty Pleasure? Communicating Sexually Explicit Content on Dating Apps and Disillusionment with App Usage." *Human Communication Research* 46, no. 1 (2020): 55–85.

Niesen, Molly. "Love, Inc.: Toward Structural Intersectional Analysis of Online Dating Sites and Applications." In *The Intersectional Internet: Race, Sex, Class and Culture Online*, edited by Safiya Umoja Nobel and Brendesha M. Tynes, 161–178. New York: Peter Lang, 2016.

Noble, Safiya Umoja. *Algorithms of Oppression: How Search Engines Reinforce Racism.* New York: New York University Press, 2018.

Nopper, Tamara. "Digital Character in 'The Scored Society': FICO, Social Networks, and Competing Measurements of Creditworthiness." In *Captivating Technology: Race, Carceral Technoscience, and Liberatory Imagination in Everyday Life*, edited by Ruha Benjamin, 170–187. Durham: Duke University Press, 2019.

North, Anna. "What It Means to Be Anti-Racist." *Vox.* June 3, 2020. https://www .vox.com/2020/6/3/21278245/antiracist-racism-race-books-resources-antiracism

O'Keeffe, Gwenn Schurgin, Kathleen Clarke-Pearson, and Council on Communications and Media. "The Impact of Social Media on Children, Adolescents, and Families." *Pediatrics* 127, no. 4 (2011): 800–804. https://doi.org/10.1542/peds.2011 -0054

Omi, Michael, and Howard Winant. *Racial Formation in the United States*. New York: Routledge, 2014.

O'Neil, Kathy. *Weapons of Math Destruction: How Big Data Increases Inequality and Threatens Democracy*. New York: Broadway Books, 2016.

Paechter, Carrie. "Rethinking the Possibilities for Hegemonic Femininity: Exploring a Gramscian Framework." *Women's Studies International Forum* 68 (2018): 121–128. https://doi.org/10.1016/j.wsif.2018.03.005

Pager, Devah, and Hana Shepherd. "The Sociology of Discrimination: Racial Discrimination in Employment, Housing, Credit, and Consumer Markets." *Annual Review of Sociology* 34 (2008): 181–209.

Panday, Abishrant, and Joyce Tian. "Algorithmic Fairness in Post-Processed Toxicity Text Classification." 1–7. 2020. https://abishrantpanday.com/documents/226.pdf

Pandika, Melissa. "Are Your Dating Preferences Racist?" *Mic*. July 1, 2021. https://www.mic.com/life/are-your-dating-preferences-racist-82343271

Papacharissi, Zizi. "Democracy Online: Civility, Politeness, and the Democratic Potential of Online Political Discussion Groups." *New Media & Society* 6, no. 2 (2004): 259–283. https://doi.org/10.1177/1461444804041444

Pardes, Arielle. "Tinder Asks 'Does This Bother You'?" *Wired*. January 27, 2020. https://www.wired.com/story/tinder-does-this-bother-you-harassment-tools/

Park, Ji Ho, Jamin Shin, and Pascale Fung. "Reducing Gender Bias in Abusive Language Detection." *arXiv* (2018): 1–6. https://doi.org/10.48550/arXiv.1808.07231

Pass, Michael, Ellen Benoit, and Eloise Dunlap. "'I Just Be Myself': Contradicting Hyper Masculine and Hyper Sexual Stereotypes Among Low-Income Black Men in New York City." In *Hyper Sexual, Hyper Masculine? Gender, Race and Sexuality in the Identities of Contemporary Black Men*, edited by Brittany C. Slatton and Kamesha Spates, 165–181. London: Routledge, 2014.

Passos, Wesley L., Igor M. Quintanilha, and Gabriel M. Araujo. "Real-Time Deep-Learning-Based System for Facial Recognition." *Simpósio Brasileiro de Telecomunicações e Processamento de Sinais (SBrT)* 37 (2018): 895–899.

Patil, Shailaja A., and P. J. Deore. "Face Recognition: A Survey." *Informatics Engineering: An International Journal* 1, no. 1 (2013): 31–41.

Phan Howard, Khoa. "The Creepy White Guy and the Helpless Asian: How Sexual Racism Persists in a Gay Interracial Friendship Group." *Social Problems* (2021): 1–17. https://doi.org/10.1093/socpro/spab052

Phillips, P. Jonathon, Fang Jiang, Abhijit Narvekar, Julianne Ayyad, and Alice J. O'Toole. "An Other-Race Effect for Face Recognition Algorithms." *ACM Transactions on Applied Perception (TAP)* 8, no. 2 (2011): 1–11.

Plummer, Mary Dianne. "Sexual Racism in Gay Communities: Negotiating the Ethnosexual Marketplace." PhD dissertation. University of Washington, 2008. http://hdl.handle.net/1773/9181

Pollock, Taia N. "With Love: Designing with Love to Create Space for Healing." MA thesis. Pratt Institute, 2021. https://www.proquest.com/openview/7fbc5d9 c58bc258cc36d70219596db63/1.pdf?pq-origsite=gscholar&cbl=18750&diss=y

Portes, Alejandro, and Rafael Mozo. "The Political Adaptation Process of Cubans and Other Ethnic Minorities in the United States: A Preliminary Analysis." *International Migration Review* 19, no. 1 (1985): 35–63.

Poster, Winifred R. "Racialized Surveillance in the Digital Service Economy." In *Captivating Technology: Race, Carceral Technoscience, and Liberatory Imagination in Everyday Life*, edited by Ruha Benjamin, 133–169. Durham: Duke University Press, 2019.

Powell, Dionne R. "From the Sunken Place to the Shitty Place: The Film *Get Out*, Psychic Emancipation and Modern Race Relations from a Psychodynamic Clinical Perspective." *Psychoanalytic Quarterly* 89, no. 3 (2020): 414–445. https://doi.org/10.1080/00332828.2020.1767486

Presidente, Giorgio, and Carl Benedikt Frey. "The GDPR Effect: How Data Privacy Regulation Shaped Firm Performance Globally." *Vox EU*. March 10, 2022. https://cepr.org/voxeu/columns/gdpr-effect-how-data-privacy-regulation -shaped-firm-performance-globally

Procope, Chavez, Adeel Cheema, David Atkins, Bilal Alsallakh, Nekesha Green, Emily McReynolds, Grace Pehl, Erin Wang, and Polina Zvyagina. "System-Level Transparency of Machine Learning." *Meta Research*. February 23, 2022. https://research.facebook.com/file/3015640278652885/System-Level -Transparency-of-Machine-Learning.pdf

Quayum, M. A. "July's People: Gordimer's Radical Critique of White 'Liberal' Attitude." *English Studies in Africa* 39, no. 1 (1996): 13–24. https://doi.org/10.1080/00138399608691243

Rafalow, Matthew H., Cynthia Feliciano, and Belinda Robnett. "Racialized Femininity and Masculinity in the Preferences of Online Same-Sex Daters." *Social Currents* 4, no. 4 (2017): 306–321. https://doi.org/10.1177/2329496516686621

Rakova, Bogdana. "Challenges for Responsible AI Practitioners and the Importance of Solidarity." *Partnership on AI*. March 8, 2021. https://partnershiponai.org/challenges-for-responsible-ai-practitioners/

Reddy, Ajitha. "The Eugenic Origins of IQ Testing: Implications for Post-Atkins Litigation." *DePaul Law Review* 57 (2008): 667–678.

Reinstein, Julia. "Tinder Will Stop Banning Users for Fundraising for Black Lives Matter and Bail Funds." *BuzzFeed News*. June 7, 2020. https://www.buzzfeednews.com/article/juliareinstein/tinder-ends-ban-blm-fundraisers

Richards, Neil. *Intellectual Privacy: Rethinking Civil Liberties in the Digital Age*. New York: Oxford University Press, 2015.

Ricks, Becca, Mark Surman, and Contributors. "Creating Trustworthy AI." *Mo-*

zilla Foundation. December 15, 2020. https://foundation.mozilla.org/en/insights/trustworthy-ai-whitepaper/

Rigot, Afsaneh. *Design from the Margins: Centering the Most Marginalized and Impacted in Design Processes—from Ideation to Production.* Belfer Center for Science and International Affairs. May 13, 2022. https://www.belfercenter.org/publication/design-margins

Riotta, Chris. "Tinder Still Banning Transgender People Despite Pledge of Inclusivity." *The Independent.* December 12, 2019. https://www.independent.co.uk/news/world/americas/tinder-ban-trans-account-block-report-lawsuit-pride-gender-identity-a9007721.html

Ritzer, George. *The McDonaldization of Society.* Los Angeles: Sage, 2013.

Ro, Annie, George Ayala, Jay Paul, and Kyung-Hee Choi. "Dimensions of Racism and Their Impact on Partner Selection Among Men of Colour Who Have Sex with Men: Understanding Pathways to Sexual Risk." *Culture, Health & Sexuality* 15, no. 7 (2013): 836–850. https://doi.org/10.1080/13691058.2013.785025

Robinson, Brandon Andrew. "'Personal Preference' as the New Racism: Gay Desire and Racial Cleansing in Cyberspace." *Sociology of Race and Ethnicity* 1, no. 2 (2015): 317–330. https://doi.org/10.1177/2332649214546870

Robinson, Russell K., and David M. Frost. "LGBT Equality and Sexual Racism." *Fordham Law Review* 86, no. 6 (2018): 2739–2754.

Robinson-Moore, Cynthia L. "Beauty Standards Reflect Eurocentric Paradigms—So What? Skin Color, Identity, and Black Female Beauty." *Journal of Race & Policy* 4, no. 1 (2008): 66–85.

Robnett, Belinda, and Cynthia Feliciano. "Patterns of Racial-Ethnic Exclusion by Internet Daters." *Social Forces* 89, no. 3 (2011): 807–828. https://doi.org/10.1177/2329496516686621

Rudder, Christian. *Dataclysm: Who We Are (When We Think No One's Looking).* New York: Crown, 2014.

Rushton, J. Philippe, and C. Davison Ankney. "Whole Brain Size and General Mental Ability: A Review." *International Journal of Neuroscience* 119, no. 5 (2009): 692–732.

Ryu, Hee Jung, Hartwig Adam, and Margaret Mitchell. "InclusiveFaceNet: Improving Face Attribute Detection with Race and Gender Diversity." In *Workshop on Fairness, Accountability, and Transparency in Machine Learning (FAT/ML 2018)*, 1–6. Stockholm, Sweden, 2018. https://doi.org/10.48550/arXiv.1712.00193

Sap, Maarten, Dallas Card, Saadia Gabriel, Yejin Choi, and Noah A. Smith. "The Risk of Racial Bias in Hate Speech Detection." In *Proceedings of the 57th Annual Meeting of the Association for Computational Linguistics*, 1668–1678. Florence, Italy, 2018. https://doi.org/10.18653/v1/P19-1163

Scharff, Darcell P., Katherine J. Mathews, Pamela Jackson, Jonathan Hoffsuemmer, Emeobong Martin, and Dorothy Edwards. "More Than Tuskegee: Understanding Mistrust About Research Participation." *Journal of Health Care for the Poor and Underserved* 21, no. 3 (2010): 879–897.

Schuman, Howard, Charlotte Steeh, Lawrence Bobo, and Maria Krysan. *Racial Attitudes in America: Trends and Interpretations*, 2nd ed. Cambridge, MA: Harvard University Press, 1997.

Sen_Mendoza. "How Race Affects the Reply Rate Among OkCupid Members." Reddit: r/dataisbeautiful. March 24, 2014. https://www.reddit.com/r/dataisbeautiful/comments/217vtn/how_race_affects_the_reply_rate_among_okcupid/

Shapiro, Thomas M. *The Hidden Cost of Being African American: How Wealth Perpetuates Inequality*. New York: Oxford University Press, 2004.

Sharfstein, Daniel J. "Crossing the Color Line: Racial Migration and the One-Drop Rule, 1600–1860." *Minnesota Law Review* 91 (2007): 592–656.

Shaw, Frances. " 'Bitch I Said Hi': The *Bye Felipe* Campaign and Discursive Activism in Mobile Dating Apps." *Social Media+ Society* 2, no. 4 (2016): 1–10. https://doi.org/10.1177/2056305116672889

Shek, Yen Ling. "Asian American Masculinity: A Review of the Literature." *Journal of Men's Studies* 14, no. 3 (2007): 379–391. https://doi.org/10.3149/jms.1403.379

Siju, V. "A Survey on Machine Learning Algorithms for Face Recognition." *International Research Journal of Engineering and Technology* 7 (2008): 1072–1075.

Silvestrini, Molly. " 'It's Not Something I Can Shake': The Effect of Racial Stereotypes, Beauty Standards, and Sexual Racism on Interracial Attraction." *Sexuality & Culture* 24 (2020): 305–325. https://doi.org/doi:10.1007/s12119-019-09644-0

Skinner, E. Benjamin. "The Fight to End Global Slavery." *World Policy Journal* 26, no. 2 (2009): 33–41. https://www.jstor.org/stable/40468631

Smith, Jesús Gregorio, and Gabriel Amaro. " 'No Fats, No Femmes, and No Blacks or Asians': The Role of Body-Type, Sex Position, and Race on Condom Use Online." *AIDS and Behavior* 25, no. 7 (2021): 2166–2176. https://doi.org/10.1007/s10461-020-03146-z

Smith, Jesús Gregorio, Maria Cristina Morales, and Chong-suk Han. "The Influence of Sexual Racism on Erotic Capital: A Systemic Racism Perspective." In *Handbook of the Sociology of Racial and Ethnic Relations*, edited by P. Batur and J. R. Feagin, 389–399. New York: New York International Publishing, 2018.

Smith, Jesús Gregorio, Andrew J. Sage, Maggie McGlenn, Janai' Robbins, and Sheldon L. Garmon. "Is Sexual Racism Still Really Racism? Revisiting Callander et al. (2015) in the USA." *Archives of Sexual Behavior* 51, no. 6 (2022): 3049–3062. https://doi.org/10.1007/s10508-022-02351-2

Sood, Reema. "Biases Behind Sexual Assault: A Thirteenth Amendment Solution to Under-Enforcement of the Rape of Black Women." *University of Maryland Law Journal of Race, Religion, Gender* 18, no. 2 (2018): 405–428.

Stacey, Lawrence, and TehQuin D. Forbes. "Feeling Like a Fetish: Racialized Feelings, Fetishization, and the Contours of Sexual Racism on Gay Dating Apps." *Journal of Sex Research* 59, no. 3 (2022): 372–384. https://doi.org/10.1080/002244 99.2021.1979455

Stevenson Jr., Howard C. "The Psychology of Sexual Racism and AIDS: An Ongoing Saga of Distrust and the 'Sexual Other.'" *Journal of Black Studies* 25, no. 1 (1994): 62–80.

Stewart, Kristian D., and Daniela Gachago. "Step into the Discomfort: (Re)orienting the White Gaze and Strategies to Disrupt Whiteness in Educational Spaces." *Whiteness and Education* 7, no. 1 (2022): 18–31.

Strubel, Jessica, and Trent A. Petrie. "Love Me Tinder: Body Image and Psychosocial Functioning Among Men and Women." *Body Image* 21 (2017): 34–38.

Suyemoto, Karen L., Alissa L. Hochman, Roxanne A. Donovan, and Lisbeth Roemer. "Becoming and Fostering Allies and Accomplices Through Authentic Relationships: Choosing Justice over Comfort." *Research in Human Development* 18, no. 1–2 (2021): 1–28.

Telzer, Eva H., and Heidie A. Vazquez Garcia. "Skin Color and Self-Perceptions of Immigrant and U.S.-Born Latinas: The Moderating Role of Racial Socialization and Ethnic Identity." *Hispanic Journal of Behavioral Sciences* 31, no. 3 (2009): 357–374. https://doi.org/10.1177/0739986309336913

Thai, Michael. "Sexual Racism Is Associated with Lower Self-Esteem and Life Satisfaction in Men Who Have Sex with Men." *Archives of Sexual Behavior* 49, no. 1 (2020): 347–353. https://doi.org/10.1007/s10508-019-1456-z

Thompson, Laura. "'I Can Be Your Tinder Nightmare': Harassment and Misogyny in the Online Sexual Marketplace." *Feminism & Psychology* 28, no. 1 (2018): 69–89.

Thompson, Martie, Dylan Sitterle, George Clay, and Jeffrey Kingree. "Reasons for Not Reporting Victimizations to the Police: Do They Vary for Physical and Sexual Incidents?" *Journal of American College Health* 55, no. 5 (2007): 277–282. https://doi.org/10.3200/JACH.55.5.277-282

Timmermans, Elisabeth, and Ellen De Caluwé. "Development and Validation of the Tinder Motives Scale (TMS)." *Computers in Human Behavior* 70 (2017): 341–350.

Tkach, Benjamin, and Apryl A. Williams. "Mobile (in)Security? Exploring the Realities of Mobile Phone Use in Conflict Areas." *Information, Communication & Society* 21, no. 11 (2018): 1639–1654. https://doi.org/10.1080/1369118X.2017.1348531

Tsunokai, Glenn, Allison R. McGrath, and Jillian Kavanagh. "Online Dating Preferences of Asian Americans." *Journal of Social and Personal Relationships* 31, no. 6 (2014): 796–814. https://doi.org/10.1177/0265407513505925

Vincent, James. "Google 'Fixed' Its Racist Algorithm by Removing Gorillas from Its Image-Labeling Tech." *The Verge.* January 12, 2018. https://www.theverge.com/2018/1/12/16882408/google-racist-gorillas-photo-recognition-algorithm-ai

Wade, Ryan M., and Gary W. Harper. "Racialized Sexual Discrimination (RSD) in the Age of Online Sexual Networking: Are Young Black Gay/Bisexual Men (YBGBM) at Elevated Risk for Adverse Psychological Health?" *American Journal of Community Psychology* 65, no. 3–4 (2019): 504–523. https://doi.org/10.1002/ajcp.12401

Waldman, Ari Ezra. "Law, Privacy, and Online Dating: 'Revenge Porn' in Gay Online Communities." *Law & Social Inquiry* 44, no. 4 (2019): 987–1018. https://doi.org/10.1017/lsi.2018.29

Waldman, Katy. "A Sociologist Examines the 'White Fragility' That Prevents White Americans from Confronting Racism." *The New Yorker.* July 23, 2018. https://www.newyorker.com/books/page-turner/a-sociologist-examines-the-white-fragility-that-prevents-white-americans-from-confronting-racism

Wang, Mei, and Weihong Deng. "Deep Face Recognition: A Survey." *Neurocomputing* 429 (2021): 215–244.

Whitlock, Dominic. "Bumble Makes Users Take Pledge to Support Black Lives Matter." *Global Dating Insights.* June 25, 2020. https://www.globaldatinginsights.com/news/bumble-makes-users-take-pledge-to-support-black-lives-matter/

Whyte, Stephen, Ho Fai Chan, and Benno Torgler. "Do Men and Women Know What They Want? Sex Differences in Online Daters' Educational Preferences." *Psychological Science* 29, no. 8 (2018): 1370–1375.

Wilkinson, Betina Cutaia, and Emily Earle. "Taking a New Perspective to Latino Racial Attitudes: Examining the Impact of Skin Tone on Latino Perceptions of Commonality with Whites and Blacks." *American Politics Research* 41, no. 5 (2013): 783–818. https://doi.org/10.1177/1532673X12464546

Williams, Linda Meyer. "Race and Rape: The Black Woman as Legitimate Victim." 1986. https://files.eric.ed.gov/fulltext/ED294970.pdf

Wong, Hoo Keat, Ian D. Stephen, and David R. T. Keeble. "The Own-Race Bias for Face Recognition in a Multiracial Society." *Frontiers in Psychology* 11 (2020): 1–16. https://doi.org/10.3389/fpsyg.2020.00208

Yancey, George. "Homogamy over the Net: Using Internet Advertisements to Discover Who Interracially Dates." *Journal of Social and Personal Relationships* 24, no. 6 (2007): 913–930.

Yosso, Tara J. "Whose Culture Has Capital? A Critical Race Theory Discussion of Community Cultural Wealth." *Race Ethnicity and Education* 8, no. 1 (2005): 69–91.

Zembylas, Michalinos. "Affect, Race, and White Discomfort in Schooling: Decolonial Strategies for 'Pedagogies of Discomfort.'" *Ethics and Education* 13, no. 1 (2018): 86–104.

Zheng, Robin. "Why Yellow Fever Isn't Flattering: A Case Against Racial Fetishes." *Journal of the American Philosophical Association* 2, no. 3 (2016): 400–419. https://doi.org/10.1017/apa.2016.25

Zhou, Zhiqiu Benson. "Compulsory Interracial Intimacy: Why Does Removing the Ethnicity Filter on Dating Apps Not Benefit Racial Minorities?" *Media, Culture & Society* 44, no. 5 (2022): 1034–1043. https://doi.org/10.1177/01634437221104712

abstract liberalism, 44
accountability, 66, 146–47, 169–70, 180
affordance, 76–77, 79
African American English (AAE), 152
Alexa, 151
algorithmic reparation, 172
algorithms, xii–xiii, 6, 23, 36, 57, 114,
    165–66, 170; attractiveness scores,
    2–3; bias in, 14, 18–19, 24, 114;
    commonality score, 72–73; covert
    nature of, 19; credit scores, 20; in
    dating apps, 37; dating and intimacy
    platforms, 4, 107, 140; discrimina-
    tion, ix, xi; facial recognition
    software, 60–63, 67–68; Google
    searches, 15–16; "hot or not," 51; ick
    factor, 150–53; implicit racial bias,
    168; insurance industry, 21; manipu-
    lation of users, 84–85; offline dating
    processes, replicating of, 2; optimal
    fit, 37; pornography industry, 15–16;
    profile matching, 53; public good,
    threat to, 168; racialized construc-
    tions of beauty, rooted in, 11;
    racialized sorting, 7, 37, 70, 81, 114;
    racially curated sexual marketplace,
    22; ranking of, 71; of search engines,
    167–68; sexual racism, 17, 24, 37, 76,
    80–81; structural inequity, contrib-
    uting to, 20–21; swipe-based dating
    apps, 21, 51–52, 58, 63–64, 68–69;
    toxic language, 152; transparency,
    171; user bias, 1; user demand, 107–8;
    user feedback, 68; user preference,
    68–69
algorithm studies, 25–26
All Cops Are Bastards (ACAB), 147–48
Amazon, 36–37
American Civil Liberties Union
    (ACLU), 60
anti-Asian sentiment, 135
anti-Blackness, 130, 137; in Asian
    communities, 132–33, 135; dating
    markets, predicated on, 136

Anti-Defamation League (ADL),
    145–46
anti-Latinx immigrant sentiment, 130
anti-miscegenation laws, 34, 43–44,
    165; as unconstitutional, 6–7; White
    racial superiority, rooted in, 6
anti-racist thought, 110–11, 144–48, 164
Anzari, Aziz, 1
Arbery, Ahmaud. 143
artificial intelligence (AI), ix, 18, 37,
    150–51, 152, 172, 179; accountability
    and collective well-being, as central
    to, 170; ethical AI, xii; ethics, 171
Asia, 31, 130
Asian American men and masculinity:
    16, 27, 30
Asian Americans, 16, 134
Asian community: Asian fetish, 159;
    "fancy Asians," 133; interracial
    dating, 133; "jungle Asians," 133
Asian men, 4, 7–8, 13, 42; racial traits,
    30; sexual racism, experiencing of,
    41; stereotypes of, 128; as threat to
    U.S. society, 16; White women, as
    threat to, 16
Asian women, 4, 105, 124, 129; cute
    ideal, 125–26; as exotic, 106; in
    hentai, 128; racial fetishization of,
    128; sexual racism, 125, 128; stereo-
    types of, 15, 125–26, 128
assimilation, 131; racial sexual desirabil-
    ity politics, reinforcing of, 134
attractiveness, 2, 11, 29, 50, 52–54, 63,
    73; attractiveness scores, 1, 3, 6–7, 51,
    68, 70–72; conceptualizations of,
    21–22; ELO, use of, 55; evaluating of,
    14, 70, 176; facial recognition
    software, 68; ideals about, 3; as
    mechanism of control, 79; as
    racialized, 120; ranking algorithms,

6; as socially constructed, 4, 55;
    standards of, 55; White European
    aesthetics of, 6, 20–21. See also
    beauty
Aunt Jemima trope, 15
Austin Justice Coalition, 145
automated eugenics, 13, 24–25. See also
    eugenics
automated sexual racism, 6, 17, 21–22,
    24–26, 48, 68–69, 76, 80–81, 83, 108,
    112, 130, 140, 177; concealing of, 85;
    cyclical nature of, 85; effects of, 113;
    individual sexual racism, converging
    with, 113; normalizing of, 165; safety,
    176. See also sexual racism

beauty, 14, 70, 112–13; in eye of beholder,
    56; European aesthetic, rooted in,
    55–56, 130; norms of, 3, 67–68; as
    racialized aesthetic, 11, 68; standards
    of, 55–56; White Western aesthetic
    of, 6, 21–22, 40, 43, 55–56, 79, 92, 101,
    103, 119, 130–31. See also attractiveness
Benjamin, Ruha, 84, 140–41; discrimi-
    natory design, 20; New Jim Code,
    19–20, 25, 80, 166, 177
big data, 19
Black Americans, 145
Black bodies, 123; tropes of, 15–16
Black communities, 135, 143; colorism
    in, 134; lighter skin, 134; skin
    bleaching, 130
Black femininity, 15; Black feminist
    thought, 14
Black feminism, 14, 23; resisting oppres-
    sion, purpose of, 13
Black Feminist Thought (Collins), 14
Black liberation, 14
Black Lives Matter (BLM), 60, 110, 120,
    135, 143–45, 147–48, 177–78

Black masculinity, 30

Black men, 4, 30–32, 44, 65, 108–10, 114, 120, 132, 134, 156; fetishization of, as dehumanizing, 42–43; as hypersexual, trope of, 16

Blackness, 17, 116–17, 132; appropriation of, 136; denial of, 136; regulating of, 136; sexuality of, 32

Black sexual bodies, 93

Black women, 12, 80, 113–14, 135; angry stereotype of, 36; attractiveness, 7–8; Black mammy, image of, 36; as docile, 40; fetishization of, 15; objectification of, 121–22; as property, 14–15, 31; "laying their edges," 43; as public property, 33; "queen" colloquialism, 120–21; racial fetishization of, 118–19; racist stereotypes about, 4–5, 15, 44, 123; sexual harm, victims of, 123; sexual tourism, 120

Black women sexuality: as public property, 33

Black Women's Health Imperative, 145

BLK, 171

bodily tourism, 116, 118

Bonilla-Silva, Eduardo, 43–45, 88, 90

bootstrap mythology, 97

Boston (Massachusetts), 60

Brown v. Board of Education, 80

Bumble, 51–52, 76–78, 120, 126, 146, 158, 164, 166; anti-racist pledge, 144–45, 147; ick factor algorithm, 150; "Microagressions & Fetishization" resource page, 153; Private Detector, 150; racial justice, commitment to, 145; safety, 149

Bumble BBF, 120, 149, 179

Bumble Bizz, 120, 149, 179

Butler, Judith, 3, 38

California, 11, 170

Canada, 31, 67, 176

capitalism, 65; appropriation of Blackness, 136; denial of Blackness, 136

Central America, 31, 99

Chispa, 171

citizenship, 96–97

civility, 89–90

civil rights movement, 90

Collins, Patricia Hill, 3, 14–15, 29, 33, 36

colonization, 45, 90, 133, 136

color-blind racism, 43, 45, 88–90, 96; naturalization frame of, 103

colorism, 46, 99, 109, 131, 135; in Black communities, 134

computing systems: master-slave filing system, 83–84

conservatives, 89; interracial dating, 98–99

Consumer International, 170

consumerism, 48

controlling images, 22; of Black mammy, 36; of Black women, 15, 33; men of color, 16; racialized myths about, 36

Cooper, Bradley, 55–56

COVID-19 pandemic, 135

credit scores, 20

critical Indigenous theory, 14

critical internet studies, 13, 23

critical Marxist thought, 14

critical race theory, 20

critical social thought, 14

cult of true womanhood: domesticity, 14, 33; piety, 14, 33; purity, 14, 33; submissiveness, 14, 33

cute aesthetic, 127

cyber dating abuse, 138

cyber stalking, 138

data privacy: as human right, 168

Dataclysm (Rudder), 7–8

dating: racialization of, 25–26; racial logics, cultivating of, 137

dating companies, 178–79; algorithms, 85

dating culture, 123; commoditization of, as predicated on anti-Blackness, 136; patriarchal violence, 139

Davis, Viola, 36

decency, 89

Denmark, 67

Design from the Margins (Rigot), 25, 173–74

Detroit (Michigan), 60

DiAngelo, Robin, 41, 88, 90, 111

digital dating apps: rape culture, link to, 138–39

digital sexual racism, 47–49. *See also* sexual racism

digital technologies, 47–48, 76

Digital Trust and Safety Department, 175

digital violence, 138

discrimination, 6, 25, 27, 34, 41, 44, 80; age, 170; algorithmic, ix, xi; ethnic, 65; housing, 91; racial, 48, 51, 65, 108, 144, 165; structural, 97

disenfranchisement, 20

dog-whistle politics, 89–90

Du Bois, W. E. B., 35

Egypt, 174

eHarmony, 2, 149; safety, 149

ELO, 50, use of, 55

exoticism, 15, 104–7, 115, 119, 121–22

eugenics, 6, 31, 70; albeism of, 65–66; biological superiority of White race, 68; Nazi science, 65–67; negative, 64; one-drop rule, 34–35; positive,

65–66; profile-sorting process of, 68; as race biology, 64; racialized science, 83; sterilization, 65. *See also* automated eugenics

Europe, 170, 176

European Union (EU), 173, 176

European Union Digital Services Act (DSA), 176

exchange relations, 136

Expatriation Act, 97

Facebook, 2, 59–60, 63, 78, 167, 170, 176, 179; Facebook Dating, 149, 162–63

facial recognition, 176; accuracy of, 61; algorithms, 60–63, 67–68; attractiveness, 68; Black individuals, 60–61, 63–64; local binary patterns (LBP), 62; non-White faces, 70; skin reflectance, 61; software, banned in policing, 60

Fanon, Frantz, 94

Feagin, Joe, 30, 89, 142

femininity, 3, 28–29, 38, 40, 49, 74, 166; socially constructed racialized beliefs of, 4

fetishization, 25. *See also* racial fetishization

First Amendment, 141

Flesch Kincaid Grade Level test, 66–67

Flesch Kincaid Reading Ease test, 66

Florida, 21; Cuban population, conservative views of, 99

Floyd, George, 143, 146

Foucault, Michel, 39

Full Metal Jacket (film), 15

Gebru, Timnit, 172–73

gender, 3, 49, 53, 74, 166; and race, 38; as social construct, 28

General Data Protection Regulation (GDPR), 176

gendered other, 40

gendered performance, 38; shaped by race, 39

gendered power relations, 37

Get Out (film): Sunken Place, as metaphor, 115–17, 120, 122–23

Global North, 135–36

Gone with the Wind (film), 36

Google, 59–60, 80, 151, 167–68, 173, 175; Counter Abuser Technology Team, 152; Jigsaw, 152; Perspective Application Programming Interface (API), 152; as profit driven, 15–16; toxicity scoring, use of, 152

Gosling, Ryan, 55–56

Gramsci, Antonio: hegemony, concept of, 29

Grindr, 163, 174–75

Guatemala, 131–32

Gunning Fog Index, 67

Gunning Fog score, 66

harm reduction, 142, 153, 158, 164, 172, 175–78

Harvard University: Cyberlaw Clinic, 54

hate speech, 144, 153

hegemonic femininity, 39

hegemonic masculinity, 38–39

Help, The (film), 36

Hemings, Sally, 35

Herd, Whitney Wolfe, 166

Hinge, 7, 22, 102, 158, 171; swipe-based, 58

Hispanics, 135. *See also* Latinx

homophily, 4, 45–46, 54

How to Be an Antiracist (Kendi), 108, 111

hypermodernity, 79

hypodescent, 35

imperialism, 45, 90

India, 133

inequity, 29, 36, 123, 135, 145; algorithmic, 19–20; racial, 90, 144, 178; social, 25, 89; structural, 20–21, 37; systematic, 19

information studies, xi

Instagram, 60, 63, 78, 126–27, 167, 179; DMs, 59

insurance industry: risks and mortality rates, 21

intelligence tests, 66–67

internet, 83; implicit bias in, 21; internet dating culture, controlling images, 16; matchmaking and sorting, 13; as network of networks, 13; Whiteness, as default, 21

internet and digital media studies, xi

interracial dating, 13, 25, 43, 85–86, 95–97, 165; in Asian communities, 133; conservative view of, 98–99; eugenics, exercise in, 34; hierarchy of desirability, 101

interracial marriage, 8–9, 34, 45, 80; prohibiting of, 32

intimacy apps, 2, 13

intimacy platforms, 49; Black feminist thought, 14; online dating experience, 4; as profit driven, 21; race and algorithms, 17; race and gender bias, 13–14; sexual racism, 28; White normative standards of attraction, reliance on, 6

Iran, 174

Japan, 127

Jefferson, Thomas, 35

Jezebel trope, 15

Jim Crow laws, 80

Kendi, Ibram X., 108, 111
Kincaid Reading Ease test, 67
Klobuchar, Amy, 175
K-pop, 27, 128, 159, 161

language detection systems: bias in, 152
Latin America, 131–32
Latina and Latino critical theory, 14
Latinx. 129–30, 134; sexual racism, 129;
    as White adjacent, 99; Whitening
    effect in, 99. See also Hispanics
Lebanon, 174
LGBTQIA+, 56, 174
light skin, 130, 133–34; social privilege,
    131
Loving v. Virginia, 6–7, 34
loyalty, 168
lynching, 156; as social control, 31–32

machine learning systems, xiii
mammy trope, 15
marginalization, 14
marginalized users, 25, 81, 142, 173–74;
    protection for, 140, 163–64, 175;
    protective affordance for, 101;
    reducing harm to, 150, 176–78;
    sexual racism, protection from, 149
masculinity, 3, 28–30, 38, 49, 74, 166;
    socially constructed racialized
    beliefs of, 4
Match.com, 7, 52–54, 58, 76–77
Match Group, 7, 24, 36, 55, 59, 64,
    76–77, 148, 150, 156, 164, 167, 171;
    commonality scores, 69–70, 80;
    Harry and Sally example, 71–73, 75;
    patent of, 51–54, 56–57, 63, 66,
    69–75, 79–80, 85, 108, 166, 177;
    profile matching, 53; safety, 139. See
    also OKCupid
Madea character, 15

Mateen, Justin, 166
Martin Luther King Jr. Day, 121
matchmaking, x, 2, 13, 136; automated
    systems of, 54
McDaniel, Hattie, 36
McDonaldization, 79
Meetic, 171
Meta, 59–60, 169, 171, 175
meritocracy, 19, 144; myth of, 20, 44
Mexico, 32, 99–101
Microsoft, 175–76
Middle East, 130
Middle East/North Africa (MENA),
    174
military-industrial-academic complex,
    17
minimization of racism, 91
mirrored matches, 169
miscegenation, 16
misogynoir: sexual racism, rooted in,
    155–56
misogyny, 29–30
Modern Family (television series), 15
Mozilla Foundation, 170–71; "Privacy
    Not Included" project, 169
myth of neutrality of choice, 48–49, 76;
    racist logics of desirability hierar-
    chies, concealing of, 107
myth of neutral personal preference, 94

National Association for the Advance-
    ment of Colored People (NAACP)
    Legal Defense and Education Fund,
    145
naturalization, 44, 90
naturalization frame, 46, 90–91; of
    color-blind racism, 96, 103; in tech
    culture, 45
natural language processing (NLP),
    151–52, 164

neoliberalism, 48, 141; neoliberal
    individualism, 148
neutral performance preference:
    anti-Blackness of, 137; myth of, 94;
    sexual racism, 137
New Jim Code, 19–20, 25, 80–81, 140,
    166, 177–78
Noble, Safiya, 15–16, 18–19, 80, 167–68
non-racialism, 45
non-Whiteness, 27–28
Noonlight, 156–57
Northeastern Network Science
    Institute, 126

OkCupid, 1–4, 7–9, 50–51, 53, 56, 58,
    68, 76–77, 101, 149–50, 171, 183–84n7.
    See also Match Group
one-drop rule, 34–35, 165
online dating apps, x, xiii, 13, 106, 112,
    158–59; habitual nature of, 115;
    modern dating practices, mimicking
    of, 2; myth of neutrality of choice,
    48–49; objectifying women, 103; for
    racialized sexual tourism, 105; as
    rape culture, 139; reporting mecha-
    nisms 162; sexual racism, perpetuat-
    ing of, 37; sorting algorithms, 37;
    swipe based, 21, 51–52, 58, 63–64,
    68–69, 86–87, 102–3, 180; user
    privacy, disregarding of, 169; White
    users of, 4
online dating industry, 1, 3, 52, 56, 75,
    141, 167, 176, 179–80
online dating platforms, xi, xii, xiii, 8,
    11, 26, 31, 46, 55, 76, 86, 122–23, 141,
    146, 167, 171–72, 179; algorithmic ma-
    nipulation and sexual racism,
    intersection of, 17; algorithms, 1, 71,
    107; anti-racist thought, 144;
    artificial intelligence (AI) features,

150–51; automated sexual racism, 6,
    85, 113; beauty standards, 68; black
    box problem, 50; commonality, 85;
    commonality scores, 84; commod-
    itizing of, 12; conceptualisms of
    attractiveness, White European
    aesthetics of, 21–22; daters of color,
    4; embodiments, 56–59, 71;
    eugenicist logic, 6, 67, 70; explicit
    racial bias on, 24; facial recognition
    software, 67; feedback loop, 28, 112;
    filtering by race or ethnicity, 101;
    gameplay design of, 79; gamification
    of, 77, 79; hierarchal racialized
    system of, 74; ick factor algorithms,
    153; intelligence, 67; master-slave
    role play, 117; misogyny, 29–30;
    personal preference, as neutral, 84;
    questionnaire based, 56, 77; racial
    bias, 25; racial fetishization, 113, 121;
    racial filters, 102; racial flavors,
    trying out, 104; racialized desirabil-
    ity hierarchy, 101; racialized ranking,
    6; racialized sorting processes, 70;
    racially curated sexual marketplace,
    104, 107–8, 137; racial preference, as
    neutral, 23; racial taboos, 13, 107; and
    racism, 4, 168; racist sorting and
    ranking algorithms, 165; reporting
    mechanisms, as unsatisfactory, 160;
    safety, 138–40, 148–49, 158, 163–64;
    safety mechanisms, absence of,
    161–62; sexual preferences, 47;
    sexual preferences, as neutral, 113;
    sexual racism, 28, 36, 39, 47–48, 101,
    113, 140, 158, 161, 164–65; shared
    database of racial harassers, 164;
    social control, as method of, 79;
    straight White men and women,
    users of, 4; swipe-based, 56, 77, 84,

online dating platforms (*cont.*)
112; trans fetishization, 153; transparency, 53; transphobia, 153, 162–63; user activity, 59; user choice, 75; user feedback, and votes, 75; user profiles, 77; violence, strategies to prevent, 156; White normative standards of attraction, reliance on, 6; White tech bros, led by, 165–66
otherness, 40, 83, 107
Our Time, 171

Pairs, 171
pariah femininities, 39
patriarchy: hegemonic, 39; tradition of, 97; Whiteness, inherent in, 97
Peele, Jordan, 115
peonage, 45
people of color, 25, 42, 45, 91, 93–95, 109, 111, 123, 143, 155, 172–73; as commoditized, 102, 104; dating culture, patriarchal violence, 139; home ownership and investing, 20–21; oppression of, as tied to anti-Black racism and colonialism, 136; safety, 158; sexual racism, 130
personal preference, 6, 10
personal racialized preference, 114
Perry, Tyler, 15
Pinterest, 175, 179
Plenty of Fish, 7, 171
police brutality, 177–78
policing: facial recognition software, 60
Pornhub, 121
pornography, 15–16, 121; hentai cartoons, 128
Portman, Rob, 175
post-modern societies: calculability, 79; control, 79; efficiency, 79; predictability, 79

post-racialism, 94
power: disciplinary domain of, 29, 36–37, 48; hegemonic domain of, 29, 35–36, 38; interpersonal domain of, 29, 33–34; structural domain of, 29, 34–35, 48
privacy: illusion of, ix; and trust, 168; violations of, 168
ProPublica, 138
public good, 168

queer, 41
queer theory, 14, 37

race, xiii, 4, 6–9, 13, 20, 44, 49, 53, 74, 85, 136, 166; avoidance of, 41; and gender, 38; as socially constructed, 10, 17, 28, 64, 109; and White people, 89, 111
Race After Technology (Benjamin), 140
race neutral, 84
race play, 107, 116
racial colonization, 136
racial disenfranchisement, 111
racial fetishization, 12, 22–24, 101–2, 106, 108, 112–13, 115–18, 123–24, 143, 153, 161, 164; of Asians, 128; idolization aspect of, 119; language of, 141; negative outcomes of, 121–22; power to harm, 142; sexual tourism, 120–22
racial filtering, 22
racial harassment, 113, 153, 164; digital sexual racism, unique to, 49
racialization, 16; of dating, 26
racialized bodies, 29, 74; consumption of, 22
racialized social control, 6
racially curated sexual marketplace, 22, 85, 101, 112; automated, 107; as commoditized, 22; dating platforms,

23, 104, 107–8, 137; designed for play, 102; racial fetishization, 104; racial filters, 23; racist tropes, influenced by, 22; swiping, as expression of taste, 114, 165; Whiteness, as desirable, 23. *See also* sexual racism

racial politics, 17–18, 31; of statistical sorting, xiii

racial preference, 4, 10–11, 26, 107; in dating profiles, 41; as "just the way things are," 43–44; as neutral, myth of, 5, 23–25; as racialized, 5, 9

racial sexual desirability politics, 134

racial sexual tourism, 23

racial stereotypes, 43, 88, 116, 161, 168; internalization of, 10

racial terrorism, 31–32, 165

racism, xiii, 4–6, 10, 18–19, 25, 30, 42–43, 82–83, 85, 88–89, 96, 110, 124, 128, 135, 140–41, 178; anti-Black, 136; benefits of, 94; biracial and multiracial women, 120; casual, 11, 101; cultural, 44, 90–91; in dating culture, 113; explicit, 155; global, 3; implicit, 168; internalized, 99, 132; minimization of, 44, 90; in online dating, 8, 168; as private, 165; racist adjacent, 90; safe from, 143; as sexual racism, 40–41, 113, 153; as social tool, 17; structural, xii, 29; upward mobility, effects on, 97; White people, undoing harms of, 108; as White people problem, 173

Reconstruction, 16, 31–32

Rad, Sean, 50, 53

rape culture: dating apps, 139

Reddit, 9–10, 175, 183–84n7

relationship support, 95

reparations, 135–36

respectability politics, 133

revenge porn, 138–39

rightness, 101

Rigot, Afsaneh, 25, 163, 173, 175; edge cases, 174

Rudder, Christian, 1, 7–9, 50, 68

safety, 25, 90, 122, 141, 176, 180; anti-racist approaches to, 164; of Black people, 143, 146, 148; on dating platforms, 78, 123, 138–40, 149, 153, 162–63, 178; definition of, 148; designing from the margins, 163–64; features, 156–57; manual reporting, 158; of marginalized users, 142, 149, 162–64, 173; measures and mechanisms of, 148–50, 157–58, 161, 164, 174–75; for people of color, 144–45, 158; public health definition of, 139; of White cisgender women, 138; for women of color, 123

San Francisco (California), 60

segregation, 90–91

settler colonialism, 131

sexism, xii, 19, 29, 110

sexual harassment, 140–41, 158–62, 173

sexual preference on dating platforms, as neutral, myth of, 113

sexual racism, xii, 13, 27, 32, 45, 74, 83, 86, 90, 112, 139, 173–74, 177–78; algorithms, 17, 24, 37, 76, 80–81; anti-Asianness of, 137; anti-Blackness of, 137; anti-Blackness capitalism, tied to, 137; Asian men, 42; Asian women, 125, 128; bodily and emotional harms of, 122–23; color-blind narratives, 43; commoditization of, 21; concealing of, 94; as covert, 28, 48; cross-cutting harm, 43; and darker skin, 120; dating apps, 37; dating platforms, 6, 28–29,

sexual racism (*cont.*)
 101, 140, 158, 161, 165; as defined, 6,
 28; digital nature of, 48–49;
 dimensional nature of, 104;
 domination, matrix of, 33, 37–38,
 47–48; domination and oppression,
 rooted in, 29; as everyday aspect of
 online dating, 113; exoticism of, 104;
 fetishized sexual attraction, 116;
 gendered bodies, marginalizing of,
 37; gendered bodies of color, as
 docile, 39–40; as harmful, 24;
 hegemonic gender roles, rooted in
 40; hypodescent ideologies, rooted
 in, 35; impact of, 115; as internalized,
 40–41, 46–47, 109, 130–32; intimacy
 platforms, 28; Jim Crow rules, 80; as
 last outpost of racist thought, 18;
 Latinx people, 129; marginalized
 users, 149; meaning making via
 inaction, 140; micro-level expressions of, 34; misogynoir, rooted in,
 155–56; negative mental health
 outcomes, 42, 115; neutral, masquer-
 ading of, 94, 137; normalizing of, by
 dating platforms, 24; normalizing
 of, by Whites, 114; online dating, 36,
 39, 47–48, 164; othered by, 104;
 people of color, 130; as personal
 choice, 165; personal taste, 172; as
 proprietary, 166; psychological
 distress, 43; race filters, 179; as
 racism, 113, 153; racism, rooted in,
 40–41; reporting of, 158–59; risky
 sexual behavior, 43; and safety, 162;
 society, shaped by, 30; sorting and
 ranking systems, 107–8; swiping
 behavior, 69; as systemic and
 personal issue, 49; thriving of, 18; as
 tool, 17–18, 48; by White men, 124;
 and Whiteness, 18, 28; White
 normative standards of attraction,
 reliance on, 6; White racial politics,
 17–18; White supremacy, 18. *See also*
 automated sexual racism, racially
 curated sexual marketplace, racism
sexual terrorism, 31
sexual tourism, 12, 23, 105; racial
 fetishization, 120–22
Silicon Valley, xii, 19; as Whitening
 machine, 83
Siri, 151, 155
skin bleaching, 130
slavery, 6, 32, 35, 44–45, 90, 115, 137;
 chattel, 14–15, 135; cognitive
 dissonance, 15
slave trade, 31, 44–45
Snapchat, 154
socialization, 47
social capital: as commodity, 136;
 White racial aesthetics, as desirable
 and valuable, 136
social control, 80; rape of Black women
 and men, 31
social media, 47
social networking sites: data-informed
 matching, 59; lawsuits, 59–60
social psychology, 92
social safety nets, 65
social segregation, 19
sociological imagination, x, xii
South America, 31, 99
Southern Poverty Law Center, 145
Spotify, 167
Sri Lanka, 133
sterilization, 66–67
structural racism, xii, 29
surveillance, ix; by police. 174; by state,
 67
Sweden, 67

swipe-based dating apps, 21, 24, 53, 56, 58, 76–77, 102, 166; objectification of women, 103

symbolic interactionism: notion of self, 47

systemic racism, 90–91, 110–11, 142, 146; neutral racial partner preferences, 83

Taylor, Breonna, 143

tech bro culture, 170

tech companies, 141, 176; edge cases, 163–64, 174; neoliberal ethos, committed to, 180; social policies, 19; unregulated, 84

tech industry, 175; embedded with coded racial bias, 84; as unjust, 179

tentacle porn, 127–28

Tinder, 2, 7, 11–12, 22, 51–52, 53, 59, 63, 76–77, 102, 107, 117, 126, 146–48, 153, 154–55, 160–61, 163, 166–67; age discrimination suite, 170; attractive users, monetizing of, 56; ELO scoring algorithm, use of, 50; encryption security, lack of, 170; ick factor algorithm, 150; Noonlight, 156–57; sex offenders, 138; super likes, 56, 78; swipe based, 58; Tinder Plus, 170

toxicity scoring, 152

trans fetishization, 153

Trans Lifeline, 153

transphobia, 6, 153, 158, 162–63, 173–74

tropes: Black brute, 16; Jezebel, 15; mammy, 15; yellow peril, 16

trust, 170; privacy, violations of, 168; and transparency, 171

Tumblr, 153

Tuskegee syphilis trial, 65

Twitter: racial and dialectical bias of, 152; toxicity scoring, use of, 152

unfitness, 64–65

United Kingdom, 67

United States, 3, 6, 12, 14–15, 17, 19, 24–26, 30–31, 34, 38, 43, 55–56, 62, 64–65, 80, 83–84, 89–90, 92–93, 97, 101, 111, 115, 123, 131, 133, 135, 137, 155, 157, 170, 173, 176; anti-immigrant sentiment, 129–30; forced sterilization in, 67; immigration to, 99; racialization in, 16; slave labor, built on, 45

University of Washington: Network Security Lab, 152

Vergara, Sofía, 15

Virginia, 32

Warcraft (video game), 50–51

WhatsApp, 122

When Harry Met Sally (film), 71–75

White men, 8, 14, 22, 31, 39, 61, 104, 107, 124, 129, 169; bootstrap mythology, 97; hegemonic space, occupying of, 41–42; power, in public sphere, 33; Whiteness, maintaining of through marriage and mating, 97

Whiteness, 19, 20, 30–31, 34, 38, 40–41, 68, 93, 108, 132, 148; algorithms, 17; as assumed natural social order, 83; dating, as desired category, 46–47; goal of, 94; guiding principles of, 89–90; on internet, 21; Latinx and Hispanic individuals, as adjacent to, 99; living free of racial tension, 90; maintaining of, 99–100; marrying into, 134; as morally right, 101; as most desirable aesthetic, 70; as nonracial social standard, 83; as norm, 143; "not white," 17; as pathological, 89; patriarchy,

Whiteness (*cont.*)
  inherent to, 97; perpetuating of,
  though familial marriage, 96–97;
  racial frame of, 23; as safe, from
  racism, 143; as sexual racism, 18, 28;
  as social default, 92; status and
  privilege associated with, 131
White people, 65–66, 83, 85, 95, 111, 130,
  152, 155, 173; anti-racist, 110, 144;
  benefits of racism, familiar with, 94;
  with conservative views, 98;
  discomfort, unfamiliar with, 90; as
  global minority, 92; making sense of
  race, 89; and naturalization, 44;
  not-being-racist, 110; race-based
  interactions, as free from, 143; as
  racially illiterate, 90; racial narratives, controlling of, 89; racial
  preferences, as neutral, 5; racial
  status quo, allegiance to, 94; racism,
  unwilling to confront, 89; racism,
  undoing harms of, 108; racist
  thoughts, uncomfortable acknowledging, 88; status and privilege of,
  131; status quo, maintaining of, 22;
  use of racial myths to justify
  nonracialism, 45; White-adjacent,
  125; White American values, 89;
  White beauty, 43; White choices,
  142; White discomfort, 93–94;
  White femininity, 46; White
  fragility, 41, 93–94; White gendered

performance, as standard of
  gender normativity, 40; White
  genocide, 7; White guilt, 93; White
  masculinity, 28, 30, 46; White
  privilege, 21, 94, 101, 110, 144, 146,
  148
White power movement, 7
White racial frame, 89–90, 94, 102, 110,
  111; Blackness, 93; internalizing of,
  96; normalizing work of, 92, 101;
  hate speech protections, 142
Whiteness Studies, 89
White superiority, 30, 131; myth of, 136
White supremacy, xi, 6, 19, 25, 30–33,
  49, 64, 179; Black deaths, 147; as
  normative, 101; sexual racism, 18
White women, 4, 14, 16, 31, 32–33, 35,
  92, 96–97, 104, 108, 123, 126, 131, 137,
  160–61
Williams, Serena, 36
women of color, 14–15, 22, 33, 40, 123,
  153; controlling images of, 33;
  exoticizing of, 105; Madonna-whore
  complex, 112; racial fetishization of,
  106; as sexual commodities, 34;
  subordination of, 35; Tinder, use of,
  107. *See also* people of color

xenophobia, 25

"yellow fever," 124
"yellow peril" trope, 16